NEW FOUNDATIONS THEOLOGICAL LIBRARY

General Editor
PETER TOON, MA, M.TH, D.PHIL

Consultant Editor
RALPH P. MARTIN, MA, PH.D

NEW FOUNDATIONS THEOLOGICAL LIBRARY

Other volumes in preparation

LIBERATION THEOLOGY

*An Evangelical View from
the Third World*

J. ANDREW KIRK

JOHN KNOX PRESS

ATLANTA

Copyright © J. Andrew Kirk 1979

Published simultaneously by Marshall, Morgan & Scott
in Great Britain and by John Knox Press in the United
States of America, 1979

Library of Congress Cataloging in Publication Data

Kirk, John Andrew.
  Liberation theology.

  (New foundations theological library)
  A revision of the author's thesis, London University.
  Bibliography: p. 228
  Includes indexes.
  1. Liberation theology. 1. Title. 11. Series.
BT83.57.K52   262.8   79–5212
ISBN 0–8042–3704–2

Extracts from the following books are quoted by permission of the publishers: *Being
and the Messiah* by J. P. Miranda, ET John Eagleson, © 1977 Orbis Books,
Maryknoll, USA. *Marx and the Bible* by J. P. Miranda, ET John Eagleson, © 1974
Orbis Books, Maryknoll, USA (SCM Press, London). *A Theology of Liberation* by
Gustavo Gutierrez, ET Sister Caridad Inda and John Eagleson, © 1973 Orbis
Books, Maryknoll, USA (SCM Press, London).

John Knox Press
Atlanta
Printed in Great Britain

To all my many friends of
the Latin American theological fraternity
who have helped and stimulated me
to add one tiny grain of sand
to their reflection on the relevance of
biblical Christianity
to the extreme needs of their suffering
and yet ever-expectant continent.

May your expectations be turned to hope
and your hope to the joy of receiving
from the Lord of Hosts
the fullness of his salvation
'when he will wipe away tears from all faces
and take away from all the earth
the reproach of his people'.

CONTENTS

PREFACE

The main part of this study of the Latin American theology of liberation attempts to explain and evaluate its general approach to the use of Scripture. It is followed by a discussion of another, different answer to the agonising question insistently raised by Christian thinkers in Latin America today: how should theology be done in a situation marked by exploitation, institutionalised violence and increasing poverty?

The theology of liberation is a recent phenomenon, tracing its beginnings roughly to the year in which Vatican II ended. In the first part of our analysis we look at its historical background within a Church marked by a persistent and deep political involvement. Here, we trace and explain the diverse influences which led to its 'left-wing' commitment. Then, in three subsequent chapters, we offer a brief description of the principal characteristics of a theological method which claims to be a major departure from other methods which have been elaborated over centuries, principally in Western Europe. We try to pay particular attention to the distinctive aspects of its development in order that its unique stance and contribution to theological methodology and reflection may be fairly judged.

The second part is devoted to a description of the writings of the five most influential thinkers within the Roman Catholic Church, paying particular attention to their individual approach to the theological task, their particular hermeneutical procedure and, where applicable, to actual examples of their exegesis. The third part looks closely at the exegetical handling and application to the Latin American situation of those biblical themes selected by the theology of liberation in general as most relevant to the fresh task they have set themselves.

The fourth and final part attempts to raise afresh, in discussion with the theology of liberation's special approach to the use of the Bible, in the light of the historical and theological influences which have moulded its thought and in a way relevant to the Church's modern mission, the fundamental issues affecting the relationship between the interpretation of God's revelation and specific Christian obedience in a real, suffering and violent world.

This book is a revised form of a thesis presented to London University. In general, even where there are now English translations, use has been made of the original Spanish editions. English translations when used are as credited.

I am grateful to Mrs Eunice Thorpe for typing the manuscript and to Dr Peter Toon for checking and editing for me.

J. ANDREW KIRK

Argentina, Easter 1978
London, Trinity 1979

PART I

THE PRINCIPAL
CHARACTERISTICS

CHAPTER ONE

HISTORICAL BACKGROUND

'At the beginning of the nineteenth century the Church in Latin America was at the apex of its power and its privileges.' However, the seeds of an open and protracted conflict between Church and State characteristic of the years during and following Independence, were already sown.[1]

I. THE CAUSES OF INDEPENDENCE AND THEIR INFLUENCE ON SUBSEQUENT DEVELOPMENTS

After nearly three hundred years on the South American continent, without any serious threat of rivalry and with the constant abetment of the civil authorities, it would seem that in 1800 the Church had no reason to fear for its peaceful and united development. The French Revolution had taken place eleven years earlier and the North American one a few years before that. Napoleon was beginning to consolidate his power in Europe, and his subsequent invasion of the Iberian peninsula was an important contributory factor to the timing of the Independence movements in the Americas. Finally, the ideas being disseminated as a result of the intellectual renewal in Europe, known as the Enlightenment, were beginning to reach the New World, influencing certain groups among the creole population.[2] Each of these historical events worked away at the hitherto homogeneous society within Latin America, bringing to an end the unity *between* Church and State, and the internal unity *of* both Church and Society.

Direct antagonism to the Church was probably not one of the contributing factors to the Independence movements, at least initially. The real causes are complex, because mutually interdependent. According to the findings of the first Hispanamerican historical congress in Madrid in 1949, there were six principal motives.[3] They are important because they either show irreversible historical tendencies, with which the traditionally conservative Church had to come to terms, or else they directly impinge upon the Church's subsequent attitude to political involvement. They are:

1. the diffusion of the theory of the French Encyclopaedists;[4]
2. the absolute authority wielded by the Peninsular Spanish, particularly their economic monopoly, which provoked the hatred of the creoles;
3. the many gross errors committed by the Peninsular government in its colonies, and its rapid decline as a force in world politics;
4. the encouragement given by the rising nations, particularly England, who were looking for new markets for their trade, to the creoles' bid for Independence;
5. the inbred individualism of the Hispanic race;
6. the growing unrest amongst the pre-Colombian peoples.

The congress was careful to state that only when taken together do these factors really explain why the cause of Independence, in spite of strong organised opposition, persevered sufficiently to see final victory.

If the rising against Spain and Portugal did not originate in an hostile attitude to the Church as such – indeed a number of its leaders were creole priests – nevertheless the Church, as a whole, adopted a largely negative attitude to Independence. A century of mutual misunderstanding and political conflict between itself and the leaders of the new, self-determined, nations was a direct result.

2. THE POSITION AND REACTION OF THE CHURCH AT THE TIME OF INDEPENDENCE

The Church's basic problem at the moment of Independence was its chronic lack of preparedness. Some of the reasons for its essentially anaemic condition were the nominal adherence of the majority of its members, a shortage of national priests[5] as a result of failure to indigenise leadership under colonial conditions, the inferior quality of the priests sent from Spain and, above all, the suffocating system of the Royal Patronage of the Indies.

The Royal Patronage was crucial to the formation of the relationship between Church and State, leading to the establishment in Latin America of a Spanish national Church controlled from Madrid, rather than a Catholic Church controlled from Rome. Due to its global strategy, 'the Church's activity is beyond that of saving souls'; it includes 'the legitimate function of creating the Kingdom of divine justice on earth'.[6] This notion, inherited, as E. Dussel suggests, from the strong drive to unify Church and State in fifteenth-century Spain,[7] has profoundly influenced the Latin American Church in its self-identification. Spain, like Israel of old, saw herself as an elect nation, destined to save the world. Propagation of the faith would be carried out by the Church's missionaries, under the direct auspices of the State. Any possibility, therefore, of severing the unity between the mutually dependent destinies of the Church and the Spanish nation would have been unthinkable to the Church's hierarchy, most of whose thirty-two bishops and six archbishops had been born and educated in the Peninsula.

One of the most important consequences of the Royal Patronage (or, perhaps, its cause) was the principle of the divine right of kings. This principle was made the chief, though never well-elaborated, theological justification for the hierarchy's strong denunciation of the uprisings.

At the same time, the chronic nature of the Spanish monarchy's fluctuating fortunes after 1808, combined with nationalist sentiment and incipient populist theology, led many creole clerics to embrace the cause of Emancipation. It is probably an exaggeration to say that the majority of the lower clergy supported a violent break with Spain, whereas the hierarchy were against it. The Vatican's strongly negative reaction, manifested in the Encyclicals *Etsi longissimo* (1816) and *Etsi Iam Diu* (1824), the swift disciplinary measures taken by the hierarchy and the lack of a solid tradition of independent thought in the theological preparation of the lower clergy, all conspired to reinforce traditional loyalties to the crown. Nevertheless, a considerable group of younger clergy, notably in Peru, had, before studying theology, taken courses in those secular subjects now being influenced by the Enlightenment. Thus by 1820 there was a remarkable intellectual agreement between priest and layman in the direction of openness and change.[8]

The more enlightened priests wanted a revival in the study of the Scriptures, a return to the primitive Church of the first three centuries, mass in the vernacular, a 'poor' Church, freedom of conscience, reform or abolition of the Curia, relaxation of celibacy for at least some of the clergy and decentralisation of the Pope's power. All this, prophetic of the trends of the second half of the twentieth century, was denounced to Rome by the Spanish royalists, recently re-established in power after the unsuccessful liberalising policy of the years 1816–1820, as the most 'bizarre impiety'.

These examples, however, were exceptions to a prevalent and deep-seated rule. The Church, through its acknowledged spokesmen, reacted, logically, in defence of its position and its traditional mission – that of perfecting the theocratic nature of colonial rule and the Catholic religion in that part of the New World which it had fallen to the lot of sixteenth-century Christendom to subjugate and civilise. In view of its dominant heritage, it is not surprising that 'theocratic' views prevailed amongst certain Church leaders well into the twentieth century.

The privileged position of the Church was defended on several grounds. It was held that the Catholic faith had been the principal creative factor in moulding the national character. There could be no national unity unless the traditional influence of the Church was maintained. 'The happiness found in the newly acquired faith compensated for ... [any] loss of liberty.'[9] 'The property which the Church possesses belongs to it independently of the will of governments; the right to acquire, maintain and administer property does not proceed from temporal concessions but rather from the inalienable rights of the institution itself, the Catholic Church ... it is a principle derived from the natural law and which is superior to all human law.'[10] Democracy, liberty and human rights were seen as inspired by secularist liberalism (that is, they did not spring originally from the teaching authority of the Church), and were found to conflict with the interests of moral goodness and truth.

Independence would be the first move in the introduction of pluralism and tolerance into the State in which the Catholic Church would enjoy no special privilege.

As a result of this type of reasoning, the uprisings against the authorities as then constituted were condemned by the Church in sweeping and uncompromising terms. The insurgents were heretics and rebels against divine authority. They were excommunicated and, if killed in action, their bodies were deprived of proper burial. The clergy's right to be exempt from the jurisdiction of the civil courts was revoked in the case of those clergy involved in, or deemed sympathetic towards, the movements of national liberation. Finally, on pain of mortal sin, the reading of certain allegedly subversive books was forbidden.

In spite of this imposing defence of their supposedly legitimate concerns, in the event the majority of the prelates' fears were unfounded. The movements for Independence rarely showed themselves intrinsically hostile to the Catholic religion. Only in Buenos Aires, for a short time, in the Declaration of Independence by the 1813 Assembly, was there an attempt to divest the State of its special relation to the Catholic Church.

In fact, there is plenty of evidence to suggest that the majority of the new governments wanted to maintain the special position which the Catholic Church enjoyed *vis-à-vis* the State, merely transferring the privilege of patronage from Madrid to their own hands. Firstly, the extreme anti-clerical concepts of the French Revolution had few echoes in Latin America. Independence brought about little more than a change of power. The leaders, with, from about 1820 onwards, the hesitating support of some elements of the Church, took it upon themselves to establish an order advantageous to their own interests. Their ideals of liberty and democracy were mainly theoretical, simple pretexts to justify their right to govern and to trade freely. Independence was essentially a political rather than a liberal movement. As such, it was not noticeably characterised by strong anti-religious feelings. Secondly, there was initially no great move to disestablish the Church. The religious attitude of the majority of the insurrectionists was avowedly Catholic. As much as anything they recognised the Church's value in helping to maintain the unity of the new nations, which was the outstanding preoccupation of men like Bolivar. As a result, total freedom of worship did not emerge till later.[11] Thirdly, the new political leaders needed the Church as an additional ally in order to justify their actions. As might be expected, they took steps to prohibit the Inquisition and in some cases, such as the decree of Chilpancingo (1813), they re-established the Jesuit

Order. But these actions could be interpreted as only marginally anti-ecclesiastical. Their clear intentions were revealed in Mexico's first Constitution, promulgated the following year, which stated that 'the Catholic Religion is the only one which may be professed in the State.'

We would summarise the position thus:

1. The majority opinion among the influential members of the Church was hostile to Independence from the colonial powers. Urged on by the monarchist forces in Spain, supported by a clear statement of the Vatican's opinion published in two Encyclicals, and aware of their own inability to face the possible consequences of far-reaching changes, they backed the doomed absolutist monarchy against the incipient republican ideas springing up in the wake of the nationalist victories.

2. There was little evidence in the earliest period that the Church would suffer loss of its authority or of its position in society. Any moves against the Church were designed to strengthen the political power of the insurgents, and happened only where the Church clearly used its own political power to curb their influence and appeal.

3. The Church basically had only itself to blame for the increasing conflict with the *de facto* governments which broke out in the period following the decisive victories of Boyaca (1823), Carabobo and Ayacucho (1824). Even taking into consideration all mitigating circumstances, this opposition was a disastrous policy. It produced a strong negative factor in the maturing process of the new nations, vastly hindered the Church's own development and influence, and created a profound reserve of ill-feeling which has subsequently vitiated any further attempt by the Church to throw its weight into the arena of social and political change.

3. FACTORS CONTRIBUTING TO THE CHURCH'S WEAKNESS AFTER THE ESTABLISHMENT OF INDEPENDENCE

The initial period of sympathy towards the Catholic Church on the part of the new leaders did not last long. They were engaged in a life and death struggle whose preliminary success seemed to have ended by the year 1816. Thus they reacted with understandable bitterness to the growing intransigence of the Church against recognising and encouraging the rights of the Independence movement, or at least to its remaining relatively uncommitted.

Measures taken to curb the Church's almost unfettered power arose when the Church insisted on throwing its weight behind the 'loyalist' forces. When, therefore, R. Pattel states that aggression always sprang from the governments, he misrepresents matters, seemingly with the desire to justify posthumously the Church's attitude to the changes it faced. He could more easily argue that 'Hispanamerican Independence had nothing to do with the Church as such',[12] although such a remark does not explain the nature and extent of the intervention.

Reasons now need to be considered for the Church's chronic weakness and inadaptability at the outbreak of and during the campaigns, from which it took, at least in some areas, about a century to recover.

Although the Church had established various universities from an early period, they had never become great centres for independent learning. Established largely for the training of clergy, they did little more than reflect the turgid thinking emanating from Spain. It was not surprising, therefore, that 'nineteenth century Latin America did not produce an original system of thought to equal the outstanding ones of Europe'.[13] If this was true for the culture in general it was even more true of the Church's theological activity in particular. As a result of its failure to inculcate a reflective and critical attitude, the Church was incapable of meeting the new clash of ideas springing from the new modernity of the eighteenth century. It was not even able to cope with the works of such Spanish scholastics as Vitoria, Suarez and de Molina who wrote, from within a Catholic framework, against the absolute power of the monarchy.

Perhaps the Church's incapacity to deal with these specific challenges proved the deciding factor in its withdrawal-syndrome from 1810 onwards. Subsequently it has manifested the same generic inability to respond to the successive challenges of Positivism, Protestantism and Marxism. In short, during this long period stretching from Independence right up to modern times there has been a serious shortage of intellectual reserves and a lack of concern to create new ones. This vacuum seriously retarded the development of any indigenous theological thought.

I. Vallier, in his study of modern Catholicism in Latin America, seeks to discover the causes of the present fragmented Church.[14] These causes, in addition to those listed above, can also be traced directly to the events of Independence, or even earlier. From the very beginning of the Church's missionary endeavour in Latin America the Catholic religion was casually disseminated rather than carefully planted. The great distances between isolated religious centres tended to produce a series of unfortunate effects: each ecclesiastical functionary became subject to extra-ecclesiastical controls, deriving its decision-making authority from local non-religious élites without any control from a united or international hierarchy. This, in turn, led to the formation of short-term political coalitions in order to produce immediate *ad hoc* solutions to pressing problems. This strategy of survival meant that practical problems took precedence over the creation of theological principles and ethical codes. Most of the Church's energies were taken up in political manœuvrings so that slowly a gradual dichotomy appeared between the 'Church' and the 'Catholic religion'. The result of all this was a failure of preparedness, a hand-to-mouth existence based, for its relative effectiveness, on the maintenance of a static equilibrium within the existing forces. Whereas Vallier may attribute too much to purely geographical factors, his theory explains the Church's bewilderment at the time of Independence when the balance of power was altered by the substitution of new forces for the former political support of the Church.

Two decades of conflict left the Church exceedingly vulnerable and, at certain crucial moments, even threatened her survival. One of the first effects of Independence was the departure of the majority of the Church's dignitaries, leaving their sees vacant. Apart from depriving the Church of any effective leadership, their swift defection created the impression that self-interest was the controlling motive of the hierarchy's attitude and action. The grave situation was worsened by the vacillations of subsequent Popes who, refusing either to concede the right of patronage to the new authorities or to take an independent line from that of royalist Spain, delayed making any episcopal appointments for several years.

The lower clergy, too, became severely reduced in numbers. At the time of Independence there were between 40,000 and 50,000 clergy, including members of religious orders. After ten years their number had fallen to approximately 10,000. Moreover, the situation was made worse by the absence of replacements from Europe, at least until the new nations were accorded diplomatic recognition. Many of the monasteries disappeared entirely, especially in rural areas. A like fate befell some diocesan seminaries, such as those at Santiago and Concepción in Chile. The lack of bishops contributed to serious deficiencies in the training of those priests who remained.

The attitudes of successive Popes, sometimes acting against their best advisors, deepened the problems of the struggling Church. For example, Gaetano Baluffi, the first-ever papal nuncio to Latin America (1836) was still, even at that late date, prophesying restoration of the monarchy. Through his agency, Rome pushed aside or ignored all churchmen who had in any way collaborated with either Bolivar or San Martin. This meant that those bishops who were eventually appointed, after the conflicts of Independence had subsided, were more often than not of an ultramontane tendency. These bishops in their turn made sure that the 'new conservatism' was officially taught in the seminaries. Lastly, the fresh influx of monastic orders from Spain, such as the Franciscans in 1837, fleeing, by a curious twist of history, from political disorders in their own country, strengthened the influence of monarchist and ultramontane ideas.

Unable for these reasons to initiate theological and political change, the Catholic Church in Latin America, after 1830, reflected once again the intransigent opinions of Rome which some thirty years later were to issue in the 'Syllabus of Errors'.

4. THE ATTACK ON THE CHURCH DURING THE NINETEENTH AND EARLY TWENTIETH CENTURIES

The Church's stand against political and social change was rooted in many centuries of unquestionable unity and stability between throne and altar. Such an alliance was defended on the grounds of God's essential ordering of humanity. Church leaders at that time were not sufficiently sophisticated theologically to realise that this position had been a gradual and late development in the relation between Church and State, and that it represented a corruption rather than a legitimate outworking of the Gospel. Even less did they question the concept of God assumed in the theological position they defended. Finally, the changes which began to undermine the whole carefully constructed edifice did not produce a reading of the 'signs of the times' which could have promoted creative theological reflection. The Church was, with notable but sporadic exceptions, a prisoner of its time.

The Church's negative stance towards change was savagely attacked by its adversaries. These included some of the most influential political and intellectual thinkers of the period, such as Lastarria (1817–88), Bilbao (1823–65), Gonzalez Prada (1848–1918), Roca (1843–1914), Bunge (1874–1918), J. Battle y Ordoñez (1865–1929) and many others. This whole movement, by no means homogeneous, but at least united in its intense distrust of and opposition to the Church, is often referred to as 'laicism'. Intellectually, it was far better equipped than the Church to carry out a confrontation. This may help to explain why it sometimes seems as if the Church was more the object of attack than its originator.

This confrontation differed from that produced during the period of political emancipation in that its representatives made no distinction between the empirical Church and the Catholic religion as such. Bilbao expressed the indissoluble unity between the two in uncompromising terms, 'Our past is Spain. Spain is the Middle Ages. The soul and body of the Middle Ages were Catholicism and Feudalism.'[15] The Church had little answer to this sustained attack except dogmatically to restate its traditional convictions. Commenting on the first Continental Council of the Church in 1898, E. Dussel says that its posture was to 'conserve, defend and protect the faith and not, on the other hand, to pass actively to the diffusion of that faith'.[16]

The representatives of 'laicism' seized hold of every conceivable argument to mount their onslaught on the Church. Bilbao pointed out the contrast, as he saw it, between the progress and liberty of the United States of America and the stagnation and reaction of Latin American society. For him the contrast was directly related to the respective influences of the Protestant and Catholic religions. He was not a secret Protestant, however. He considered that Protestantism was the best attitude that had been adopted by any historic society, but not the best possible historical attitude. Lastarria was convinced that religion (he knew only Catholicism at first hand) was the basis of despotism instead of the promoter of civilisation, freedom and the rights of man. He proclaimed the need for the immediate separation of Church and State. Prada preached that liberty (the egalitarian liberty of the French revolution) could not exist side by side with Catholicism. Juarez justified his extensive anti-ecclesiastical reforms in Mexico (1867–72) on the grounds that the civil independence of the Church should be curtailed, clear lines of demarcation between the two realms drawn, and a totally autonomous sphere in civil affairs for the exercise of the freedom of conscience secured. By the time of Juarez' death 'the Republic had, by act of law, taken control of all acts pertaining to the civil status of the people, making these acts legally valid without any reference to any religious creeds and definitely establishing freedom of worship'.[17] The Church interpreted this as an attack on its sovereignty, independence and dignity. In fact, it was a move against the absolutism of the religious control of civil rights and towards pluralism and the 'open society'.

Originally opposition to the Church was political, in the interests of the immediate goals of Independence. By the middle of the nineteenth century, however, new classes and leaders had emerged who were interested in real reform. They began to see that the political stance of the Church was an essential aspect of its religious convictions, and also a defence of its economic privileges. At that point anti-clericalism became a political philosophy. Its most consistent base was Positivism.[18]

Positivism was to be used as the great educational weapon to change the mentality of the entire Hispanic people. Cultural emancipation from the heritage imposed by Spain had still not been achieved. Only a religion matching the one which had deeply imposed itself upon the soul of Latin America could effect the educational and spiritual renewal necessary to produce liberal and progressive policies. This 'religion' proclaimed the sovereignty of reason and of the people, the religion of law dominating the conscience of all. The conflict can be explained in terms of a dualism which was destroying Latin America. As Bilbao put it, 'the Catholic Religion is searching for its form of government, the Republic form of government is searching for its religion. The policy of the first is monarchy; the religion of the second rationalism.'[19] As a result, either Catholic theocracy or Republicanism must triumph.[20] No quarter was given in this long struggle which, in some countries, lasted into the middle of the twentieth century.[21]

5. ATTEMPTS AT RENOVATION WITHIN THE CHURCH
DURING THE TWENTIETH CENTURY

'The history of the Roman Catholic Church in Latin America has been varied. From a high degree of integration in society during the colonial period it has passed through very profound struggles and even persecution in the nineteenth and early twentieth centuries until now it has come to a position of social awareness and the assumption of certain leadership in a time of social change.'[22]

H. A. Landsberger, a student of the Church's social involvement in Chile, asks the pertinent question, 'When, if ever, can change be said to have a beginning point?' Certainly in Latin America the chronological sequence has varied from country to country. In Chile efforts were made to adjust to the plight of the working classes before the publication of the first 'social' Encyclical of the modern period, *Rerum Novarum* (1891).[23] Subsequently, the Chilean episcopate changed its position on social reform more rapidly than any other group. In Peru and Brazil concern about the 'social problem' did not become serious until the late 1950s.

This social concern was accompanied by a gradual overall renovation of the life and witness of the Church. As the influence of Positivism over the intellectual life of the continent waned, an intellectual renewal sprang up amongst some Catholic thinkers. This renewal centred on the lay philosopher, Jacques Maritain, whose classic work, *Humanisme Intégral*, was published in 1937. It is significant that theological renewal eventually came by way of an original philosophy and that 'professional' clerics in Latin America were awakened to change through the impact of one lay thinker upon largely lay groups.

The three most significant efforts at mobilising the Church to face the challenge of mission in modern Latin America have been Catholic Action (CA), the Catholic Trade Union Movement (CLASC) and the Christian Democrat Parties (CDP). The first two were founded by episcopal decision and the latter through the initiative of concerned lay people.

No extensive history of Catholic Action in Latin America exists. However, a full documentation of its activities and impact after the Chimbote gathering of 1953 has been compiled by a Chilean Protestant.[24] Catholic Action is based on the premise that the modern mission of the Church should be founded on a new and aggressive lay apostolate, which would seek to penetrate all aspects of society with an up-dated Catholic witness. The kind of programme which might be employed in the midst of rapid social change is well elaborated by F. Houtart.[25] He lays stress on the need to mobilise intellectuals, for 'it is more important to work in a university than in a new parish', and on the danger of a new form of clerical domination of lay activity. Although one of the great instruments of this contemporary renovation will be a new-style catechesis (the responsibility of the clergy), its concrete outworking in society will be entirely in the hands of the laity: 'it is vital that the laity assume their social responsibilities.'

Initially the CA organisations saw themselves as bulwarks against the materialism and atheism of communists and socialists. Stress was laid on the education of leaders. This paid great dividends, as a whole generation, with a new mentality towards spiritual renewal, evangelism and social issues, was formed. Its direct influence on concrete lay political involvement is undeniable, more particularly in the formation of the CDP and, later, in the rise of Catholic radicalism, especially in Brazil. This has been its greatest significance. Its original intention of being a renewing missionary force within Latin America has, according to some, largely failed.[26]

Alongside Catholic Action, but with an ultramontane orientation, arose the *'cursillos de cristiandad'*. Their aim, according to Vallier, is the reconversion of the indifferent into apostolic militants. They are profoundly confessional and, as a result, traditional in their orientation. Although their overt intention is spiritual and moral recuperation, their political involvement is widely known. Their recent appearance gives the impression that they are the right wing section of the Church's reaction to the new militancy springing up on the left.

Another crucial aspect of renovation concerns the hierarchy itself. No programme for renewal stands much chance of internally affecting the Church unless it manages to secure the support of at least a part of the hierarchy. The case of Chile has shown that the hierarchy may be influenced, over a fairly long period, from below.

Structurally decisive for the Latin American episcopate have been two consecutive developments, the first of which is the great increase in the number of dioceses. Since Independence over 500 new sees have been created, to match both the population explosion and its increasing mobility. Of these, nearly 150 were created in the decade 1950–60. Cohesion and planning between bishop, clergy and people were naturally enhanced by the multiplication of smaller units. Secondly, a permanent episcopal organisation for consultation, study and action, CELAM (*Consejo Episcopal Latino Americano*), was set up in 1955. This council's most effective role has been the interpretation for Latin America of certain recent key Encyclicals, especially those dealing with social issues. The bringing together of the concerns of Vatican II and a fresh socio-political and economic analysis of Latin America in the documents of Medellín (1968)[27] became a significant catalyst for the 'theology of liberation' movement.

6. THE CHURCH AND NEW FORMS OF SOCIAL AND POLITICAL INFLUENCE AND COMMITMENT

'Latin America can no longer afford the time for evolution. There is only one choice: revolution, that is, radical transformation of some kind or other.'[28] With this both the CDP and the New Catholic Left (NCL) would agree. But the means by which they hope to achieve it, their respective ideological bases and analyses of the present reality, differ widely. The continuation of the quotation pin-points these differences. '... The continent can choose a Marxist revolution. Or it can choose development through participation of the popular masses, economic planning ... and an effective and massive foreign aid. History will tell which path is taken.'

The CDP have been extensively influential only in Chile and Venezuela, although smaller groups have existed in other countries.[29] They have developed under the intellectual guidance of Maritain and have been served by organisations like the Centro Bellarmino in Santiago under the direction of the Belgian Jesuit, R. Vekemans. Their importance, according to Vallier, lies in three functions: their capacity to combine Catholic thought with programmes of extensive social reform, their espousal of a 'third way' (between communism and capitalism), and their strong leadership. Also, according to Vallier, they fulfil the double function of acting as shock absorbers between the Church and the political scene and serving as a safety valve for the more politically militant laity. Both these functions keep the Church from espousing a strong leftish programme, so creating conflict in the Church and causing the hierarchy to silence the most politically minded groups. The result of such a process would be a tendency to a dangerous 'neutral' or central position, thus legitimising the *status quo*. Vallier supports the thesis that a reformist Catholic party will help to stop the uncreative swing from left to right, and vice versa, and support meaningful and possible programmes of change.

The ideological base of the CDP is well set out by Frei in several articles.[30] It rejects the demagogic attitude of the left which proposes short-term goals to satisfy party or ideological ambitions and that of the right, marked by the unchecked selfishness of privileged groups who hold the dominant power in society. Both of these negations are to be achieved by incorporating the proletariat into the national existence. R. Shaull uses the suggestive term 'theocentric humanism' to describe its underlying theological and philosophical premise.[31] The CDP takes up the position on social change that the present social system no longer corresponds to the demands of development and hence of social justice. There is need for decisive and rapid action brought about by inspiring the motivation of Christians towards change.[32]

The survival of the CDP, or some basically non-violent development of it, will probably depend on the outcome of the struggle between the right, now in the ascendancy, and the left with its domination of the intellectual scene. Its future will depend on its ability to harness intellectuals for a less dogmatic programme of structural change, to identify itself as a party of the masses and to work with the constitution so as not to alienate unduly those who see the military coup as an ultimate defence for privilege. Time will tell whether their more long-term emphasis on change has any chance of success. For our purpose this 'third position' has been strongly rejected by the NCL, for reasons which we shall now briefly examine.

7. CHRISTIAN GROUPS AND SOCIAL JUSTICE: THE RISE OF A CONCERN FOR REVOLUTION

The Church's long-neglected concern for social justice for the poor and oppressed arose partly as a result of the challenge of communism, and partly as a result of the Popes' social encyclicals. The first of the modern ones, *Mater et Magister* (1961), springs in part from changing theological emphases, what Bishop McGrath of Panama calls, 'the Theology of Progressive Change'.[33]

Spokesmen for this viewpoint are prepared to use the word revolution in a positive sense, meaning by it fundamental reform of institutions, the overthrow of feudal structures and widespread social equalising. But they negate its overtones of violence, class struggle and dictatorial methods. They do not stress the economic factor in revolution, for social change is still a prerequisite for economic advance, and not the reverse. Change may be brought about by a social pluralism which, if unequivocally backed by the Church, would still give religious values a chance of influencing social change.

In this change of attitude, assumed mainly in the two decades stretching from 1940 to 1960, the place of the Church is ambiguous. On the one hand, there was a sincere desire to give the

Church a new image, separate it from all traditional influences and make it autonomous with respect to political activities, thus in principle creating an effective opposition to monolithic military dictatorships. On the other hand, the changes were motivated as much by confessional concerns as by radically political ones.

According to Shaull, the greatest impact of this new move in the direction of social justice and freedom was felt by the clergy and laity, only in rare instances by the episcopate. Essential to this viewpoint is the belief that economic development can take place simultaneously with structural change and social justice. However, in the face of the concrete challenge to defend the victims of reactionary military paternalism (Shaull writes in the light of the 1964 military coup in Brazil) it showed the shallowness of its conversion to the propagation of genuine social justice. In Shaull's view the Church became an unwilling victim of its own internal contradictions, due largely to an ingrained fear of Marxism and of the violent overthrow of institutions. It stated ideals but did not work toward creating the political conditions necessary to achieve such goals. It chose survival rather than risk itself in the uncompromising defence of human values. It could not deal with its own conservative elements.[34]

In synthesis, we can agree that 'the most striking aspect of Latin American Catholicism in the mid-twentieth century has been its new alignment behind popular demands for a better life in the secular sphere',[35] and that this alignment has been the result of converging forces producing a more integrated concept of historical responsibility.

However, this new impulse should be sharply distinguished from the NCL in at least three respects. It is opposed to violence to bring about changes in the present power structures of society, it springs from an idealist (i.e. ethical) standpoint, not a historically determinist one,[36] and it preaches patience in method, accusing the New Left of political ineffectiveness, due to its total approach to political change.

In spite of this unprecedented development in the Church's social concern, other groups within the Church have arrived at a decidedly different interpretation of revolution and its pressing urgency.

Whereas the older social reformers believed that change could come about by democratic, i.e. popularly elected, governments, the New Left are inclined to think that democracy and social and economic reform cannot develop simultaneously. Whereas the first group tended to put great trust in the CDP, especially in Frei's 'revolution in liberty' (1964–70) as a 'third way' between competitive capitalism and some form of communism, the second group reject all 'third ways' and tend to polarise the alternatives between violent seizure of power and maintenance of the *status quo*.[37]

Perhaps the greatest differences between the two groups can be summed up thus: the first group commit themselves as citizens with a clear Catholic stance while the second group appear to launch the Church on direct, undifferentiated paths of action in political strife. As Shaull puts it, the NCL is not concerned to 'christianise' the revolution but to be so involved in it as to 'humanise' it.

It is difficult to establish dates for the rise of a concern for revolution. Undoubtedly, the experience of Cuba would be a powerful factor in showing that great changes were possible. Among other influential factors would be the progressive failure of the much-vaunted 'Alliance for Progress' to solve the problems of the 'under-developed' nations; the beginning of personal contact by many priests with the really poor areas of the mushrooming cities, experiencing at first hand the devastatingly inhuman consequences of privilege and discrimination; contact with institutions in Europe and the influence of priests from overseas; and the example of Camilo Torres. Also, one could cite the growing wealth of writings by Latin American sociologists and economists showing, with undeniable statistics, the economic dominance of the continent by international monopolistic interests;[38] the increasing repression by military governments in such countries as Brazil, Argentina, Paraguay and Bolivia; the increasing outspokenness of the 'social' Encyclicals, the last one being *Populorum Progressio* (1967); and the influence of the Protestant group 'Church and Society in Latin America' (ISAL), especially the documents published after its initial conferences of 1961 and 1963.

8. THE PRESENT STATE OF THE CHURCH

The present state of the Church is very different from that which emerged from the upheavals of Independence. The hierarchy, numerically quite strong, is organised into relatively well-functioning local commissions and, on a continental scale, in CELAM.

Nevertheless, the Church is still weak when measured against the greatness of the task demanded of her by the current crises. These weaknesses are in large measure the effect of a certain vacillation in the face of the concrete challenge of unheeded social injustices.

The more obvious weaknesses reproduce the conditions which have been inherited since Independence. There is a rising gap between the growth in population and the decline in vocations to the priesthood. This is accentuated by the large number of foreign priests still participating in the life of the Church. As long as these sources of manpower are still available, the problems which will result from the rapid closing down of seminaries will remain shelved, and the effective indigenisation of the Church will be postponed.

This chronic shortage of priests gives rise to a particularly vicious circle. A priest is obliged to spend much of his time in cultic activities; his pastoral and teaching ministries are considered as activities for time left over and, therefore, the Church as a whole finds it difficult to give priority to the training of the laity for its mission.

But by far the most serious weakness of the contemporary Church revolves around its grave internal divisions over social and economic questions, the result, mainly, of profound disagreements over the place and function of authority, morals and theology in the contemporary Church.

F. Houtart has identified four basic viewpoints held by different sections of the Church:[39]

1. The role of Catholicism in Latin America is to support the system in doctrine and practice (the ultramontane position).
2. The existing system is good in principle but can be perfected. The role of religion is to bring correctives to the

system (a paternalistic position, based on the efficacy of works of charity).

3. The present social system no longer corresponds to the demands of rapid development and hence of social justice. It must be changed by rapid and decisive action. The Church should inspire the motivations of Christians towards change (the position of the CDP and certain Catholic centres for socio-political research).

4. The existing system is fundamentally wrong. It can be changed only by overthrowing it and bringing into being a totally new set of structures (the position of the NCL).

Finally, there remains the unresolved problem of how the Church should relate to its more radical groups. These groups owe their awareness of the unjust situation of the oppressed classes partly to the social teaching of the Church. The Church has nevertheless tended to abandon them at a time of national crisis or polarisation.

CHAPTER TWO

THE IMMEDIATE ORIGINS

Gustavo Gutierrez, the Peruvian theologian, who has written the most systematic account of the theology of liberation, has also defined it most closely: it is a theological reflection 'based on the Gospel and the experiences of men and women committed to the process of liberation in the oppressed and exploited land of Latin America; it is a theological reflection born . . . of shared efforts to abolish the current unjust situation and to build a different society, freer and more human.' The task of theology is to 'elucidate the meaning of [Christians'] solidarity with the oppressed . . . to think through our faith, to strengthen our love, and to give reason for our hope.' In brief, the theology of liberation is 'a critical reflection on Christian praxis in the light of the Word.' This latter definition is a formula continually repeated in the writings of the theologians of liberation. From the perspective of this study it is interesting to note that Gutierrez calls it 'a political hermeneutics of the Gospel'.[1]

Throughout this study it must be borne in mind that the theology of liberation is a theology in process of discovering its own identity. It seeks to break free from a past world, without yet having discovered the contours of a new one.[2] Thus it is provisional, more of a series of soundings than a *Summa Theologica*. It admits that its instruments are rudimentary, but is convinced that there is no other legitimate way of doing theology, especially in Latin America. Thus our evaluation of this 'new' theology must also be tentative, an attempt to take stock of its present position and to suggest a different way of looking at the resources for liberation contained in the biblical revelation of God.

I. VATICAN II AND THE SOCIAL ENCYCLICALS

The theology of liberation is a post-conciliar theology. It originated in 1965, the same year that the Vatican Council finished.

But it is more than a post-conciliar theology in the usual sense of the word, for its primary concern is not to up-date the Church, but to reflect upon and stimulate action in the present revolutionary process, in the light of the Church's documents of faith. Its concern is not intra-ecclesiastical formation. Thus, it has concentrated upon the Social Encyclicals which deal with the *aggiornamento* of the Church in the world, and upon those aspects of these Encyclicals which seem to promise a new methodological approach to the concrete problems of a world radically divided between the rich and the poor.[3]

Extremely significant for Latin America has been the open document written in the light of *Populorum Progressio* by fifteen bishops speaking on behalf of the Third World nations.[4] In this, they affirm that the 'peoples of the Third World are the proletariat of today's humanity'; that the Church must not be 'attached to financial imperialisms'; that property should have a collective destiny and that the Church, divested of its social and monetary privileges, should unite itself with all the exploited in defence of the recovery of their rights. The theology of liberation sets out to reflect on the theological significance of such statements.

2. EXPERIENCE IN THE COMMITMENT TO REMOVE POVERTY

Neither these documents nor the ones that were to follow would have had the influence they did on the early development (1965–70) of the theology of liberation were it not for the fact that they reflected certain atrocious situations of poverty throughout the continent, situations which had been personally experienced by various priests and laymen.

These documents were used tactically to demonstrate to the reactionary elements of the Church that official teaching on social issues was changing substantially. However, those engaged at first hand with the intractable problems of poverty were beginning to advance more radical answers than those of the official documents.

The area of the Church's greatest contact with poverty, up to the middle of the 1960s, was the north-east of Brazil where Dom Helder Camara had been made Archbishop of Recife in

1964. Those working there were greatly influenced by new thinking on the subject of underdevelopment, change and humanisation by the Brazilian Catholic educator, Paulo Freire.[5]

Freire coined the word *concientización* ('making aware') as a method for bringing change from the grass roots. He stressed that poverty was directly caused by a few people (such as land-owners), defending their privileges against the masses, and that it could be solved only as the poor *liberated themselves* from their 'dominated-conditioned' mentality and their passive despair, and freed the rich from their 'dominating-conditioned' attitudes.

At this stage, education (particularly literacy programmes) was seen as a subversive tool which would cause the dominated to demand the removal of their shackles. Many elements in the Church dedicated themselves to putting into practice Freire's method of 'education as the practice of liberty'.

3. REJECTION OF THE CONCEPT OF DEVELOPMENT AS AN ADEQUATE MEANS OF ELIMINATING POVERTY

The systematic suppression of the forces working for *concientización* which followed the Brazilian military coup of April 1964, was a cruel blow to the expectations of those Catholics who had confided in Freire's methods. Without abandoning his insights, they began to investigate more deeply the play of powers which had enabled the rightist forces in Brazil (and later in Argentina) to extinguish so easily the early hopes for a deep-seated transformation of society, the elimination of poverty and all forms of human degradation.

Catholic thinkers began to study a new generation of Latin American economists who questioned the concept of under-development elaborated in the north, rejected a functionalist approach to sociology, and began to use Marxist categories to explain the reasons behind Latin American poverty and stagnation.[6] Latin American economists and political thinkers rejected the categories of development tied to the perpetuation of a 'liberal' economy and worked out their own. They concluded that poverty was the direct result of exploitation, for dividends on investments and high-interest loans from the rich nations removed far more capital from the sub-continent than that given in aid.

It was in the light of this reality of exploitation and economic and political (as well as cultural) dependence that some Catholics began to reflect on the meaning of their Christian faith. The theology of liberation developed from this reflection, directly challenging the 'theological ideologies' of the *status quo*. The word 'liberation' was chosen for two basic reasons: it formed a direct contrast to the concept of dependence, and it had a long historical usage in biblical and Church tradition as a synonym for salvation.

When the theologians of liberation use such concepts as 'praxis', 'reality' or their equivalents, they mean the social, economic and political situation as this is analysed by means of Marxist or neo-Marxist sociological tools. It is this interpretation of the Latin American situation which has most influenced the origin and development of the theology of liberation.

4. NEW THEOLOGICAL MOVEMENTS IN EUROPE

During the 1960s most of the influential thinkers within this new Latin American theological movement studied in Europe. They were cognisant, therefore, of the recent development of the so-called 'political theology'. Certainly, their initial theological reflection owes much to such writers as Moltmann, Metz and, to a lesser extent, Rahner and others engaged in the Christian–Marxist dialogue.

The theology of liberation is both a continuation of and a rupture from this brand of political theology. For example, it has valued the emphasis on universal human history as the medium and context of God's acts of salvation. In this respect, it has accepted the criticisms of Moltmann, Pannenberg and others of the essentially ahistorical nature of theology inspired by existentialist philosophy. It has also welcomed the critical nature of this theology as a *Theologie der Frage* with its stress on the future as a constant overcoming of the present. Nevertheless, the theology of liberation tends to underline the differences rather than the coincidences. For this reason, certain authors have called it a 'theology of rupture'.

For example, it rejects the imposition of a theological programme from Europe or the United States. This is due to its generally negative assessment of 'North Atlantic' theology and its conviction that Latin American reality requires a change both in content and method from theology done in the developed countries of the West. The following, then, are its main criticisms of 'political theology':

1. The methodological starting point is philosophical idealism which has hindered its use of certain tools of socio-political analysis as a means of bridging the hermeneutical gap between past event and present reality.
2. The language concerning revolution, for lack of an adequate awareness of the essential injustice of capitalism, is vague, unrealistic and non-conflictive.
3. It makes an unjustified distinction between ethics and dogmatic theology.[7]
4. It still allows the secular realm too much autonomy, showing that it has not fully abandoned a 'theology of secularisation'.
5. Its proponents are not committed in practice to changing society, only to explaining and criticising it.[8]

5. THE MEDELLÍN DOCUMENTS

Some of the more radical statements of the Second General Conference of CELAM were both the result of and a catalyst for the developing theological reflection on liberation.

The significance of Medellín is profound, long-lasting and multiple. For the purposes of our study, it is necessary to point out that the documents, particularly those dealing with justice and peace, began to assume, at the level of the Latin American hierarchy, the new language of liberation, and condemned in concrete terms every kind of colonialism that kept Latin America permanently underdeveloped.[9]

For example, the document severely castigates the liberal capitalist system with its 'erroneous concept of the property rights of the means of production'; the current exercise of authority in Latin America, 'justified ideologically and practically', which 'frequently acts against the common good and favours privileged groups'; 'the increasing distortion of international commerce' due to 'the international monopolies and inter-national monetary imperialism' and 'institutionalised violence provoked by those who hold to their privileges'.

It makes a strong appeal for a new just social order in which man, particularly the popular classes, fully participating in the processes of government, may be the subject of his history and not the arbitrary object of speculation and 'profit without end', and also for the defence of the poor and oppressed by means of grass-roots organisations which would fight for their rights.

Most Catholic theologians consider that Medellín marks a highly significant watershed. E. Dussel sums up the achieve-ments of Medellín thus:

> Medellín uses the language of liberation, it speaks of depen-dence, domination, international monetary imperialism and allows us to begin to think differently ... it is situated on the road leading from "developmentism" to the "Theology of Liberation" ... Beyond "developmentism" a new posture is to be found which rapidly influences theology and creates a new language, a whole new economic, political and, of course, theological interpretation of liberation.[10]

CHAPTER THREE

SOME BASIC THEMES

I. THE CHURCH AS PROPHET

The prophetic nature of the Latin American Church has been both a growing fact, as witnessed to by Medellín, and a call to action. This latter, according to J. L. Segundo, is a call to insert permanently the *function* of protest into the Church's structure, the heirarchy becoming subordinate to the prophetic charisma.[1] According to many, one of the most meaningful prophetic acts would be to loosen the Church from all formal ties to the State.

Gutierrez believes that the Church's hierarchy should go even further, throwing all its influence, still considerable in many parts of the continent, against every dehumanising situation. Its denunciation should not be partial (individual acts of injustice), but global (the entire system of dependence).

The theologians of liberation consider that this prophetic voice, directed to the world's crises, is the only way in which the Church can authenticate itself before a watching world.

2. RELIGION AS CONSUMER GOODS AND AS THE 'HEROIC' FAITH OF A MINORITY

However, the theologians of liberation are not too confident that the Church will ever become the Church of the poor and the oppressed. A considerable caution has been noticed amongst many individual bishops and also national episcopates since Medellín. According to Segundo, the basic reason is that the Church is afraid of becoming a minority Church, thereby risking the loss of its prestige, and its protective power, however tenuous, over the masses. The Church has not yet escaped from the vicious circle of its traditional pastoral strategy. This will happen only if it decides for an entirely different strategy – the preaching of a gospel demanding both personal conviction and assent and a transforming presence in society in the building up of a genuine social community. In this way, the Church will doubly challenge the prevailing view of the consumer society that religion is a private matter which is expressed publicly only in the rites and ceremonies of the Church.[2]

Now the relation between the Church and the masses, and how this affects the Church's prophetic voice, is a matter of increasing polemic amongst Latin American theologians. The theology of liberation is known generally as a vanguard movement, standing against the danger of the Church's prophetic voice being assimilated and muted by short-term reformist programmes, although these might appeal to a mass conscience. As Dumas puts it: 'We have no right to submit a radical evangelical attitude to calculated strategic ends . . . there needs to be a prophetic movement which will attempt to break the world's logic.'[3]

3. THEOLOGY AS CONFLICT

Partly as a result of the radical thinkers' growing frustration with the non-implementation of the Medellín programme, the theology of liberation has become a prophetic theology (i.e. a theology of conflict) in order to keep alive the Church's real options. According to Assmann, 'the subject of conflictivity in historical and real terms has become the central subject-matter of the "Theology of Liberation" '.[4] One of its principal contributions could be the opening of a breach in the 'superstructure' represented by 'petit-bourgeois values' which both in their origin and continuance, are closely related to pseudo-Christian traditions and values. This can be done effectively only as theology, in Latin America, assumes the Marxist analysis of society as the historical scene of the class struggle.[5] In this way, theology may also point to a possible Christian presence in the transformation of the substructures.

From these brief remarks, it may be noted that the theology of liberation has moved beyond the Social Encyclicals' classification of the world into developed and underdeveloped, rich and poor, and even the more exact classification of Medellín into dominators and dominated, to approve the classical Marxist categories of oppressors and oppressed.

Theology cannot be prophetic unless it can be specific. Being specific means dropping the 'vague' language of the European 'political theology' and doing theology using the language of Marx. 'The myth of the "Christian community" [must] disappear, for it prevents the recognition of the division of society into classes.'[6]

4. VIOLENCE

It is hardly surprising that the majority of the theologians of liberation evaluate positively what Helder Camara calls the 'second violence',[7] a violence committed by 'countless human beings who suffer restrictions, humiliations, injustices; who are without prospects, without hope, their condition that of slaves.'[8] Such violence is justified according to the classical criteria for the 'just war', reiterated for example, in *Populorum Progressio* (paragraph 31), i.e. that no practical distinction can be made between the right of governments to use force to maintain order and the right of armed revolution to overthrow those governments when the order they maintain is anti-human (i.e. idolatrous). In this context, just defence is interpreted to involve the hindering of the use of the first violence in order that the process of liberation may be brought about.

5. HISTORY AS A TOTAL UNITY

According to J. Miguez, the central premise of the theology of liberation is the indivisible unity of history.[9] No type of dualism (e.g. that between faith and praxis, or between theological and ideological reflection) can be allowed.

This stress on the inner unity of history brings with it a re-evaluation of the classical concept of the history of salvation as that particular history of Israel and the Church in which God acts once for all for man's complete salvation. Particular salvation-history is subordinate to and dependent upon 'general salvation-history'; there is 'only one salvific design of creation and redemption in Christ.'[10] This concept, which we believe has profound hermeneutical consequences, sees in

Christ's salvation, wrought in one moment of history, a paradigmatic rather than an inimitable event:

> the question, [it seems to us] . . . is a matter of partial fulfil-
> ments through liberating historical events . . . Christ does not
> 'spiritualise' the eschatological promises; he gives them
> meaning and fulfilment today (cf. Luke 4.21); but at the
> same time he opens new perspectives by catapulting history
> . . . towards total reconciliation.[11]

6. REJECTION OF POLITICAL AUTONOMY

It might seem surprising that Catholic theologians, who so
strongly reject the Constantinian union between Church and
State, do not accept a complete autonomy for the political
sphere. Their stance is all the more curious when we remember
that secularisation claims to free man from metaphysical bon-
dages in order that he may realise himself more fully in this
life.

However, the rejection of political autonomy is not in the
name of a new Constantinianism, such as that proposed by
Maritain, where the Church functions in the secular world by
working towards a society built on Christian principles; the
rejection is on the grounds that any pretended neutrality the
secular order may claim for itself is already ideologically
conditioned, in that it views all religions and ethical dogmas as
relative.[12] In other words, secularisation has favoured the
continuance of those power structures which arose precisely in
the wake of what Gutierrez calls 'the distinction of planes' –
the radical separation of religious and political authority. But
these power structures are not neutral, for they use the concept
of autonomy to cover over gross injustices and situations of
oppression.

The theology of liberation does not, therefore, criticise the
notion of autonomy in the interests of a new intervention by
the Church in the organisation of society, but in the name of
'the construction of a just society' which possesses the value of
'the acceptance of the kingdom', i.e. 'of general salvation history'.

7. REJECTION OF A 'THIRD' POSITION

The notion of unitary history, where salvation today passes through human projects of political liberation, has led the theology of liberation to deny emphatically that any 'third' position between capitalism and socialism could be the mediator of this salvation.

The third position most often named is that of the CDP, based on the Social Encyclicals, which propose 'community property' and 'revolution in freedom'. However, the theology of liberation doubts that this really is a third position, for it offers no real alternative to capitalism but rather becomes absorbed by it. Its ideological base is insufficient and, as a result, it lacks the theoretical resources to put into practice a real programme of transformation.

8. THE PLACE OF UTOPIA

Gutierrez, towards the end of his study, discusses the place of utopias in the construction of a new society. He writes that 'the term *utopia* has been revived within the last few decades to refer to a historical plan for a qualitatively different society and to express the aspiration to establish new social relations among men.'[13]

Utopia, as it has been defined and used since K. Mannheim's pioneer work *Ideology and Utopia*, means the inversion of ideology, which has always worked, in the classical negative sense used by Marx and Engels, from the theoretical to the practical. Utopia has two chief functions: the constant overcoming, through a process often described as 'the negation of the negative', of historical determinisms and positivist explanations of reality, and the opening up of new vistas of a society radically different from the present ones.

Utopia, therefore, denounces the existing order, whose deficiencies announce paradoxically a wholly new order. It is a jump from the empirical reality of today to the theoretical reality of tomorrow, using that imagination which presupposes a rupture with all existing orders. Utopia is related to present reality by means of a scientific analysis of those forces at work today which anticipate this future. Thus it is not an illusion.

Nor is it merely a verbal vision, because between the denunciation and the announcement there is a real historical praxis of liberation being worked out, so that the utopia is already present in the struggle against oppression and inhumanity.

In other words, utopia is a pressure, linked to that cultural revolution which attempts to forge a new man, to challenge present society to be aware of the urgency of change and the possibility of a future society in a state of permanent revolution. The underlying theological presupposition is the concept of a general salvation history in which man (oppressed man) is capable of liberating history from opppressive structures in order to forge a new humanity. The creation of a new humanity is 'the place of encounter between political liberation and the communion of all men with God. This communion implies liberation from sin.'[14]

9. POPULAR RELIGION AND EVANGELISM

Amongst the theologians of liberation, popular religion often tends to be evaluated negatively. According to S. Galilea, popular religion, which is a 'faith conceived of as a cultural heritage, a religiosity more and more expressed in rights and divorced from ethics and life . . .', has been created by Latin American Christendom.[15] According to J. L. Segundo, popular religion is the result of a Church interested only in the task of supplying religious security through the massive and indiscriminate administration of the sacraments.[16] It is the fruit of the Church's fear of freedom which seeks to protect the masses against any radical questioning of their faith. Popular religion produces a religous conscience which obstructs the path to the total liberation of society. It reinforces the typical religious inversion of reality of which Marx spoke in his 1844 manuscripts.

When these theologians speak about evangelism they are speaking basically about a message which will lead to popular religion being freed for a new commitment to the process of liberation. Evangelisation, for Segundo, is 'the proclamation of the good news that God's liberating love in Christ is not lost on earth' in such a way that a person may come to a *personal* conviction of the liberating power of the Gospel.[17]

CHAPTER FOUR

THE IMPORTANCE OF METHOD

I. ORTHODOXY AND ORTHOPRAXIS

The theology of liberation has been defined as 'critical reflection on historical practice in the light of the Faith'. Using other terminology, it means that the verification of a theological position or formulation depends upon its conformity to the actual process of liberation which God is bringing about. In other words, the correctness of the stated position of the theology of liberation can be measured only by its ability to liberate (by the language and symbols it uses) forces for the reconstruction of a more human society.

Theology is never an abstract exercise. The theology of liberation constantly denounces any notion of a 'pure theology' deducible from an *a priori* set of principles. Theological thought, right from the beginning, is a hermeneutical exercise directed towards the Church's contemporary witness, not, as has often been the case in Europe, a self-contained academic hermeneutical procedure. It should not begin with an intellectual debate about the application of Christian faith to modern problems, but with a project to change an unjust society into a just one, using the accumulated wisdom of Christian reflection to illustrate, penetrate, challenge and modify a praxis already engaged upon.

The biblical basis for this approach is found in the Johannine concept of truth (orthodoxy) as doing the truth or walking in truth. Dumas says, for example, that 'in the light of John 3.21 a fundamental orthopraxis is required in order to remain in the faith.'[1] Two illustrations indicate how the priority of orthopraxis over orthodoxy may be worked out.

In the contemporary Christian-Marxist dialogue there can be two approaches. On the one hand, it is possible to engage in a theoretical debate of the 'philosophical' position of each 'system' in order to see to what extent there are coincidences of belief which would permit a common project in the future; on the other hand, it is possible to engage in a common project now, and allow this experience to modify and correct the theoretical philosophical position of each system. The theologians of liberation understand that the two approaches mark the difference between European and Latin American methodology.[2]

Secondly, the relationship between dogmatic theology and ethics can be conceived of in three different ways; the logical priority of dogmatics, the simultaneity of the two, or the logical priority of ethics. Classical ethics has espoused the first position, situation ethics the third, and the theology of liberation the second. This means, on the one hand, that there is no specifically Christian ethic, nor a universal ethic (i.e. absolute norms of conduct), for the price of such a position is an abstraction from the complexity of any given situation. The context of decisions and human action is indicative, not imperative. On the other hand, the Scriptures and Christian tradition provide a series of guide-lines which help to develop a human ethic. The indicative nature of ethical decision is further developed by Dussel in the concept of the *alteridad del prójimo* (the otherness of one's neighbour),[3] and given an exegetical base by J. P. Miranda.[4] However, although the otherness of one's neighbour is mediated by his concrete situation, indicated by the terms 'exploitation' and 'loss of liberty', it also issues in an imperative call to action. And this imperative, in a Christian context, is also mediated through the indicative of God's revelation in Christ.

2. PRAXIS AS THE STARTING POINT FOR THEOLOGICAL REFLECTION

From the preceding discussion, it may be seen that 'historical reality' is the privileged position from which all theological reflection must begin. Assmann states it categorically, and in polemical terms:

> The 'text', we repeat, is our situation. This is the first theological reference point. The other reference points (Bible, tradition, magisterium, history of doctrine) . . . are not the

first reference point, a 'sphere of truth-in-itself', unconnected to the historic 'now' of truth-praxis.[5]

Theological reflection is a process which demands constant change as new historical realities are faced practically in the light of God's Word. This process is particularly important in Latin America for two reasons. Creative theological enquiry has never before taken place in a situation analogous to that of Latin America today; and up until recent years theology done in Latin America has usually supported a reaction against change. Segundo emphasises, therefore, that 'interaction between social praxis and theology is the most decisive methodological factor for actual and future Latin American theology.'[6]

This means that, today, 'the only way of encountering the Christian message "de-ideologised" is to begin with reality, i.e. commitment to those exploited by the relations of production.'[7] This is a methodology already supported from within the Bible itself, for 'the only key which opens for us God's message is . . . a revolutionary commitment on behalf of the oppressed which is a biblical pre-understanding of the Bible itself.'[8] On the other hand, this will also require 'the methodological contribution of sociology'.

The use of sociology to 'de-ideologise' theology in its contact with the situation of exploitation in the Third World is likened to the methodological 'suspicion' which led Bultmann to demythologise the Gospel narratives. In fact, the importance of this hermeneutical procedure will become clear later when we demonstrate that Segundo's method is equivalent to Bultmann's, having apparently substituted Marx for Heidegger.

Nevertheless, the important difference between Bultmann's methodology and that of the theology of liberation remains. Bultmann begins from the modern existentialist analysis of 'being' in order to understand the actuality of the biblical message for existence; liberation theology begins not only from a Marxist analysis of society's structures as oppressive, but from a practical identification with a process that will change them. And this is the point where liberation theology's criticism of existentialist theology goes deeper than that of Moltmann and Metz.

The absolute priority of praxis in the theological task leads

Assmann to affirm that the theology of liberation is a 'methodological innovation', for theological reflection which today seeks
to be hermeneutically responsible cannot begin until modern
man has been historically interpreted by the human sciences.
It is also an innovation in another sense, for the Church is doing
theology from a hitherto untried situation: 'the Church has not
been born in an oppressed world.'[9]

It would not be false to liberation theology's basic concern to summarise it as a 'theology of the event' (the Latin
American equivalent of the 'theology of the signs of the times'),
the 'event' being Latin American reality. This description will
later help us to identify its characteristic hermeneutical procedure when applied to the Scriptures.

3. REVELATION AS THE STARTING POINT FOR THEOLOGICAL REFLECTION

Certain theologians, notably Assmann, consider the purity and
normativeness of revolutionary practice to be so self-evidently
true that there is little room for a contribution from biblical
revelation as the Christian's fundamental source of truth.
Others however, although they strongly criticise a methodology
which has overtones of an idealistic pre-understanding of reality
(the use of a deductive hermeneutic) are aware of the danger
of taking ideological short cuts in theology when biblical revelation is not allowed a full part in the hermeneutical process.

Segundo, in this context, criticises Assmann for failing to see
that his 'praxiological' position is just as *a priori* as the position
of those who believe it inevitable and right to take their Christian pre-understanding of reality to their revolutionary praxis.
'If the Christian contribution is hung, as it were, from a prior
revolutionary commitment, this latter appears hung, as it were,
from a correct, non-deviationary, evaluation of socio-political
praxis. One pre-understanding presupposes another. Do they
not, then, enter into a circle?'[10] As an alternative possibility,
he postulates the need to place 'the specific Christian contribution, a revolutionary commitment and a new understanding
of the evangelical message', within a hermeneutical *circle*, where
each element contributes to a correct interpretation of both
reality and the biblical message.[11]

This alternative, at least in theory, means that biblical revelation is able to make an original, and therefore critical, contribution both to the mechanisms of theological thought and to revolutionary practice. Indeed, Miranda recognises that in so far as theology is 'critical reflection on historical practice in the light of faith' it is the biblical message which must finally determine whether it is the Faith which is being talked about or some other theory. 'If there is no controllable and scientific study in depth of the Gospel message we are being arbitrary, and both conservative and revolutionary theology have an equal right to call themselves Christian.'[12]

Without this original contribution the biblical message either will not be heard at all or will be orchestrated in the interests of, at best, a partial understanding of today's reality.

Theology is a necessary mediator between faith and political commitment. Faith is reflected upon and defined within a community which seeks to hear that prophetic (and also political) word which builds the Kingdom. This community, therefore, also forms part of the hermeneutical circle, for it acts as an indispensable intermediary between the prophetic word which is heard and obeyed and any particular historical moment.

4. THE PLACE OF IDEOLOGY IN THEOLOGICAL HERMENEUTICS

In contemporary discussion the concept of ideology is being used somewhat loosely, although generally in the opposite sense to that given to it, in the last century, by Marx and Engels. For them, ideology was used as the main arm of bourgeois society to *cover over* both the real origin of capitalism, society's class structure and the misery of the proletariat: namely, capitalist ownership of the means of production. For the theologians of liberation, it is used as an arm to *uncover* the hidden theoretical resistances, especially within the Church, to revolution as an end to exploitation, oppression and dependence. Whereas Marx saw his theory as a synthesis of the real forces at work in history which sooner or later would bring about the collapse of capitalism, and ideology as the reactionary attempt to ignore or disprove the existence of such forces, the theology of liberation sees Marxism as an ideological system which lays bare the

vested interests of the present power structures, whether of the
Church or the State. By extension, the Marxist system may be
used to classify different theological methodologies according
to each one's social context.

Ideology thus becomes a hermeneutical key, both in the
interpretation of the Christian foundation-texts and in the
formulation of a new revolutionary language of faith. Every
interpretation which seeks to minimise or spiritualise the project for man's liberation in contemporary history (e.g. every
dualistic notion of salvation), is ideologically suspect for its
hidden political motivations. Yet ideology is not just a theoretical point of reference, but a theory put into practice. Thus,
theology can only be objectively 'de-ideologised' from the perspective of revolutionary practice. Only this commitment possesses the necessary force to wrench theology from its idealistic
moorings and put it to the service of a revolutionary programme.

However, ideology has its limitations as a tool for doing theology. Scannone mentions two of them.[13] Firstly, no ideology
possesses its own built-in self-justification. It cannot say why it
should be the *only* choice. Secondly, ideology works on the level
of the analysis of present social structures. In this respect it
merits consideration as an autonomous science. However, on
the question of society's future, the option is not only 'scientific,
political or technical'; a theological discernment which contem-
plates the historical movement of an integrated liberation is also
valid.

Thus theology is also capable of *uncovering* the idolatrous pretensions of absolutist ideologies. Theological hermeneutics
avails itself of a critical, revolutionary ideology, and at the same
time enters into a dialectical process with it, in order to ensure
that every future project of liberation is open-ended, pointing
towards man's total humanisation and liberty.

5. THE USE MADE OF MARXISM

According to Moncada, one of the principal results of a theological encounter held in June 1971 was a recognition of 'the
emphatic need for Marxism to contribute to the establishing of
a theological method'.[14] The extent of this contribution is evi-

denced in five important characteristics of the methodology of liberation theology.

1. The emphasis on praxis as the epistemological reference-point for all theoretical thought. Assmann, paraphrasing Marx's famous eleventh thesis on Feuerbach says, 'It is not the simple interpretation, but the transformation of the world, which occupies the central place of the theologian's concern.'[15]

2. The use of certain socio-political tools of analysis as a prerequisite in the hermeneutical task of reading the signs of the times. The refusal to accept the situation as it is, with the concomitant use of theology as an agent of conflict in the process of 'conscientisation'.

3. The use of Marxism as the most objective means of detecting and liberating every false ideology: 'The current vogue of interpreting Marxism in Latin America according to Althusser has spread the idea of historical materialism as a "science of history" which tries to free itself from all ideological elements.'[16]

4. The impulse given to the interpretation of the Christian faith in essentially prophetic terms.

5. The concept or the possibility of man being a free agent to control his future destiny in the direction of a truly human community.

PART II

SOME LEADING EXPONENTS

CHAPTER FIVE

THE GOSPEL AND IDEOLOGY

Up to this point the impression may have been given that the theology of liberation is a totally uniform system, similar shades of meaning always being given to the same concepts. Such an impression, however, would be false. Although similar areas of common interest are discussed, and a common basic theological methodology is employed, there are also, within one common framework of reference, differences of subject matter and points of view which sometimes even seem to be antagonistic.[1] In a general analysis like the present one, it is only fair to point out these differences, especially as the theology of liberation does not seek to present a monochrome position, but is rather an open-ended reflection on a changing situation.[2]

Both differences and similarities will become apparent in the following evaluation of those five (Roman Catholic) theologians who, in our opinion, are the chief protagonists of the theology of liberation and its most faithful representatives.

The subject matter of their books and articles is varied and their specialist theological fields are also different. Of the five, Assmann can be characterised as the ideologist – the one with the greatest interest in the philosophical background and implications of liberation theology.[3] Gutierrez is the systematic theologian. Segundo has dedicated a great deal of his thought to the pastoral dimensions, whilst Croatto and Miranda have contributed much to its exegetical and hermeneutical basis. Each has done creative thinking in his own right. Whilst they have undoubtedly mutually stimulated one another, they do not form a homogeneous 'school' of theology in the European sense.

Our main concern in Part II will be to discover the explicit or implicit hermeneutical procedure of each of these writers and to look at the way in which they approach or handle the Scriptures. In each case we begin with a short account of their principal concerns, and from there we analyse their own accounts of their methodological procedure.

Hugo Assmann is the first to be considered.

1. REALITY IS THE ONLY TEXT FROM WHICH TO START

We have already discussed in general terms the relation between orthodoxy and orthopraxis in a committed theological reflection, and the significance of praxis as the starting point for the theological task. Assmann has undoubtedly taken the most extreme position in this regard. It is important, therefore, to look at the particular reality about which he is concerned and what it means, hermeneutically, to begin from that alone.

In global terms, for Assmann, the overriding reality of Latin America today is that it suffers domination: 'the greatest merit of the Theology of Liberation lies, perhaps, in its insistence on the historical point of departure for its reflection: the situation of dominated [Latin] America.'[4]

In general terms, all reality is strictly political. This means that man can be interpreted only in relation to his global historical existence in society. The horizons of man's existence are drawn by his daily involvement in an historical process from which he cannot withdraw and for which he is fundamentally responsible. The meaning of his existence is totally circumscribed by his historical project: 'instead of pointing the global nature of the question "for what reason?" beyond history, man has learned to assume the question historically. He has pointed it radically inwards to his history in the world.'[5]

In more particular terms, reality is determined by two factors, the analysis of a situation and a process which is actually taking place. Assmann, developing Marcuse's insights, emphasises the imperialistic and technocratic nature of Latin America's domination: 'because of the fact that the [Third World] is now found in the context of the triumphant technification of domination-mechanisms on a world scale, the revolution in the Third World is simultaneously anti-imperialist and anti-technocratic.'[6]

The process actually taking place is the struggle for liberation. This struggle is certainly a continuation of past social revolutions, which originated in 1789 and came to their climax in 1917. However, given the differing circumstances of the Third World, inserted as an object into a history managed by the West and marked by its conflict with the communist block, 'the struggle for liberation has already overtaken the ideals of the revolutionary guidelines of 1789 and 1917.' The reason for this is that 'it embodies in itself both the struggle to secure those goods which are indispensable for a dignified human life and the struggle for man's freedom to participate at every level of social decision. It is this two-fold struggle which impresses on the primacy of the political dimension a new characteristic in Latin America.' The struggle for liberation, then, involves being engaged on two fronts: principally against all capitalist domination, but then also against the false bureaucratic corruption of the revolutionary process (exemplified, for example, by Russia) which is caused, Assmann believes, by a false confidence in the powers of technological achievement.

In the case of both the analysis and the process, reality is largely defined in negative terms. The Third World is subjected to a series of forces which it can neither control nor alter; for this reason it is both dominated and dependent. The only action open to it is to negate these forces; theoretically, by demonstrating their origin, their mechanisms and their vested interests, and practically, by resisting those internal forces (the national oligarchies) which benefit from the indefinite prolongation of the present play of economic forces.

This negative stance means that, apart from vague allusions to an autochthonous socialism, there is no definite, political-social project for the future. 'Does the rejection of one type of historical project already represent a new, different, historical project?' The answer is clearly no, for a revolution in Latin America, in order to be 'anti-developmental', must also be anti-projectoral and anti-systematic. The closed nature of the imperialist systems, even the socialist ones, makes a change of system impossible. The only hope left open for real, humanising, structural change lies therefore in the negation of the entire system.

The second point of discussion centres upon the question as to what exactly it means to begin from reality alone. Basically, for Assmann, it means the choice of those analytical instruments which alone can determine the content and form of the praxis of liberation in the sub-continent: 'there is an enormous difference between a purely descriptive analysis (which predominates in the Medellín documents) and a dialectical-structural analysis, which refers to the causes underlying the mechanics of domination: the choice of analytical instrument itself implies an ethical and political stance.'[7]

In other words, language by itself, even if it speaks of justice, exploitation, oppression, and so on, cannot give a sufficient explanation of those forces at work in modern society which continue to keep the vast majority in a state of sub-humanity. Reality is a text needing a special hermeneutical key to unlock its fundamental meaning. And at present, according to Assmann, there are only two such possible keys. There is a functionalist analysis of society which basically accepts the positive value of the capitalist system in its international phase; and a Marxist analysis based on the confrontation of classes within a society manipulated by the industrial private sector.

To understand the real mechanisms of society at the economic-political level, we have to choose between the two. The choice is an ethical one, because ultimately it is between humanity and inhumanity, between a society based on privilege and exploitation and a society based on real equality, fraternity and freedom. The reason for this ethical choice, and its meaning, even when these are in all essentials the inevitable consequence of the particular socio-analytical basis chosen, nevertheless includes, as a fact, '*an ethical element not derived from the analysis itself; man's capacity for making himself responsible for history.*'[8] This is a key quotation, summing up quite clearly Assmann's methodological point of departure which, when fully developed, produces his characteristic approach to biblical/ theological hermeneutics.

In brief, the only text from which hermeneutics may legitimately begin is reality, not in a 'chemically pure' state (as Assmann himself would say of theology), but interpreted in terms of a certain *a priori* way of looking at man in history. Because this point fundamentally affects the way the Christian texts are used, we shall develop it later in more detail.

2. THE DILEMMA OF A THEOLOGY OF LIBERATION

Because of Assmann's almost totally one-sided epistemological emphasis, it has been hard for him to explain adequately the meaning and relevance of theological reflection for the praxis of liberation.

His cataclysmic 'de-ideologising' programme has left him without even a minimal content for faith, as one of the reference points for theological reflection. Or, put in another way, his concern to see theology as a genuine reflection on reality, historically mediated, has led him to insert so many intermediary steps between theology as a reflection on faith and theology as a reflection on the praxis of liberation, that the content of faith has almost disappeared. As a consequence, the specific nature of Christianity as a world-view, with an irreducible message addressed to every age, is seriously questioned.

It is to Assmann's credit that he is aware of this dilemma and has tried to grapple with it. In the first place, it is hardly necessary to emphasise that Assmann is not interested in theoretical answers. The specific contribution of Christian theology to liberation is in terms of the quality of its practical commitment to what Assmann describes as the 'only historical process of liberation in Latin America'.[9] Nevertheless, revolutionary practice requires revolutionary theory, and Assmann is almost convinced that Marxism, in spite of its penetrating dialectical-structural analysis of society, cannot finally supply this: 'a truly historical reading of the Bible, particularly of the message of Christ, leads to a whole series of radical questions to which Marxism has not paid sufficient attention.' He mentions the radical alienation of death as the most important of these questions.[10]

Although Assmann entirely dismisses theological thought as an adequate instrument for analysing reality, since it possesses no *a priori* basis from which to function in this respect, he is prepared to concede that it may contribute something to the question of how the only praxis of liberation should be carried out. It has nothing to say about the point of departure but something to say about the journey. The distinction between the Christian and the simple humanist ought not to be looked for, of course, in a separation of tasks for the humanisation of history, but rather in an excess of intensity and critical ability in the liberating commitment; not in the criteria of simple doctrinal orthodoxy, but in the criteria of orthopraxis.

In other words, theology is a useful exercise as long as it enables a Christian to deepen his commitment to the radically historical task of humanisation. Here, so it seems to me, Assmann follows the insistence of Moltmann and Metz that the Christian faith's radical commitment to the historical process enables it to challenge every ideology or process which deflects history from its consummation in a radically new order.[11] This is what Assmann means when he talks about a 'unique Christian project'. 'The existence of criteria for making human experience more historical, criteria of a constant and wholly-human liberation, derived from Judaism and Christianity, continues to be valid, and can hardly be found with such force in other revolutionary texts.'[12]

Summarising, we can point to a still unresolved conflict in Assmann's epistemology. On the one hand, he wants to be able to say that there is a specific Christian contribution to the praxis of liberation, which in some way, is deducible from the primary texts of the Christian faith: 'Isn't theology trying to speak from the basis of the gospels, of revelation, of the essence of Christianity...?' On the other hand, he categorically denies that there is a specific, a priori, Christian starting point which is essentially different from any other contribution: 'Isn't theology trying to speak ... at the same time from the secular sciences, elevating their data as prime facts and indispensable sources of reference,' relating itself to these as an indispensable point of departure? There is no such thing as a 'Christianity in itself' which is not mediated through an historical analysis of actual reality.[13]

3. THE HERMENEUTICAL PROCEDURE

Assmann does not find it easy to establish valid hermeneutical guidelines in order, as he says, 'to bring together interpretations of present-day reality and a discovery of relevant criteria in the history of Judaeo-Christianity.' Indeed, he believes that one of the two greatest gaps in liberation theology is in the field of hermeneutics; the other is Christology. We would agree. However, in spite of the essential difficulties presented by Assmann's 'praxiological' methodology, he is well aware of the need for an adequate hermeneutic if 'a critical reflection upon man's historical praxis is going to be theological'. The search for this hermeneutic accompanies his whole theological discussion.

The hermeneutical question is neatly posed in the statement by Gutierrez that 'a critical reflection upon man's historical praxis will be theological in so far as in this praxis it detects the presence of the Christian faith.' This must mean, at the least, that 'Christian faith' or the near-equivalents 'gospel', 'revelation', have some detectable reference-points. For Assmann the reference-points are the Bible and the Church's historical confessions.

However, no sooner does Assmann admit this than he begins to qualify the meaning of 'reference-point'. The detection of the Christian faith is to be understood typologically (i.e. as a distinguishing sign) and not in an exclusive sense. There are two separate, but carefully interrelated reasons for this. Firstly, the only exclusive reference-point is actual reality. This is the text; this contains the first word. Secondly, 'the Bible is not a direct text full of criteria, but rather the history of successive configurations of these criteria, always partial, dialectically conflicting amongst themselves.' This means that, in practice, we cannot bring to theological reflection conceptual realities which, in themselves, can be used as *a priori* points of comparison.

In the light of this strong initial caution, it is scarcely surprising that Assmann never engages in any real textual exegesis of the Bible. In this he is unique amongst the chief protagonists of the theology of liberation. Nevertheless, he does allude to biblical exegesis. He quotes serious exegetical studies as a corrective to immediate and superficial applications of the Scripture to today's reality and he talks of making the biblical texts speak.[14]

The central hermeneutical problem is precisely how to make the biblical texts speak in such a way that, on the one hand, they are not used as simple ideological legitimation, and on the other, they contribute their subversive language of liberation to the global processes actually under way. In order to resolve this problem satisfactorily, it is necessary to reject the classical hermeneutical procedure. This procedure, according to

Assmann, seeks to begin exclusively from the biblical data, and to work from there to some kind of contemporary application. However, this method fails to take into account either the need for the biblical message to be historically mediated today through scientific data, or the urgency of today's praxis of liberation. In a word, it is a hermeneutical procedure without a hermeneutical key.

In order to explain the meaning of this fundamental criticism he compares the hermeneutical procedure of Metz to that which he believes is characteristic of the theology of liberation. For Metz, it is necessary to take into consideration the historical foundation of the global society in order to arrive at a satisfactory political ethic of change. This can be done only by using an adequate 'hermeneutic' of past texts. The key concept of this ethic is the 'dangerous memory', which is discoverable only through a careful interpretative investigation of the past. This in turn can be carried out only by separating oneself, as objectively as possible, from any false present influences which may betray the hermeneutical task. For Assmann, hermeneutical methodology should pursue an opposite course. The why and the wherefore of a political ethic can be decided only on the basis of a structural analysis of the present. This is also the only perspective from which the past can be adequately interpreted. 'There is no manoeuvering to try to separate oneself from the ambiguity of praxis. For, is it not the contextual hermeneutic of action, in the concreteness of today, which really interests us? This is not the same as the hermeneutic of historical elements from the past...'15

So Assmann falls back on present reality as the primary text which needs to be clarified before we can successfully measure the Bible's contribution to present praxis. However, the rejection of one kind of hermeneutic does not automatically produce another. What Assmann wants to do is reasonably clear. It is 'to reflect upon present historical practice and rescue, for its sake, significant processes of praxis from the Jewish-Christian past.' How to do this still remains an enigma.

The first step, evidently, is to discover the right hermeneutical key. This key, as we have already had reason to suspect, is a revolutionary theory which comes to us in the language of liberation.16 It is only this language, the result of a particular historical praxis, which can liberate biblical hermeneutics from 'hidden ideological positions'. The language enables us to arrive at an 'effective historical hermeneutic whose centre of concern is actual history, and not simply history of the past, of the Word of God'. This hermeneutic might well be called a 'hermeneutic of liberation'.

This hermeneutic of liberation, whose content is decided by the scientific analysis of modern society, is then used as the key for a 'second reading' of the Bible (it being understood that a 'first' reading cannot supply us with any form of biblical or primitive Christianity). 'Man's capacity to "listen" to the challenges of his history gives him an intuition of what others have previously "listened" to in the same radical historical way. Then he lays himself open to revelation.' Conversely, 'what others have listened to', expressed at the deep level of symbols and myths, becomes concrete only in the light of today's revelation.

If the theology of liberation is critical reflection on historical practice in the light of faith, the hermeneutics of liberation is critical reflection on historical documents in the light of present reality. The sources do not speak on their own. 'They have to be "made to speak", even as texts, through the secular sciences.'[17] The perspective from which it is possible to read Christian sources anew, in a significant way, is determined by the situation and choice of the one who reads, every reading being, of necessity, also an ideological-political reading.

This means that the verification of a correct hermeneutical procedure cannot depend on criteria which are extracted from the sources themselves, but solely on the concrete historical mediation of love, understood politically. It cannot be stressed too strongly that Assmann has turned classical hermeneutics upside down. There is only one history – present day history, and only one interpretation of that history – the Marxist one.

As we noted earlier, Assmann is not directly interested in the concrete content of the Bible, or exegetical methodology, or the challenge of the biblical message to today's reality. On at least two occasions, however, he shows the way in which he uses biblical symbols in order 'to recuperate a dimension of truth about the earlier language, the dimension of praxis' and to discover 'the original intentions of the Christian sources, coincidental with the practical, original purposes of the myths'.

In the first place, he examines the idea of the people of God. From the perspective of present reality in itself, we may not talk in exclusivist terms of a 'history of salvation' with its point of articulation in the Jewish-Christian experience of history as the history of the election and liberation of a special people. Rather, we must speak of 'general salvation-history' or the 'salvation of history'. The biblical base for this would be the 'one and only salvific plan of creation and redemption in Christ ... the omnipresence of the mystery of Christ through the wide span of evolving history'. And from the perspective of 'general salvation-history', 'the people of God is the whole of humanity'. The people of God, in the sense of Israel the Church, is only of secondary importance. It is a body conscious of the one history of the world, which purpose it is called to serve, but not to identify with its own existence and future.

In the second place, he takes the cross of Christ as 'the symbol-reality of love's final fulfilment' and shows how this, interpreted from the perspective of love as politically efficacious, both interprets and motivates the most profound liberating praxis. But the perspective of present 'reality in itself' demands 'that the theology of the Cross be liberated from its alienating mystifications' (for example, the interpretation of the Cross in terms of reconciliation, void of conflict) in order to give back to the *man* Jesus the integrity of his human condition and to his *death, the historical and political dimension which it had,* in order, from that point, to rediscover, in the light of challenges not yet understood, that which is hidden within the Christian symbols of the New Testament'.[18]

CHAPTER SIX

A NEW THEOLOGY AND
A NEW FUNCTION

I. THE NEW TASK FOR THEOLOGY

The theology of liberation is careful to distinguish itself from the political theology currently being written in Europe. Certainly, it shares with the latter the rejection of all political theologies where the political reflection has been merely tagged on to the gospel as an appendage in response to the pressure of a particular and passing fashion. Rather, the so-called political dimension is a factor which springs necessarily from the interior of the gospel itself. The gospel is political in the total structure of its message.[1]

Nevertheless, in reply to a question about the difference between the theology of liberation and the theology of revolution, Gutierrez replies:

The Theology of Liberation does not intend so much to justify a commitment as to reflect upon the faith as it is lived by a committed Christian. Thus, as it attempts this reflection it plays a critical role from within the commitment. The Theology of Liberation tries to be a theological vision which arises *after* a certain amount of commitment. The Theology of Liberation has been concerned to restate the problem of the theological task: what does it mean to do theology? In the Theology of Revolution it is not like that. This latter starts out from principles which it applies to the political sphere. What the Theology of Liberation tries to do is the exact opposite, begin from a faith lived out in a commitment and reflect upon that. It is for this reason that it puts the methodological question: how should theology be done?[2]

Summarising this difference, which is fundamental for an understanding of the biblical hermeneutics of the theology of liberation, Gutierrez states: 'the Theology of Liberation offers us not so much a new theme for reflection, as a *new way* to do theology.' And the methodology of this new way is compressed into a succinct statement, which again reminds us of Marx's famous eleventh thesis on Feuerbach, that it is 'a theology which does not stop with reflecting on the world, but rather tries to be part of the process through which the world is transformed'.[3]

Gutierrez is not so polemically critical of European theology as is Assmann. Nevertheless, he is just as clear that the Latin American situation calls for a radical rethinking of the whole universal task of theology: 'Another fundamental difference ... is that the Theology of Liberation tries to be a theology of salvation in the concrete historical circumstances lived out in Latin America. For this reason it insists on the relationship between the three different levels, aspects or dimensions of the process of liberation.'[4] The theology of liberation then, is a theology done 'in a Latin American perspective'.

In order to understand more fully the new task which Gutierrez proposes for theology we need to explore in more depth the reasons for these differences.

European political theology springs from the accumulative effects of the industrial and technological revolutions, the result of man's domination of nature through the natural sciences. The positive result of this process is that 'contemporary man has acquired the consciousness that he is capable of radically modifying the conditions of his life and has clearly and stimulatingly affirmed his freedom with regard to nature.'[5] The negative result is that man has been progressively replaced by the machine. And this result has created the so-called 'reserve industrial army', an increasing mass of marginal peoples not reabsorbed into the system. This, in turn, has tended to sharpen the already glaring contradictions within advanced modern societies.

On the other hand the French Revolution, which historically coincided with the beginning of the modern, scientific revolution, 'represented the experience of the possibility of a profound transformation of the existing social order ... As in the former case [the domination of nature] we are confronted with a new affirmation of man's freedom, this time it is in relation to his social organisation ... But this democratic structure of society, in order to be real, presupposes just economic conditions ...'[6]

In this way we can trace briefly the scientific, social and

political consciousness of Europe over the last two hundred years. Theology, naturally, has had to respond to the anti-religious challenge inherent in this consciousness, a challenge which has led, as Gutierrez notes, to the fact that a good deal of contemporary theology seems to have set out from the challenge of the *non-believer*. Moreover, the new political theology has arisen partly as a response to the actual crisis of confidence and expectation with regard to the future, caused mainly by over-confidence in the ability of technical planning to solve all of man's pressing problems.

The Latin American consciousness, however, is notably different: 'In a continent like Latin America the challenge does not come in the first place from the non-believer but from the *non-man* . . . The non-man does not question so much our religious world, as our *economic, social political and cultural world*.' 'The question, then, will not be how to speak about God in an adult world but how to announce him as Father in a non-human world.'[7]

The answer to this latter question will spring from a third consciousness which, perhaps, only man in the Third World possesses to any strong degree. 'To transform history necessarily presupposes the simultaneous transformation of both nature and society. In this transforming praxis there is more than a consciousness of the meaning of economic activity or political action, there is a new manner of *being man* in history.'[8] In other words, theological reflection in Latin America has to be done from a subversive liberating praxis which is committed to struggle for the transformation of the *non-man* (those who suffer misery and exploitation) into the *new man*.[9] In concrete terms the function of theology is to act as a mediator between a new way of living one's faith and its communication; it is to reformulate the gospel message from the praxis of liberation which implies 'reflecting upon a truth which is done, and not only affirmed.'[10]

Finally, theology, in so far as it is a rationale of a faith lived out in a praxis of liberation, needs to avail itself of certain scientific instruments of analysis which will enable it to penetrate more profoundly into the *origins* of that reality in which faith today is inevitably incarnated. Only then will it be able to contribute to the process of transformation. This latter must be seen as the future justification of all theological thought in Latin America. 'If theological reflection does not vitalise the action of the Christian community in the world by making its commitment to charity fuller and more radical, if ... it does not lead the Church to be on the side of the oppressed classes ... it will have been of little value.'[11]

2. LIBERATION IS SALVATION ON VARIOUS LEVELS

One of the chief tasks of the theology of liberation for Gutierrez is to reflect on the relationship between salvation and the historical process of man's liberation.

Salvation is the key concept which explains the work of Christ as liberation. The biblical message of salvation provides a reference point for an interpretation of the signs of the times in terms of conflict in human history.

Liberation is the key concept which identifies the process through which history must pass in order to be rid of its conflicts and contradictions. It is the radical removal of all causes of alienation which prevent man from being fully man.

Man's liberation is one united process, for history is one and indivisible. Nevertheless, it occurs at different levels of man's history.

It occurs at the level of man's socio-economic and political life. Man needs not only to be free from economic and political dependence, but to free himself. The consciousness of his situation leads man to protest against it. But man has not reached his status as free man until he is able to forge a new society which will be free from every alienation and servitude: 'through the dialectical process man constructs himself and attains a real awareness of his own being; he liberates himself in the acquisition of genuine freedom which through work transforms the world and educates man'.[12] This is what Gutierrez calls *external* liberation.

Liberation also occurs at the level of man's psychic life. Man needs to be free from the internal conflicts which have been analysed and catalogued in the Freudian notion of repression. As in the first level of liberation, becoming aware of the situation is a major step in the conquest of freedom. This is what Gutierrez calls *internal* liberation.

Finally, liberation occurs at the level of man's root problem, sin. Man needs to be free, by God's grace, from a fundamental alienation. Sin, for Gutierrez, is 'absence of brotherhood and love in relationships among men, the breach of friendship with God and with other men, and, therefore an interior, personal fracture'.[13] Freedom from this root alienation is the condition for the integration of exterior and interior liberation.

It is true that Gutierrez emphasises the deep-rooted and objectively-structured nature of sin, salvation from which is a *sine qua non* of any kind of liberation. Therefore we must accept, at least at the level of intention, the desire to integrate liberation from sin with political and other human liberations. Nevertheless, in his exposition of liberation Gutierrez very rarely goes beyond the external liberation, summed up in the reconciliation of man with man through a new and just ordering of society's structures. Even when he does mention radical sin, he sets it in the context of its political manifestations and its conquest by man through 'all struggle against exploitation and alienation, in a history which is fundamentally one, [which] is an attempt to vanquish selfishness, the negation of love.'[14]

In spite of developments in his thinking, Gutierrez still has to explore in depth the fundamental relationship between Christ's once-for-all salvation and the historical process of liberation. Part of his difficulty, in our opinion, is that he has not yet seen clearly the dilemma inherent in the championing of man as the free agent of his history. In part, it is the methodological problem of his hermeneutical procedure.

3. MAN'S DILEMMA AS A FREE AGENT OF HISTORY

Together with Gutierrez's emphatic denial of all dualism, an obsession which tends to blind him to the opposite perils of a monistic position, there is his confidence that man is ultimately the agent for the free transformation of his social and political structures. Certain quotations, taken from different parts of his major work, will make his position clear:

> What is at stake . . . is the possibility of enjoying a truly human existence, a free life, a dynamic liberty which is related to history as a conquest.

Man gradually takes hold of the reins of his own destiny. He looks ahead and turns towards a society in which he will be free of all alienation and servitude.

In the current statement of the problem, one fact is evident: the social praxis of contemporary man has begun to reach maturity. It is the behaviour of man ever more conscious of being an active subject of history...

The Latin American, by participating in his own liberation, gradually is taking hold of the reins of his historical initiative and perceiving himself as master of his own destiny.

The liberation of our continent means ... in a deeper sense, to see the becoming of mankind as a process of the emancipation of man in history. It is to see man in search of a qualitatively different society in which he will be ... the artisan of his own destiny.[15]

One may ask why this should be a dilemma for Gutierrez. Clearly, it would not be so for a strictly Marxist interpretation of the role of the proletariat in shaping a new society of freedom and equality. But Gutierrez is writing a theology of liberation, not a sociology of liberation, and in this role, from a position of faith, he is convinced that 'theology never uses a rational tool without criticising and modifying it ... If theology modifies the rational tool ... it does it because faith itself speaks about man ... To speak about a science as something totally independent from a committed person, or from present faith, seems to me naive.'[16] In other words, Christian faith reveals something about man which is true, but inaccessible to sociological analysis. It reveals the presence of a power in man which seems to frustrate every project for self-liberation, in which man finds himself caught, even in modern revolutionary processes, in a vicious circle which turns newly-won freedoms into new kinds of tyranny. It also reveals a scheme of salvation, in which the basic problem of sin is solved only by the free gift of Christ.

Nevertheless, in discussing the relationship between man's responsibility for effecting change (temporal progress) and Christ's gift of salvation (the growth of the kingdom), Gutierrez almost always opts for the first as the best explanation of the mystery of liberation in history. In this respect he criticises the

Church's Social Encyclicals, because they 'block the question about the ultimate meaning of man's action in history'. He further speaks of 'the liberating and protagonist role of man, the lord of creation and co-participant in his own salvation ... Only the concept of the mediation of man's self-creation in history can lead us to an accurate and fruitful understanding of the relationships between creation and redemption.'[17]

Gutierrez seems to find a possible solution to the dilemma in Christ's incarnation in the oppressed. Here we shall merely place alongside each other two quotations, and, in Chapter 11, follow up Gutierrez' line of thought.

> It is the poor who must be the protagonists of their own liberation.[18]

> There is neither substitution nor representation but rather identification between Christ and the poor.[19]

4. THE HERMENEUTICAL PROCEDURE

It is evident, from Gutierrez' writings, that he is aware of the hermeneutical problem raised by liberation theology's new methodology. He places the debate within the context of the relationship between faith and reason which, in its turn, gives rise to the epistemological question of the theory of knowledge.

The general problem can be stated in terms of the point of departure for theological reflection: 'From what place does the theologian speak? For what reason and for whom does he speak?' The particular problem can be stated in terms of which tools are to be used to mediate between the gospel and present reality. On the one hand, the basic task of theology is to inquire into the meaning of God's Word for us in today's history, i.e. to return to the source of revelation in order to place all pastoral action in the widest possible context. On the other hand, theology must be on the look-out for new rational structures in order to discover new ways of reformulating the Word. The difficulty lies in the fact that the gospel can be heard only from a particular historical perspective, which is inevitably mediated to us through the use of certain analytical tools. Yet this gospel cannot be identified with any one method of analysing society nor with any one philosophical perspective concerning man, because in its own light, as a liberating message, it performs its own permanently creative and critical task.

Although Gutierrez is aware of the hermeneutical problem, he has not given it much systematic attention. For this reason we run the risk, in giving only a brief summary of what appears implictly or explicitly to be his general line of thought on the subject, of simplifying or even misrepresenting his position.

With this risk in mind, we can detect two lines of approach which Gutierrez has not yet really brought together. They reflect his dual concern both for the coming of the Kingdom and for the transformation of society; both of which he is concerned to integrate, if not to identify, in the one unitary, cosmic liberation which Christ brings. The principal hermeneutical problem is the relationship 'between the Kingdom of God and the building up of the world ... The task of contemporary theology is to elucidate the current state of these problems, drawing with sharper lines the terms in which they are expressed.'[20]

The first line of approach is that which is characteristic of liberation theology in general: all hermeneutics begin from the Christian's commitment to eliminate poverty and oppression. In the participation in the process of liberation there will be heard 'nuances of the Word of God which are imperceptible in other existential situations.' 'Exegesis of the Word, to which theology desires to contribute, is done from within the facts.'

This is the negation of the type of hermeneutics which, beginning from biblical or theological principles, seeks, as a second step, to apply them to praxis. In Gutierrez' scheme the third step of theology, 'critical reflection on praxis', governs the first two, namely 'theology as wisdom' and 'theology as rational knowledge'.[21]

This first approach means, therefore, in terms of the task of biblical exegesis, that we must 'reformulate the gospel message for our contemporaries' and for the Church. Gutierrez does not concern himself much with formal exegesis, but where he does so, he gives us some idea of how his hermeneutical procedure affects the transmission of the text to our cultural reality. Two examples of this would be: (a) his use of the Exodus narrative; (b) his extended treatment of the Parable of the Last Judgment. At this stage we shall mention only the results of the procedure. Later, in Part III, we shall describe the process.

a. *The Exodus*

'The memory of the Exodus pervades the pages of the Bible, and inspires one to reread often the Old as well as the New Testament.' The Exodus experience is paradigmatic for two reasons.

Firstly, the work of Christ is both part of this re-interpretation and also its perfection and fulfilment. Secondly, the relevance and actuality of the Exodus are underlined by the fact that God's people today are passing through similar experiences. The work of Christ, as the interpretation and fulfilment of Israel's liberation ('a liberation from sin and from all its consequences: despoliation, injustice, hatred'), creates 'a new chosen people, which this time includes all humanity. Our experiences, being in a direct continuum with those of the Hebrews in Egypt, permit us to see that the new people are those who today are oppressed (economically, politically, culturally) and struggle to become free.

In this brief attempt at a hermeneutical re-interpretation, Gutierrez considers that 'the liberation from Egypt linked to and even coinciding with creation, adds an element of capital importance: the need and the place of man's active participation in the building of society.'[22]

This final conclusion does not spring from a direct reading of the text, but from a new interpretation of the Exodus motif based on a new pre-understanding of the meaning of Christ's universal work of salvation in the historical process of man.

b. *The Last Judgment*

After an extended exegetical study of the passage Matthew 25.31–46, with attention to the principal commentators, Gutierrez concludes that there are three principal emphases in the parable: 'the stress on communion and brotherhood as the ultimate meaning of human life; the insistence on a love which is manifested in concrete actions, with "doing" being favoured over simple "knowing"; and the revelation of the human mediation necessary to reach the Lord'. By a further process of deduction, Gutierrez arrives at the conclusion that these principal emphases can become effective and meaningful today only in a concrete commitment of love within the world of poverty and exploitation. Firstly, it is possible to encounter

Jesus Christ only in the poor and down-trodden, those with whom he has been pleased to identify himself in a special way and secondly, 'to offer food or drink in our day is a political action; it means the transformation of a society structured to benefit a few who appropriate to themselves the value of the work of others'.[23] These conclusions likewise spring from a reformulation of the gospel from within our praxis.

Gutierrez' second line of approach to the hermeneutical problem appears to contradict the first. It is probably true that the contradiction is more apparent than real. Nevertheless, there is greater emphasis on allowing the biblical faith, as this is exegetically discovered, to speak its unique message to the present situation without any *a priori* claim to a special illumination and avoiding the temptation of an easy harmonisation of the biblical text with today's reality.

The key statement in this approach comes after an extended discussion of the relationship between the historical Jesus and his political environment. The discussion begins with a warning that the task of revising the presupposition that Jesus was apolitical has to be undertaken 'without forcing the facts in terms of our current concerns. If we wished to discover in Jesus the least characteristic of a contemporary political militant ... we would deprive ourselves of what his life and witness have that is deep and universal and, therefore, valid and concrete for today's man'.[24] In this quotation Gutierrez appears to be using a hermeneutic which unashamedly argues from the universal to the particular, from principles to actual cases.

At the end of his discussion of the question of Jesus' relationship to the Zealots, Gutierrez concludes that 'the deep human impact and the social transformation that the Gospel entails is permanent and essential because it transcends the narrow limits of specific historical situations and goes to the very root of human existence: the relationship with God in solidarity with other men.' In Gutierrez's first approach, such a statement would be out of the question for it would be impossible to understand the 'essential' nature of the gospel except from a particular historical situation as a necessary mediation. The quotation finishes by expressing in even stronger language the unique political content of the gospel which is discoverable apart from any particular modern commitment: 'The gospel does not get its political dimension from one or another particular option, but from the very nucleus of its message.'[25]

The fact that Gutierrez is here proposing a different kind of hermeneutic can be verified by the fact that his disagreement with Cullmann[26] is of a different order from that earlier made with respect to Metz.[27] With Cullmann there is a disagreement about how to understand the biblical text exegetically. With Metz there is a disagreement, arising from an ideological split, about theological hermeneutics in general.

5. THE PRAXIS OF A NEW 'PASTORAL' FOR LATIN AMERICA

Of all the main protagonists of a theology of liberation, Segundo is probably the one most concerned with the radical renovation of the structures and practice of the Latin American Church: 'Segundo, in contrast to other theologians ... shows a great interest in the "internal life" of the Church and proposes a concrete alternative to traditional pastoral practice.'[28] The reason for this is that Segundo believes that a 'new' Church has a vital role to play in God's design for the humanisation (or hominisation, a term he borrows from Teilhard de Chardin) of the whole creation.

Because the Church, ultimately, is the only organism which can act as a catalyst and permanent symbol of all true paths to final salvation (liberation), its renewal is a pressing necessity. It can fulfil these functions only when it maintains itself faithfully as one pole of what Segundo calls history's 'entire dialectical process'. This process is a constant struggle between two opposing forces: mankind's 'majority tendency' which looks for easy and short term solutions to its problems and the 'minority tendency' which looks for richer and more creative syntheses on a long-term basis.

The Church's supreme function is to represent the more difficult path of the richer syntheses which alone lead to real and *permanent* transformations of society. At the end of the fifth and last book in his series, *A Theology for Artisans of a New Humanity*, Segundo summarises his thought in this way: Christ 'did not set up his Church as a community "alongside" the human community, as a parallel community dispensed from the latter's concern to move evolution forward and to arrive at the creation of a more human society... The gospel expects the Christian community to perform a function (within the entire dialectical process) that is equivalent to one of the two poles of this dialectic: the minority one.'[29] Without a profound change of consciousness and practice, the present Church has no chance of playing this role, because throughout its history on the Latin American continent it has allied itself with the opposite pole of the dialectical process, namely the majority one.

In *Latin American Pastoral Action: its hidden motives*, Segundo analyses the Church's traditional stance and attitudes and proposes some far-reaching changes. The Church, by not concerning itself with the personal commitment of faith of its individual members, has allowed itself to be dominated by the idea of the closed religious society, fruit of the theocratic notions of the Church's original expansion in Latin America. This attitude has developed into a pastoral practice which has basically been concerned to preserve the faithful against loss of faith in the Church as the vehicle of salvation, due to the pressures of change in society. Segundo is convinced that it is this concern, rather than an innately conservative political stance, which has led the Church to ally itself so often with those political authorities which have guaranteed the inviolability of both its institutions and moral teachings.[30]

However, Segundo also shows that this practice has been totally superseded by the advent of the consumer society which fundamentally questions the monolithic claim of any human institution to possess the whole truth. A further characteristic of the consumer society is 'the making private and, finally, the relativising of all radical values and options.'[31] For this reason, if the Church is not to lose its members for lack of a personal, intelligent conviction, it must alter its pastoral programme to form members 'who are ready ... victoriously to undergo contact with other ideas and concepts of life.'[32]

But there is a second aspect of the consumer society which gives added urgency to the change of pastoral practice in the Church. When all values and commitments are private and relative, in the interests of maintaining the unity and inviolability of the consumer society, the effect is to maintain the *status quo* and to silence the voice of those who believe that the present structures of society are unjust. 'The very nature of the means and function of mass-communication is to place itself at the service of consumer majorities and not of *ideological minorities.*' In other words, the vast majority of modern societies, even when they are not able to avail themselves of the consumer society's goods, are exploited by its ideals and in its interests. These interests are class interests and thus the blatant injustices and oppression which they bring can be removed only through class struggle. The 'silent majority', largely unaware of the fact that it is being used in the interest of a small group of powerful and rich people, constitutes one of the poles of history's entire dialectical process. The opposite pole is not only, nor in Latin America most importantly, the Marxist, for 'There is a "conscientisation" which is brought to pass in the name of the gospel.'[33]

The Church in Latin America, if it is to change from a majority to a minority institution, needs to be re-evangelised. The purpose of evangelism, then, will be precisely to bring people to a personal and heroic faith, which has social significance because it is committed to the global transformation of society. The theology of liberation has arisen to help stimulate, orientate and advance this vital task of evangelisation which will once for all remove from the Church its *'psychological* fear ... when confronted with freedom, its *theological* fear for the salvation of the unprotected masses, and its *pastoral* fear of being unable to attract men with nothing else but the Gospel.'[34]

6. THE 'SALVATION OF HISTORY' AND THE 'ENTIRE DIALECTICAL PROCESS'

Segundo's theological thought belongs within the general framework of liberation theology. Nevertheless, he introduces other, unique elements which make his thought rather more subtle and, as a consequence, more difficult to synthesise.[35]

One of these elements is the influence of Teilhard de Chardin.[36] One might describe Segundo's theological thought as the result of a creative synthesis between Teilhard's evolutionist, Christophanic vision of the world, and the Latin American

Church's pressing need to be wholly at the service of a dialectical process of change which will lead to greater justice and solidarity among men.

It would seem, therefore, that the foundation of his entire thought is the Teilhardian concept of evolution. Every aspect of his thought is built into this framework. He takes over from Teilhard three paramount ideas.[37] The first of these ideas is that the Church is the self-consciously 'Christified' portion of the world. This means that, as the extension of Christ, it represents the firstfruits of the whole creation. Secondly, the entire universe is, from its beginning, Christified. It thus follows an evolutionary pattern which is always initiating new and higher evolutionary cycles. This pattern progressively opens itself up to the plenitude of Christ's life and love, already inherent within its movement. Thirdly, the Christification (or recapitulation in Christ) of the entire universe passes through the Church, which is the spiritual or Christic pole of the ascending spiral of hominisation.

Now, the anthropocentric, optimistic philosophy of history which pervades all Teilhard's writings can, without too much difficulty, be synthesised with the Marxist, eschatological vision of man as the creative subject of his ultimately free historical process.[38]

What Segundo has borrowed principally from Marx is his analysis of the evolutionary process as conflictive and dialectical. This scarcely occurs in Teilhard who, according to Segundo (following P. Roqueplo, *Expérience du Monde: expérience de Dieu?*) found the language of biology, which speaks in scientific terms of 'trajectory, convergence and structure' incompatible with the language of revelation, which speaks in terms of sin and guilt.[39] However, Segundo finds in Teilhard's writings an allowance for evil in the principle of loss or destruction: 'What is gained on one side is lost on the other. Nothing is built except at the price of an equivalent destruction.' In other words, the richer syntheses, needed by the evolutionary process, are gained only by the equivalent destruction of immediate solutions which, in turn, respond to a deterministic rather than a dialectical concept of progress.

Segundo makes an unqualified transposition from the biological to the moral-theological plane when he says that 'egotism, sin and enslavement to the world and the flesh make up the negative vector of evolution. This is the obstacle that evolution must overcome so that what is new and positive can make its way to complete fulfilment, i.e. to its recapitulation in Christ.'[40]

Sin is defined, then, as anything and everything which hinders the upward progress of human history towards full humanisation in Christ. It must be removed; man must be freed from its weight and destruction. On the other hand, within the evolutionary, ascending concept of human history, sin is also a negative inevitability without which 'a new synthesis, qualitatively different and superior', would be impossible. The evolutionist concept concludes that guilt is no more than one error in an ever-increasing movement. The satanic element in the Gospels is revealed not so much as an independent evil power as the negative, but necessary, basis in order that God's humanising power may bring the whole process to completion. 'The sin with which the New Testament is familiar is ... that brand of egotism in which the richer, less immediate synthesis is sacrificed in favour of the more immediate, impoverished syntheses.'[41]

Salvation can be understood only within the context of sin and evil, defined as the negative pole of an inevitable, upward process of history. Segundo defines salvation, made possible by Christ's gracious, spontaneous act of self-sacrifice, as freedom from every kind of evil force. It is a salvation universal in its scope, intra-worldly in its effects and progressive in its outworking.[42]

Each of these aspects of salvation is related to the Church's role in the entire dialectical process of 'the salvation of history'. Although total and absolute salvation is a process in which the whole of humanity is involved, there is a sense in which salvation without the Church is not possible. This is so, because salvation is granted only to those who open themselves freely and effortlessly to the one who saves, Jesus Christ. For only the person who accepts salvation as a free gift, not available through law keeping, can work effectively for those higher syntheses which keep the evolutionary process from capitulating to the pressures of majority structures.

In other words, the Church, as the body of those who are

aware of the universal process of Christification and are consciously working to bring it about, comprises the only group of people who have responded to that dynamic of grace which makes evolution into a process of ever-increasing love and upbuilding.

The nub of Segundo's synthesis of Teilhard's evolutionism and Marx's dialectic, within the perspective of a theology of liberation, is the distinction he makes between a deterministic and a dialectical evolution. He criticises Teilhard for not seeing the conflictive nature of the process and Marx for not seeing its complexity.[43] The difference between determinism and dialectics is the difference between the 'mass-orientated' and the 'minority' stance with regard to what Segundo calls 'salvation in the dominion of time', that is, a 'political maturity' which 'will entail putting all the elements of the universe in the service of the humanisation process. It will mean gradually stripping them of their determinant character in both the physical and moral sense, so that they can be put in the service of liberty.'[44]

It is at this point that Segundo disagrees with what he regards as the more mechanistic views of Assmann with regard to the relationship between personal Christian commitment and the change of structures.[45] The Church must realise that its commitment to the changing of structures is through a critical, complex, long-term and minority stance which rejects the 'messianic' role of the masses on the one hand, and the tendency to the absolutisation of structures on the other, for both are the fruit of a deterministic philosophy of history or, to use the Johannine terminology, of the *kosmos* as an impenetrable circle.

Segundo's evaluation of his own position is that 'a kind of symbiosis between Christianity as a minority position and Marxism as the science of the leadership of the masses is one of the most important pastoral facts of Latin American Christianity'.[46] Salvation of the evolutionary process from the threat of destructive forces will be possible only as history is kept open by the creative force of Christians, under the control of the spontaneity and unpredictability of grace, acting as a group with a determinedly minority orientation.

7. THE HERMENEUTICAL PROCEDURE[47]

Because the Christian Church is the conscious part of the evolutionary process which, by a dialectical struggle against short-term, majority solutions, seeks to put itself at the disposal of creative solutions leading to full humanisation, it will need to use biblical hermeneutics as one tool in this struggle. 'The Church is a whole community which, under the guidance of the Holy Spirit, should unceasingly be about the work of creatively translating the message, *spoken* in different circumstances, in terms of the problems that are posed today by human beings who are subjects of history.'[48]

This creative translation, or re-interpretation, of a word spoken in a *particular history of salvation* to the problems of a *general salvation history* is made partly possible by the word spoken today in God's final incarnation within the Church. We are discovering the word within us, through which Christ is today communicating his good news concerning our history, in order to fill it with meaning.[49]

It is made more obviously possible by the conscious discovery of an adequate hermeneutical key, corresponding to the reality of the Church's call in a particular situation. This key, in agreement with Segundo's development of the 'dialectics/determinism' tension, will be that of 'masses/minorities' or, as Segundo prefers to put it, 'mass man' and 'minority man'. The key is needed precisely because the hermeneutical process does not consist of a simple application of data, discovered through a neutral exegesis. The simple transposition of the interpersonal categories in which Jesus expressed the good news and his demand for conversion, to an age, like ours, which is very different, where both love and sin take on effective dimensions which are more and more social and political, is not, according to Segundo, a valid exegetical procedure.

At this point Segundo adds to the biblical hermeneutical task a new dimension not explicitly found in our other writers. The problem of transposition is not simply that of reading biblical categories in the light of our own ideological prejudices, thus inoculating ourselves against the biblical text being able to speak a new word (as Miranda stresses). The problem is rather that the biblical message itself is already impregnated with a

certain ideological slant. The suspicion of an ideological interpretation, which can be logically applied to historical theology,
penetrates to the sacred writings themselves. Why should these,
being already essentially interpretation, be free of ideology?[50]

Segundo mentions two ideological slants in Scripture: first
that the emphasis on the personal aspect of free love in the
teaching and ministry of Jesus works against the efficacy of love
in a more complicated, more conflictual, contemporary social
situation; and second that the entire Scripture is written, as
is logical, within a fixed (in contrast to evolutionist) mentality,
which is completely ignorant of the slow process which constitutes divine creation.

In order to overcome the double ideological influence (as he
sees it) in contemporary biblical exegesis, Segundo proposes 'a
hermeneutical circle in which there is a unity of interpretation'
between 'a revolutionary commitment and a new understanding of the gospel message'. The two halves of the circle are
designed to complement each other. On the one hand, revolutionary commitment, starting out from a Marxist analysis of
society, as a pre-understanding of the biblical text, will by a
'de-ideologising' process (somewhat equivalent to Bultmann's
'demythologising' methodology) attempt to remove all those
elements in the biblical (New Testament) message which dis-
play a theological justification for the Church's feeling of political impotence within the Roman Empire. On the other hand,
a new understanding of the gospel message, which arises from
the questions being asked in the new, contemporary, hermeneutical situation, is able to challenge, correct and re-direct
the ideological pretension of a unitary and uniform revolutionary process. In other words, only by listening to the 'de-
ideologised' word of the gospel, but with the expectation of
receiving a new orientation, will the Christian Church be able
to close the hermeneutical circle and use the hermeneutical key
in the interests of an open-ended, non-determined, efficacious
love.[51]

CHAPTER SEVEN

THE IMPORTANCE OF INTERPRETATION

I. THE CENTRALITY OF THE 'EVENT'

With the object of establishing the theology of liberation as something more than a mere programmatic and ephemeral movement, Severino Croatto has applied himself to the elaboration of an adequate hermeneutic. In the introduction to his book, *Liberación y libertad* (*Liberation and Freedom*), he notes that the richness of the various works on liberation 'is immense, and our own future will say how much they have contributed to the formation of a "critical Latin American conscience" from the angle of Christian faith or philosophy. However, they also stimulate a desire to complete them with some hermeneutical guide-lines which may serve as a support, rather than as a criticism.' The hermeneutical procedure which he has elaborated is Croatto's main contribution to Latin American theological thinking. As befits an orientalist and Old Testament scholar, it is developed with due regard to the actual exegesis of texts.

The procedure can fairly be described as a 'hermeneutic of the Event', for the 'Event' is his fundamental starting point. The 'Event' is God's action or activity in history. It is the way he reveals himself. This emphasis on God's presence in historical events comes, in part, from a desire to subordinate orthodoxy to orthopraxis. For Croatto, orthodoxy springs from a static, intellectualised, contemplative notion of revelation which fundamentally has to do with a theology of mythical tendency. In contrast he sees biblical faith precisely in terms of a radical break with all mythological discourse: 'in biblical revelation it was the "God of the Event" who stirred into being a theology which broke with mythical discourse and created a constant tension between archetypal language ... and that of the "*Deus praesens*" of subsequent history'.[1]

The importance of this for understanding biblical history and faith is that the meaning of history follows on from the events themselves. Man captures revelation through an act of illumination as he reflects on what has happened. In more precise terms, 'the primacy of the event is essential, in that it "shows the intention" of the Promise ... The God of the "Promise" [on the level of "meaning"] comes later than the salvific event.'[2]

As far as Israel was concerned, God spoke first through historical events. Later these events were converted into a Word. In the subsequent history of Israel, the people were summoned both by the language of history and by that of the archetypal Word of the past event. The Promise, which is the teleological way of expressing the saving-event as election, is not historically prior to the event, as the Word-story was not contemporary with it. Rather it follows after it and is a new form of 'making the meaning more radical'.[3]

The Event is recognised as a 'sign of the times' first in a long process of mature reflection; later, in a centralised tradition; later still, in the written Word. Finally, it becomes a *message* for the whole of mankind. It becomes this message because the God of the Event continues to make himself known in contemporary 'signs of the times'. And the 'faith-recognition', which is operative today in the same way, produces a complete hermeneutical 'circulation'. This means that today, God speaks to us from two word-sources: contemporary history (the reality of man's history) and a word already spoken.

> The 'recognition' of God in the salvific-theological event is not instantaneous ... rather man causes this *profound presence* of God to surface in so far as the Event continues to hand over its 'meaning'. This being so, the articulation of event and meaning is at the centre of the whole hermeneutical problem.[4]

2. THE SEARCH FOR A NEW LANGUAGE

One of the principal conditions for engaging in a contemporary hermeneutic of the Word of God is the discovery of an adequate solution to the modern problem of language. Part of the problem lies in the different language-systems of religious over against scientific language. Religious language is essentially symbolic, allusive, intuitive, profound, for the sacred cannot be limited by time and space. On the other hand, logical and scientific language is so limited.

Language is the vehicle of revelation, and revelation, the profound meaning of the Event, spontaneously 're-creates' a double polarity: towards the past (its first realisation) and towards the present. 'The problem of the interpretation of language is born at this point. Why? Because the first realisation of revelation is made in mythological or symbolical language, which in order to become the expression of a second realisation, needs to be interpreted.'

Mythical language, according to the researches of P. Ricoeur,[5] 'does not describe a factual event but a search-for-meaning of a present situation'.[6] The movement is always from the present to an *archē* which is transempirical. Hermeneutics, then, is done primarily from my situation and involves not only an interpretation of symbolic language but rather its reinterpretation, in which the meaning of a text is projected on to my existence, not as a simple application of a text but rather as it 'tunes in' to my situation. 'Hermeneutics demands not so much a reformulation of language, as its re-creation from the vantage point of God's present salvific-liberating Event.'[7]

The primacy of the actual Event-reality does not mean imposing a modern language code upon the symbolic language of Scripture. Even less does it mean reducing the latter to the former in terms of a positivistic frame of reference, for symbolic language could not break the limited structure of scientific language to contribute its 'reserve of meaning' to the present praxis of liberation.

Hermeneutics is a dialectical process in which the biblical expression in symbols is used as a meta-language in a two-way process of communication. Communication is not simply the transmission of an archetypal message but conversion of the Word of God, which is reinterpreted through the communicator.

3. THE PLACE AND AUTHORITY OF THE ORIGINAL TEXT

The original text is the point at which the original revelation of the God of the Event has been captured, after a long process of meditation arising out of the results of the Event itself. The revelation is God's archetypal manifestation in history, which culminates in the Christ-event. This is the definitive revelation of Love in Jesus Christ and there cannot be another, either superior or parallel. It is the permanent sign by which we may recognise God. This means, for example, that the 'liberating' God of the Exodus cannot contradict himself by accepting oppression in another historical situation. This syntony with the archetypal revelation is based not on the unity of mankind but on the unity of the 'saving history' of God's design ('saving history' being an equivalent idea to Assmann's 'general salvation-history').

As God continues to act in man's unitary history so he continues, by this act, to reveal himself. Man today, as Israel and the Church yesterday, needs to discover this new manifestation in 'the signs of the times', i.e. in today's process of liberation. But the value of this process is still related to, and in some sense controlled by, the archetypal revelation. Nevertheless, the Bible records no finally definitive salvific act, for each act still needs completing by the *parousia*. Thus, God completes his salvific purposes at each stage of man's history until the final act takes place.

The relationship between the 'signs of the times' and the authority of the original texts is well summed up in the following passage:

> To recognise the signs of the times, or to read God's presence in the world's events means, at least, that there must be a very deep 'syntony' between the latter and the Christian message. This is so because first, God is discovered *in the Event*, from which one goes back to the archetypal message, as a guarantee of the faithfulness of the 'meaning' of that event and as a summons from faith itself. The opposite procedure, on the other hand, may be no more than a situational adaptation of the message to the present event or, what is worse, may miss the richness of the message as it is received through God's new manifestation in history...[8]

4. EXEGESIS IS HERMENEUTICS

Croatto does not attempt to conceal the fact that for him 'pure' exegesis is of little value for a faith which is committed to the praxis of liberation in Latin America. He makes a fairly strong distinction between what he calls traditional exegesis and the hermeneutical art of 'unveiling the challenge of the sacred Scriptures for a particular historical moment in the present, the search for an illuminating word for the contingencies of time.'[9] The methods of analysis generally associated with modern exegesis can be only a very preliminary step in the discovery of the real meaning of a text, for literary analysis only allows us to rediscover the history of a text, and redactional criticism only helps us to arrive at the end of redactional process of re-interpretation.

Nevertheless, the interpreter of a text realises that even through traditional exegesis he is entering into a hermeneutical process which has already been begun within the text itself. The purpose of this exegesis is, therefore, to capture, beyond the actual traditions used, the intention of the final editor through the elaboration and universalising of the work. But, the scientific apparatus used in traditional exegesis is only instrumental and peripheral. It discovers the meaning of a text, but only at one level, not at the level in which the text reaches me in my particular real situation today.

Therefore, exegesis must be complemented by a hermeneutical procedure. And not only complemented, but actually directed by a whole process of understanding. Exegesis is hermeneutics, for Croatto, because there are in fact three rather than two dimensions to the interpretation of Scripture.

Traditional exegesis has worked with only two registers, first an historical-critical exegesis, which has tended to claim an autonomous 'scientific' individuality, separating it off from commitment to the text studied; and then an attempt to apply what has been discovered 'scientifically' to a modern situation or context. However, Croatto rejects this method, which often makes the biblical passage accommodate itself to the contemporary situation. Rather, he maintains, the latter ought first to be studied, and then taken into prior consideration as an integral part of the original biblical interpretation.

Hermeneutics, therefore, must work with three registers. First, there is the archetypal event through which God manifests his salvific design and teaches man what ought to be his fundamental attitude of faith. This is the *ontological* or historical reference-point. Second, there is the mediation of language which condenses the event in a non-scientific and, therefore, more penetrating communication and also connects two horizons, that of the text to be interpreted and that of the interpreter. This is the *aesthetic* reference point. Finally, there is the present event, including contemporary reality and personal decision, or the *existential* reference-point.[10] It is the interaction of these three reference-points which Lapointe calls 'the hermeneutical circulation', and Gadamar 'the syntonising of horizons'. The basic hermeneutical problem is how to fuse together the three registers.

In tackling the hermeneutical problem from the standpoint of present reality, Croatto takes for granted certain presuppositions which, within the contemporary hermeneutical debate, give his solution a certain originality. He presupposes:

1. That present reality is primarily political, and thus hermeneutics has to be political in order that the spiritual liberation which Christ made possible may, today, be understood politically.

2. That the biblical text always says more than can be discovered by the methods which seek out the *sensus literalis*. This 'more' is a 'reserve of meaning' or a meaning 'in suspense', of the original word or the original interpretation.

3. That this 'reserve of meaning' is transmitted in a *continuum* of tradition which may be understood as an 'accumulation-of-meaning'.

4. That the 'reserve of meaning' can be disengaged from the text only from the standpoint of new acts of liberation; it can be discovered only as God's revelation is unfolded in new circumstances.

5. That the uniquely privileged position from which to understand the biblical references to liberation is that of the oppressed nations of the Third World.

6. That the new situations of oppression and liberation which are being experienced today continue to complete the meaning of the original acts of oppression and liberation. The Exodus, for example, is the ontological origin of its present reality in an interpretative continuum which we are called to prolong.

7. That the interpretation which we give, from within this continuum, does not annul the original event but enriches it with a deeper vision. For example, the biblical *kerygma* of the Exodus underlines the value of the concept of 'people'. This value is not lost in the process of the disengagement of its profound 'intention'. However, something remains over 'in suspense', which is discovered in the reality of the present, namely that true liberation also reaches the oppressor.

The rest of Croatto's discussion of hermeneutics is an attempt to explain further and justify these presuppositions. We shall try to follow him in the process.

The concept of a hermeneutical continuum stretching from the original text to the interpreter's present moment is, according to Croatto, a thoroughly biblical one. Within the Scriptures, already in the development of the Old Testament, and more particularly in the New Testament's exegesis of the Old, a continuous reinterpretive process of the original text in the light of the new event is going on. For example, at the time of Israel's greatest unfaithfulness, when power had become centralised and corrupted and when the central event of her history ('I am the Lord your God, who brought you out of the land of Egypt, out of the house of bondage') was no longer a 'dangerous memory' for the nation, the prophets arose as new interpreters of Israel's liberation from Egypt.[11]

Even more is this true of the New Testament's interpretation of the Old Testament in the light of the Christ-event: 'the Christ-event takes over and extends the *kerygma* of the Exodus.'[12] It does this in at least three ways: by using the vocabulary of the Exodus (e.g. 'redemption', 'liberty', 'salvation', 'mercy-seat'); by exploring new dimensions of man's liberation through Christ (e.g. Rom. 5–8); and by leaving the way open for further hermeneutical explorations of liberation (e.g. what it means to be rescued from sin, death and the law in today's prophetic present).

In other words, the new Christ-event reveals new levels of meaning in the already-given text. There is a messianic 'plus' revealed in the historical Christ which goes beyond every messianic prophecy when taken in its natural historical sense. And

this 'plus' even transmutes the original meaning of the prophecy, for, 'the innovation of the Event reverses the "meaning"
of the past revelation which ceases to be such when it does not
syntonise with the former.'[13]

What this means, in practice, is that in the New Testament
the Event could not be contained in structures inherited from
the past. It was precisely the attempt to enclose Christ in a traditional frame of interpretation which caused the Pharisees and
Scribes to be blind to God's new self-disclosure within his
people. 'Evidently, the *interpretation* of Scripture is ambiguous:
it either frees one from the author, considering within its
"meaning" the Event of the reader-interpreter [hermeneutical
process], or it alienates once again in a "no-donation" of meaning [pharisaical interpretation and every kind of legalism].'[14]

Now the hermeneutical continuum did not cease with the
apostles. It is absolutely clear from Croatto's writings that he
believes that the modern interpreter, from the position of his
faith and commitment to the same revolutionary praxis as that
initiated by God in the Exodus, may continue to draw out new
meanings from the inexhaustible supply of the text's 'reserve
of meaning'.

Thus the paradigmatic Event, in this case supremely the
Exodus, possesses a reserve of meaning which is captured and
condensed in the 'myth'. The myth tends to be hermeneutical
in that it is not exhausted in the primal event but takes on
meaning also in my existence, which itself 'modifies' the primal
event. In turn the primal event is enriched in its perspective
of significance and converted, by the interaction of the two
horizons,[15] into a new archetype which can then be taken into
a future hermeneutical process, done from a different and a new
reality.

There are two roads to this contemporary re-interpretation
of the text: either the new Event is 'read' (i.e. interpreted from
our vantage point) and, in the light of this, the traditional
message is re-formulated (exegesis has now become hermeneutics): or the original word is heard in order that the believer may be yet more open to actual salvific events in the
world.[16]

From this particular discussion, it should now be clear in *what*
way the present Event controls the hermeneutical procedure.

In summary, the whole process leads us to conclude that Jesus Christ is to be understood, today, supremely in the light of his new epiphanies in history (the hermeneutical key is given in John 16.12–15), and from the vantage point of an efficacious praxis of love.

This will take place when God's revelation in Christ is made present in a new praxis of liberation which enables us, for example, to understand the meaning of Christ, not just as the man for others, but more particularly as the man for the poor, weak and exploited, or to understand what the Latin American 'new man' ought to be.

The hermeneutical process outlined above is not intended to minimise the crucial nature of the original content of revelation. Indeed, Croatto criticises Bultmann's demythologising programme as a total emptying of content, substituting for it a remythologising process in which the nucleus of original content is left intact. This process means, on the one hand, that the spiritual liberation which Christ effected by his self-offering, interpreted by Paul from the situation of the religious oppression experienced by his people, is still a reality and a necessity. On the other hand, it means that the cultural and economic oppression, ignored by Paul, may also be taken into the total redemption effected by Christ.

It is this hermeneutical procedure which enables us to rediscover the political and social dimensions of the Exodus liberation, as they are taken over and transformed, first in the paschal mystery of Christ, and secondly in the new Christ-event, incarnated in the actual praxis of liberation and interpreted, within the hermeneutical continuum, in syntony with all past liberating acts.

5. THE CHALLENGE OF MARX TO BIBLICAL STUDY

According to José Miranda, if the biblical scholar is to take seriously the challenge of Marxism to contemporary theology, he will be obliged to change his methodological approach to Scripture and give priority in his exegesis to certain biblical subjects. Miranda's two principal works, *Marx and the Bible* and *Being and the Messiah*, are attempts to respond exegetically to this challenge.

Firstly, then, it is necessary to evaluate positively the dialectical method of knowledge, as this has been understood and used by Marx. By this method, taken over from Hegel and transformed, Marx understood that true knowledge must be found beyond mere facts discoverable by the sciences. Real knowledge has to do with human relationships in a society whose present conflicts are directly caused by unjust structures inherited from the past and exacerbated by the capitalist system. Real knowledge, then, can be acquired only by partially abandoning the 'ideal of objectivity' which is, in a certain sense, the result of Greek culture.

Applying the dialectic to the world of man, we discover that economic sciences (begun in the modern era by Quesnay, Adam Smith and Ricardo), because they are simply the application of western epistemology to a new object, have, for all their objectivity, ignored the most important fact of economic reality: 'the crushing of man'.[17]

Applying the dialectic to theological understanding, we discover that Marx's method is, now, the best way into a fresh contemporary understanding of the biblical text. Marx alone among modern philosophers shares the prophetic faith of Israel: both his messianism and his passion for justice come from the Bible. More than anyone else, he saw dialectically that reality, analysed by science, is moral. His method, therefore, springs from the same basic appreciation of reality as that of the Bible. 'Marx and the Bible coincide in this affirmation of incalculable importance: Sin's achievement of an institutional systematisation in a flawless civilising structure is what was historically needed before mankind could change its epoch.'[18]

In other words, because of the uniform use made today of Greek rationalistic epistemology, within the total scientific endeavour of Western civilisation, the only way we can capture afresh the message of an essentially non-Greek book, is by reconsidering the positive contribution of dialectical epistemology.

Miranda denies that this contribution implies a necessary search for parallels between Marx and the Bible. It simply aims at producing a new understanding of the Bible, from its own perspective (i.e. from within its own view of reality as conflictive) rather than from a so-called neutral but, in fact, ideologically determined standpoint. 'What Marx criticises in

Western science is the same thing that today prevents it from being challenged by the fact, which is recognised by this science itself, that to a great degree Marx coincides with the Bible.'[19]

Secondly, from a dialectical standpoint, certain biblical ideas should be allowed a privileged position as the chief hermeneutical keys for understanding the Bible's true liberating message:

(*i*) *The totality of evil.* 'Marx and Paul coincide in their intuition of the totality of evil: Sin and injustice form an all-comprehensive and all-pervasive organic structure. Paul calls this totality *kosmos*. Marx calls it "capitalism".' Nevertheless, Miranda also chides Marx for a lack of depth in his dialectical analysis, for he fails to see that 'capitalism is the consummation and deepening of the oppression which was inherent to human civilisation since biblical times.'[20]

(*ii*) *The centrality of God's justice for man.* 'The first and decisive affinity is that Marx believes that dialectics will produce justice in the world, and the Bible believes that faith will produce justice in the world.'[21] The question of God's justice becomes the pivotal point for the whole of Miranda's discussion of salvation or liberation in the Bible. We shall comment on this in Parts III and IV.

(*iii*) *The eschaton.* 'The meaning of *mišpāṭ* as the elimination of oppression and the realisation of justice ... is accentuated in the definitive *mišpāṭ*, affirmed by the whole Bible. There is an *ultimum* in human history, and this *ultimum* is defined and characterised, as in Marx, by the complete realisation of justice on earth.'[22]

6. THE CENTRALITY OF JUSTICE IN THE OLD TESTAMENT

Marx and the Bible begins with a discussion of how it came about that the Church's Social Encyclicals defended the right to private ownership of the means of production. The first chapter attempts a definition of the meaning of private property, first of all in the contemporary discussion and secondly in evidence adduced from the Bible and from the patristic period. From this discussion Miranda concludes that 'before Christianity became compromised with the prevailing social systems, that is, up to the fourth or fifth century AD, there were never any misrepresentations or evasions with regard to the biblical testimony concerning the inescapably unjust origin of differentiating ownership.'[23]

Miranda bases this judgment on an exegetical study of the meaning of justice in the Old Testament. This leads him to believe that the prophetic denunciation of injustice is based on the fact that differentiating property is acquired only by violence and spoliation: 'The fact that differentiating wealth is unacquirable without violence and spoliation is presupposed by the Bible in its pointed anathemas against the rich; therefore almsgiving is nothing more than a restitution of what has been stolen, and thus the Bible calls it justice.'[24]

He sees the value of this conclusion for the theory of right, in the programmatic statement: 'For the Bible . . . law consists in finally achieving justice for the poor and oppressed of this world . . . The realisation of justice . . . demands that we abolish the State and the law.'[25] Later he follows up this statement with an extended study of the word-groups *ḥese̱d s̱ᵉda̱ḵa̱h* and *mišpa̱ṭ*; firstly in their relationship to the theme of knowing God.

The God of the Scriptures is the only God who cannot be objectivised, because he is understood essentially as the demand for righteousness. When he ceases to summon man (being neutralised, for example, through elaborate rituals) he ceases to be God. To know this God, then, is to realise justice for the poor. God is only known in the clamour of the poor and weak who cry out for justice.[26] Likewise, it is knowledge of Yahweh which makes the Messiah defend the cause of the poor with justice (Isa. 11.2–4; Hab. 2.14 ff.).

A similar argument is advanced to explain the problem of the prophetic denunciation of the cultic rites. According to Miranda's understanding of the relevant passages, the prophetic anathemas cannot be reduced to exhortations to reform worship, nor even to the idea that Yahweh demands interpersonal justice *as well as* the cultic structure (Amos 5.21–5). Miranda thinks that it is clear that Yahweh requires justice *in place of* rites (Isa. 1.15). This is precisely because the whole difference between the biblical God and other gods lies in the implacable demand for righteousness. In other religions, worship is used to neutralise this demand. Miranda even goes so far as to say that 'the prophets deny ... that cultus and prayer could put the people in contact with Yahweh while injustice exists on earth.'[27]

At the centre of Miranda's understanding of the knowledge of God lies his rejection of Greek epistemology as primarily concerned with the ontological question of God's existence as Being. Rather, he says, to know God biblically is to know him dialectically in the conflicts of history as justice is being struggled for. 'What is at the bottom of all this is a different God. And the difference goes far beyond all metaphysical questions ... [for] such a question moves on the level of being, while the God of the Bible is known in the implacable moral imperative of justice.'[28] Miranda's position is wholly consistent, then, when he argues that God cannot be worshipped as *Being* until the *eschaton* of total world justice (the final suppression of the dialectical process) has been achieved.

A study of the words used to translate 'righteousness', 'judgment' and 'justice' (particularly *mišpāṭ*, its root *šphṭ* and its derivatives, such as *šāpaṭ*) reveals a uniform meaning in terms of salvation. The judgment of God revealed through these words is a judgment which protects and saves, not a legalised retribution. 'When the Bible speaks of Yahweh as "Judge", or of the judgment whose subject is Yahweh, it has in mind precisely the meaning which we have seen for the root *šphṭ*: ... to save the oppressed from injustice. This is the meaning of the Last Judgment awaited down through all the centuries of expectation in the Old and New Testaments.'[29]

Thus the God who reveals himself only in response to the absolute cry of the downtrodden is also the God who brings justice (or salvation). The plan to save from injustice and from oppression determines the complete description which Yahweh makes of himself. This salvation is God's supreme work. It is made necessary because man has been unable either to produce justice for the oppressed or eliminate the oppressors. 'The hope is for the definitive establishment of the kingdom of justice on earth. This is the justice of God, not of men, for it is supposed (and is expressly verified) that men have not been able to achieve justice. This is also Paul's theology.'[30]

7. SALVATION ACCORDING TO PAUL AND JOHN

a. *Salvation in the Epistle to the Romans*

Before analysing Miranda's exegetical study of Romans in *Marx and the Bible*, it is necessary to remind ourselves again that, from the point of view of a dialectical methodology, Marx agrees with Paul that evil is a total structure, called by Paul the *kosmos*. As Miranda sees it, 'the decisive step in human liberation was taken by the biblical authors when they intuited that evil consisted in an organic and cohesive totality, that sin had a unity, that it was structured into civilisation and therefore had gained control of the very essence of the law.'[31]

Miranda, then, sees salvation in Romans essentially in terms of liberation from the law. He begins his exposition of this thesis with the section Romans 1.18–3.20, which is the compositional basis of the entire letter: 'the wrath of God is already in operation in the world against all *adikia*.' *Adikia* is the dominating concept of the whole passage (e.g. 1.18,29; 2.8; 3.5). It is inter-human injustice, perpetrated every day, which impedes knowledge of God (1.28). The gospel is salvation because in it is revealed God's justice which saves us from his wrath against *adikia*.[32]

The central question posed by Paul's argument, then, is 'How does God's justice save?' Miranda answers, 'If evangelisation and faith [he refers to the thesis of 1.16–17] make us to *be* the justice of God [cf. 2 Cor. 5.21], it is obvious that this saves us from the anger that has been concretised in history in terms of interhuman injustice. It saves us by making us to be no longer injustice, but justice.'[33] By interpreting the conflict between the knowledge and wrath of God strictly in terms of the concepts of justice and injustice, Miranda shows that he believes that Paul views salvation largely in terms of salvation from *adikia*.

Adikia, which affects both Jew and Gentile alike (cf. especially 3.9), is the essential meaning of 'sin' in Romans 4–11. We are saved from it by the *dikaiosunē Theou*. What is God's justice? According to Miranda, Paul's view is entirely founded upon and completely coterminous with the Old Testament understanding of the word.[34]

It is not surprising that from such a pre-understanding, Miranda concludes that his interpretation of the meaning of salvation in Romans drastically alters the usual one. Basing himself on Romans 2.13–15, 26–9, he believes that Paul is arguing here that there are Gentiles who already possess God's true justice; and that it is the same justice which Paul is trying to promote through the gospel.

This is the eschatological justice which the entire world has been anxiously awaiting. It is corporate and not individual.[35] It is necessary because sin has become incarnated in social structures (in the *kosmos*),[36] becoming entrenched there through the medium of law (Rom. 4.15; 5.13 and 7.7–13; 1 Cor. 15.56). But the law cannot effect justice in the world, for it is precisely through the works of the law that man realises he cannot fulfil the eschatological justice which God requires of him: that justice which will become incarnated in social structures. The law has become totally identified with this present civilisation; in order for there to be a new civilisation (a new aeon), the law must be eliminated. And it is eliminated, basically, when men respond in faith to the fact that, in the gospel, that justice of God is revealed which activates a true justice in man through a change of his heart.[37]

This justice comes (and, for Miranda, it has nothing to do with 'imputed righteousness') through the death and resurrection of Christ, which gives faith 'its capacity to make men just': 'For us to be free from the law it was necessary that the law crucify Christ before our eyes.' 'When before our eyes the law crucifies ... the only man who did not know sin, God destroys sin and the law for ever. At this point the justice of God begins in history and the "justice" of the law ends.'[38]

Miranda implies that men are saved from God's wrath against *adikia*, which is ingrained in the very structures of civilisation, by the righteousness of a faith which makes men just. The righteousness *of* faith is both objective genitive – what God has established by raising Christ from a death caused by the law, and thereby inaugurating a new aeon without law; and subjective genitive – what man does, believing that, with Christ, the new aeon has already been established and that he is, therefore, free from the law to practise that real justice (i.e. that love of the neighbour) which eventually will bring in, through man's commitment to man, the eschatological kingdom. In short, 'faith is salvation'.[39]

It is not surprising that, when Miranda starts from the dialectical position assumed by Marx, he finishes his exegesis of the Old and New Testaments by almost equating biblical and Marxist hope. What for Marx is possible through a conscious understanding of history as dialectical, is possible for the Bible through faith which acts on the assumption that the new age is already here: 'The Gospel is war to the death against the motive of acquisition ... There is nothing in strict exegesis which authorises us to postpone its elimination to another world.'[40]

Miranda implies that faith in the dialectical process is equivalent to biblical faith in God, in the sense in which we have just outlined the latter. Marx's basic problem is not his atheism but his lack of faith in the unlimited possibilities of the dialectic. In the last resort, however, it is God acting through Jesus Christ to bring in the *eschaton*, who makes possible the dialectic of history, rather than an 'eternal return'.

b. *Salvation through the Johannine Christ*

In his later book, *Being and the Messiah*, Miranda explains, on the basis of the Johannine literature, how the *eschaton* of God's total justice has been brought forward into history through the historical Jesus Christ. The realisation of the *eschaton* by Jesus Christ *here and now* constitutes the novelty of the New Testament.

The central thesis of this book, which is then elaborated exegetically, is the statement in chapter 3 that 'Time is ethical, and it can be known only in an ethical resolution. History is made of the outcry of all the oppressed; in this it consists.' It is not time as we understand it quantitively, but rather the condition for resolving ethical issues is a qualitatively different kind of time in the future. That is to say, it is the future which belongs to the Messiah, and this alone delivers us from cyclical history. Messianic time is the full arrival, in the person of the historical Christ, of the *eschaton* of God's universal kingdom. 'The *eschaton* of the Bible ... is *in this world* ... The biblical *eschaton* is not beyond history, but rather the final and definitive stage of history.' In the arrival of the *eschaton*, the clamour of the oppressed will be heeded, injustice will be finally abolished, 'the meek shall inherit the earth' (Matt. 5.5).

The latter half of the book attempts to explain the meaning of Christ's messianic activity. Miranda starts with the results of an earlier analysis of John's prologue, in which he argued that it was not the Messiah but the Word (the absolute ethical demand for justice and compassion) which was pre-existent and became incarnate in Jesus of Nazareth (chapters 6–7). According to this analysis, Christ's messianic activity consists in representing perfectly in the world the pre-incarnate *Logos*.

Through an analysis of 1 John 4.2–3; John 8.30–40; 2.24–3.1; 15.1ff. and 1 John 2.19ff., Miranda reaches the conclusion that both the Gospel and the First Letter of John state a remarkable paradox, namely that certain people simultaneously believe on Jesus Christ and yet do not believe that he is the Messiah. They are Christian believers, but they betray Jesus. They remain Christians, but they do not produce fruit. To deny that Jesus is the Messiah is to deny that with him the end of history has arrived, that the true light is already shining (1 John 2.8). The Christians prove their betrayal of Jesus by the fact that they have not thrown themselves into the realisation of a world kingdom of love and justice. They believe on Christ but they make him into an atemporal, unreal image. Thus, they reject God and his salvation.[41]

Miranda goes on to discuss his thesis that 'John did not write a history of salvation, neither in his Epistle nor in his Gospel; he affirms that history has arrived at its end and the end is already here.'[42] This is what Miranda calls Jesus' radical alteration of the traditional Jewish eschatological hope (cf. John 11.23–6; 4.25–6; 9.35–7; 1.41; also 1 John 2.18–19), proclaiming that in the Messiah all that the Old Testament means by the Kingdom is here in its fulness: 'John's message is now.' A fully realised eschatology means that even the physical world can be transformed; now even death can be abolished (cf. John 5.24–5; 10.28; 6.39; 12.25; 17.12). Miranda accuses Bultmann and others, by demythologising the *eschaton*, of having emptied it of any content. He, for his part, has radically 'de-futurised' it.

The announcement of the arrival in Jesus of the *eschaton* is more imperative than indicative. In Johannine thought, truth is active and faith is love:[43] 'the news that the *kingdom arrives* means that we must *make it arrive.*'[44] Jesus brings salvation because only in him can the realisation of the kingdom be announced and made effective. This is how Jesus Christ becomes contemporary for us; it is the meaning of our faith in him. Any other approach to Christ converts him into an idol, denies God's revelation of himself, and becomes a religion domesticated by the powers of the old aeon.[45]

So the modern Christological problem is not solved by a demythologising programme but by authentic, objective exegesis, by understanding the incarnation of the Word in Hebrew terms rather than in terms of a Greek world view. This means that exegesis is at the service of truth *which demands to be realised.*

8. THE HERMENEUTICAL PROCEDURE

Miranda's approach to the task of interpreting Scripture for today appears to be both orthodox and polemical. It is orthodox in the sense that he is convinced that the historical-critical method of exegesis is objective, rigorous and controllable: 'Objectively to investigate the precise nature of [the solution given by the New Testament writers] is a task to be carried out on the basis of demonstrable documentary evidence, which is the basis for the exegetical method.'[46] Through this method Miranda believes that it is possible to discover the Scripture's particular mode of thought. This is a way of thinking which does not admit of any easy harmonisation with modern thought, not even with that of Marx.[47]

At this point, Miranda becomes polemical. For although he is convinced that the historical-critical method is in itself objective, he is equally convinced that almost all those who use it today are hindered, by the adoption of a non-biblical, Greek way of thinking, from understanding the central message of the Scriptures and obeying it. He continually emphasises that the biblical method of knowledge is entirely different from that of the Greeks. But it is precisely the Greek method which has dominated in the conclusions derived from exegetical study: 'The western absolutisation of the ontological point of view makes us believe that this instrument of cognition is superior to that of the Bible.'[48] It is only by immersing ourselves in the biblical world and being prepared to accept biblical thought-forms that we will ever hear the biblical message.

The problem with modern hermeneutics is that it approaches its task with an *a priori* bias against biblical thought. 'To brand the biblical authors as primitive is a value judgment, not objective exegetical work. What is in question is precisely Western morality's alleged superiority to biblical morality. To base oneself on this superiority in order to reduce biblical thought to Western thought, is an extraordinarily unscientific methodology.'[49]

The result of this bias, according to Miranda, is two-fold. Firstly, it produces a false interpretation of relevant biblical texts: 'Applied to biblical exegesis, such progressivism is revealed as absurd, the negation of hermeneutics.' For a healthy hermeneutic in the objective understanding of documents from other eras, we need to rid ourselves of this *a priori* progressivist prejudice. 'To distort the meaning of the Bible on pretext of "correcting" it, making it conform to extra-biblical criteria, is not sound exegesis.' 'Extrabiblical data allow us – at the very most – to conclude that the Bible is mistaken. Period. In no way do these data allow us to distort what the Bible says so that we may comfortably profess our "belief" in it while denying its real meaning.'[50]

Secondly, this biased view does not allow the text to act as a critical control over the philosophical and ideological presuppositions which the exegete takes to his task. 'To interpret in this way is to adopt precisely the hermeneutical position in which understanding becomes impossible. If we consider the prophets to be exaggerating, we suppose ourselves to know Yahweh and revelation better than they ... Then the Bible really cannot modify our hierarchy of values, which means that it cannot tell us anything new.'[51]

Summarising, we could say that Miranda's hermeneutical procedure is both *optimistic* (the real sense of Scripture *can* be uncovered by objective methods) and *suspicious*. His discussion with other exegetes has taught him to suspect that their exegetical conclusions are more likely to be based on false ideological premises than on sound methodology.

Miranda sees the hermeneutical circle as a two-way process in which we may discover, either from the biblical text or from today's reality, that man's history is profoundly moral and needs changing: 'Though idealistic anthropology denies it, the most outstanding characteristic of our time is the demand for total justice. This does, indeed, impose conditions of possibility. For a message, any message, to deserve attention, the kingdom of justice must be achieved.' Both processes mutually enforce each other: today's reality makes the doing of justice an inescapable obligation; the biblical text helps us to know how this is possible.

However, he who does not approach Scripture with a dialectical concept of man in history will not even be able to enter the hermeneutical circle. He will not understand the message of Scripture: 'They may indeed see and not perceive, and may indeed hear but not understand.' Exegetical knowledge, then, comes through correct methodology, but even more through obedience.

PART III

THE PRINCIPAL BIBLICAL THEMES

CHAPTER EIGHT

A PRIVILEGED TEXT:
THE EXODUS

Before entering upon an exposition of how the Exodus narrative has been used within the theology of liberation, it it necessary to clarify several points. None of our authors has undertaken an exegetical study of the passages, in the accepted sense of the word. Most of them are aware of, and draw upon, some of the results of contemporary exegetical studies. However, they use them more as an interpretative 'launching pad' than as a conscious creative tool. As a result, most of them make no attempt to verify exegetically the correctness of either their method or their use of the text. The controlling factor, therefore, in their understanding of the text is not a particular exegetical methodology, which might be open to dispute, but rather the requirements of the situation to which the text must be addressed.

The hermeneutical procedure (i.e. the interpretative use of the text) is carried out, consciously or not, on at least five levels. These levels will form the main divisions of our study. The exposition given here of liberation theology's interpretation of the Exodus narrative is synthetic, in the sense that we have tried to include, in broad terms, most of what has been said on the subject. The views expressed do not, therefore, pertain to any one person in their entirety.

I. THE FIXING OF THE NARRATIVE IN
ISRAEL'S HISTORY

The basic approach of liberation theology to the Exodus story can be summed up as follows. The present text of the Exodus is the result of a long interpretative process (or hermeneutical procedure) in which the original salvific event is explored and completed in the light of subsequent events experienced by the Hebrews. The fixing of the narrative, then, is already a hermeneutical process in which one event is seen to possess new meanings which gradually become added to the original 'story'. The text is not so much narrative as message. Beginning from the hypothesis, accepted by most liberation theologians, that the Exodus marks the real commencement of Israel's history, three important conclusions are drawn.

The first conclusion is that the people of Israel, before the Exodus, were not aware of their peoplehood. They were an ethnic mixture, unconscious of any past history. Secondly, the Genesis narrative which recounts certain promises to Abraham is seen as a retrojection which arose as the result of the hermeneutical procedure following the Exodus event, for in fact, according to Croatto, 'the people were a long way from knowing about some ancient "promise" or presence of God in their history.'[1] Thirdly, the praxis of the Exodus is seen to be historically both prior to the promises given by God to the people and the word spoken by God which brought about Moses' vocation as leader.[2]

2. THE ORIGINAL STORY OF THE EXODUS

If the present narrative is largely interpretation, it should be possible to recover an original historical nucleus, which later became elaborated. Where this is done by the theology of liberation, we are normally given the end result of the process without having the process explained.

The original history, it is argued, concerns certain Semitic groups which had emigrated from Syria and infiltrated into the north of Egypt between the eighteenth and sixteenth centuries BC. These groups were used as cheap slave labour, according to the practice of the Pharaohs of the time, to construct their cities. They could have been any group, and their oppressors could have been of any kind. The oppression was, in fact, political and social, practised against a foreign ethnic minority.

This people, because of their very extreme situation, cried out in their bondage. The cry from the depths was the beginning of a spontaneous process of 'conscientisation' which eventually led Moses to assume responsibility as a political leader. His task was to strengthen the people's awareness of the depths of their bondage and of the possibility of their liberation. This he did, in spite of his different upbringing, by identifying himself with his own people in their exploitation and internal divisions. Later, the plagues were also used as a convenient means for showing the people that their liberation really was possible. Nevertheless, Moses had to struggle continually to keep open the option for liberation, for the people were still mentally dominated by their oppressed conscience.

It is characteristic of the majority of our theologians that they stress the political aspects of the people's liberation as a necessary preliminary to any other form of liberation.[3] Though it is true that God's inspirational word to Moses, within the process of leading a liberation movement, is allowed a certain programmatic place in the initiation of the struggle, the majority of commentators insist that God's intervention took place only after the Hebrew people had become conscious of the possibility of liberation.[4]

The liberation theologians' inclination to see, in the final form of the narrative, a complete hermeneutical process at work has led them to emphasise firstly that Yahweh's role in the narrative belongs largely to secondary sources, although some kind of activity of a god of the original semitic groups in the process of liberation must be taken into account; and secondly that the exodus was largely the task of the people themselves.[5]

3. THE FIRST HERMENEUTICAL LEVEL: THE TEXT ITSELF

According to the theory that the liberated people engaged on a subsequent and prolonged interpretation of their own origin, it is assumed that the original story of the Exodus soon became largely forgotten and a different account of what happened arose in its stead. This account largely reversed the importance of the two facts noted above, so that Yahweh, and not either Moses or the people, now becomes the chief protagonist of liberation.

Israel's God is the God of the Exodus, the one who revealed himself and acted only because of the people's clamour under bondage: 'The God who originally revealed himself to Israel was the God of the Exodus, and his self-revelation was simply an obligatory intervention on behalf of the oppressed against their oppressors.... It is the "outcry" of the oppressed (cf.

Exod. 3.7) that makes this God intervene to revolutionise history.'[6]

God's intervention in order to save a people from an oppressive slavery caused by the indiscriminate use of naked power, is interpreted at the level of the present narrative in four distinct but complementary ways.

Initially, through the Exodus, God began to form a new people. The 'no people' became a new nation. According to Miranda, 'When God intervenes his principal activity is directed to the conscience. And through people's consciences he achieves his true intervention ... The God of the Exodus is the God of conscience. The liberation of the slaves from Egypt was principally a work of the imperative of liberty and justice implacably inculcated into the Israelites.'[7] There are two basic things that can be said about this God in connection with the formation of a new people. He is a God of the future who, in consequence, calls for the formation of a people according to the possibility of what they may become in the future, and he is a God who guarantees the future freedom of his people.[8] The people themselves become conscious of their responsibility, in the light of this great act of liberation, to commit themselves to God's will. The state of liberation is dependent, therefore, upon keeping the terms of the Covenant. But even more, nationhood, which means the formation of a people out of slavery for freedom, is based on the experience of an oppression which can never be allowed to recur in the midst of the new nation.

The Exodus is completed by an 'entry'. Liberation is the first stage of a double process which must lead to freedom: '*Salvation* is identified with the possession of *freedom*. This is fulfilled in a 'liberation' in its double-aspect of "going out" from the oppression of Egypt and "entering" into the land of Canaan'.[9] The 'going out' from Egypt is only one moment in a continuing history. The correlative purpose is an *eisodus*. 'Liberation/salvation takes in exodus/eisodus ... The Exodus is liberation, for it is the prior and indispensable step for entering the Land where it will be possible to serve God'.[10] 'To leave Egypt is an illegal act in Pharaoh's eyes, for Pharaoh does not allow liberation; on the other hand, it is a supremely good act, because it fulfils the law ... of a new order'.[11]

The Hebrew people were allowed to leave Egypt only as the result of a series of violent acts on the part of Yahweh: 'God, far from agreeing with Pharaoh, listens to the oppressed and desires to liberate them (3.9, 16ff.; 6.5ff.). The most notable fact is that he acts against the "divine" authority of the king and with all the violence which characterises the God of the "holy war" ... (3.19ff.; 6.6)'.[12] The violence was necessary as a last resort, not as an end in itself, but because of Pharaoh's inflexibility, which in turn is due to his oppressor mentality. Pharaoh cannot exist without the oppressed, for it is they who complete the circle of his power (Exod. 14.5).

Liberation gained from slavery in Egypt was no guarantee of a continuing process of liberation. For Israel, in her new-found freedom, the doubly-liberating history which begins with the Exodus 'liberates the Hebrews from the fetters of cyclical time and from enslavement to the Egyptian Pharaoh. But it continues on with a very peculiar structural element, embodied in the constant and growing tendency of the Israelite people to infidelity. In other words, they continually tend to shun the liberation they have received, and to return to the cultic practices of the nature religions.'[13] In order to counteract the tendency to flee from freedom, the great feasts were instituted, especially that of the Passover. These were a kind of enacted theology which would cultivate in the liberated people a 'liberating freedom' (Deut. 15.15; Lev. 25.39ff.; Deut. 16.12; Exod. 12.14).

4. THE SECOND HERMENEUTICAL LEVEL: THE BIBLICAL REINTERPRETATION OF THE EXODUS

Many of our authors stress the fact that the Exodus became a paradigmatic event for the whole of Israel's subsequent history: 'the month of new things associated with the Exodus ... perpetuated in the Passover liturgy', remains as 'the basic structure of the whole history of the God who saves', and as 'the definitive reference-point for every prophetic interpretation of God's liberating action in the world'.[14] It was an event whose reinterpretation became transmitted first of all in the liturgy of the people (e.g. the Song of Triumph, Exod. 15), and secondly in their moral and ceremonial laws.

The fact that the 'memory of Egypt', to use Gutierrez's phrase, 'impregnates the pages of the Bible and inspires many reinterpretations both in the Old and New Testament' is eloquent testimony to the fact that the Exodus was not just an act of liberation, but the preparation of an entire people to live in freedom. For example, the going out from Egypt, from the nation with its sacred monarchy, reinforces the idea of the 'desacralisation of social praxis'.[15] In other words, the Israelites' experience of oppression in Egypt, and their great deliverance, means that they are no longer at liberty to adopt the same kind of national structure as their erstwhile oppressors. The Exodus is a constant call to live out a totally new present in the light of the past; to be a people where before there were no people; to separate themselves from the nations, precisely because the sacral order practised by the latter justified and perpetuated division and oppression.

The memory of the Exodus gave to Israel a profound sense of the importance of history. Their God is not captured at the level of the cosmogonies of other religions (i.e. 'the penetration of sacrality into the *kosmos*') but at the level of the transformation of man's situation: 'the Exodus always signified for them the ontological "origin" of their present reality and became a challenging "memory" whenever they ceased to be free.'[16]

In brief, the Exodus became for the biblical writers the archetypal event through which they interpreted their entire history as 'salvation-history'. Later, as we shall see, the universal concept of God as Creator was also interpreted through the experience of the God of salvation. In this way the whole of history was given a salvific substructure.

Because of the particular nature and centrality of these many reinterpretations of the Exodus, the theology of liberation emphasises that 'liberation is not some newly-arrived concept but the very centre of the biblical *kerygma*'.

5. THE THIRD HERMENEUTICAL LEVEL: THE EXODUS AND ITS UNIVERSAL HERMENEUTIC

According to liberation theology's view of biblical hermeneutics, biblical reinterpretation of the Exodus is only the first part of a similar process which extends forward to our day.

The Exodus is not only paradigmatic for Israel's faith with a limited 'salvation-history' but 'the paradigm for the interpretation of all space and time', i.e. for the on-going, global 'salvation of history'.[17]

This means that the Exodus is not only 'a tempting term for comparison with the manifold situations of injustice and oppression experienced today ... the source and quarry of images such as: going-out, punishment, Moses the leader of an insurrection, Israel an enslaved people',[18] but the *primal* event of liberation which has to be understood afresh from our contemporary stand-point:

> The historical and religious experience of the Exodus is the first kerygmatic 'core' for a theology of liberation ... If we are to undertake a genuine hermeneutic of the Exodus-event, from which we should 'disentangle' other events which are really future to it, then its present *re-interpretation* is essential. For this reason it is not 'exhausted'. It possesses other connotations, which remain hidden until the 'situation' brings them to light. For example: the Exodus was a political (social) happening, but it is also evident that it is an event which inspires every economic and cultural liberation.[19]

As an inspiring event the Exodus is, in Assmann's words, 'a permanent motive' for the 'institutionalisation' of a critical conscience and a permanent cultural revolution, on the basis of a constant liberating struggle. The actual moment decides which aspect of the Exodus is going to be emphasised and used in re-interpretation. However, Croatto goes even further in his understanding of the hermeneutical re-interpretation of the Exodus-event. For him, a proper understanding of the text can take place only at the experiential level of human beings who are actually oppressed and dominated or, as in the case of Moses, of those who deliberately and sacrificially identify with them (Heb. 11:24–6, 'an exodus from security, the bourgeois spirit and everything created by man to avoid risks'[20]). 'Today, we can only interpret the Exodus from our position as dependent peoples.'[21] The Exodus is converted into an inexhaustible reserve of meaning. For this reason its 'donation-of-meaning' is unlimited; its hermeneutical possibilities are *unique* for Latin American theology.[22]

Croatto affirms that the Exodus-event has never ceased. It is not an event which took place simply at one point in history, but an event which, because it inspired a constant re-interpretation in terms of God's successive acts of salvation, has become a projected message for all people at all times (i.e. it is *kerygma* now).

> The Exodus is an Event full of meaning (as the biblical narrative and Israel's experience show) which even now has not been *concluded*. If our recalling of the biblical *kerygma* has any relevance, the 'memory' of the Exodus becomes, for us – oppressed peoples of the Third World – an inciting Word, the announcment of liberation. It remains for us to prolong the Exodus, for it was not an event for the Hebrews but the manifestation of God's liberating design for all peoples. Within a hermeneutical treatment it is perfectly legitimate to understand ourselves *as from* the biblical Exodus and above all to understand the latter *from within* our situation of peoples in economic, political, social and cultural slavery.[23]

Croatto, conscious of the need to justify his hermeneutical methodology, interprets the hermeneutic of the Exodus as follows.

1. The God of the Exodus reveals himself as the God of an oppressed racial minority.
2. Through subsequent re-interpretations of the Exodus he is seen as the God of all oppressed peoples, particularly those who live dehumanised lives as the direct result of the play of economic, political and social forces beyond their control.
3. The oppressed peoples of today are the poor of the Third World, the proletariat class on a global scale.
4. The God of the Exodus cannot deny himself. He still listens to the clamour of the downtrodden. He still stoops down to rescue them with 'an outstretched arm and with great acts of judgment' (Exod. 6.6). He still inspires movements of protest and revolution against those powers that have hardened their hearts against every cry for the recovery of rights.
5. God's present 'salvation-history' no longer passes through Israel or the Church but directly through suffering

humanity, who supremely constitute, today, God's elect
nation, his special people.

6. It is this oppressed humanity who will be the agent for
the 'reconciliation' of the entire *kosmos*, for only the
oppressed can liberate the oppressors.

The advantage of this hermeneutical methodology is that it
can be read in either direction. The interpretation of 'salvation-
history' as the 'salvation of history' means that we have a
concrete tool for interpreting the 'signs of the times' as God's
continuing succession of intervening salvific acts in the present.
Croatto summarises his thought thus:

> We do not deny that the patriarchs may have experienced
> a vocation or the Hebrew slaves in Egypt a call, but the
> Promise, or Vocation, *as they are written*, presuppose the ex-
> perience of liberation and Israel's existence as a people in
> the land. The Promise expresses, in the form of design, the
> event which, in reality, brings it to birth as 'word'. Such is
> the richness of the Promise, or of the language of 'vocation'.
> It says something profound, not captured at the moment of
> Abraham or Moses. Do we not use similar language when
> we affirm or discover an 'historical vocation' in the Latin
> American people ... precisely because the language of voca-
> tion (or promise when used in a religious context and
> expressed in religious language) is a way of 'expressing' the
> deepest meaning of an *event* itself. We conclude, therefore,
> that the Exodus is the programmatic Event of Israel's reli
> gious experience which establishes the value of the Word-
> story and the Promise.[24]

This particular methodology establishes the oppressor/
oppressed conflict as the chief hermeneutical key for unlocking
the contemporary meaning of the text. There follow some
examples of how this key is then used in the application of the
text to contemporary events.

The attempt to exterminate the Hebrew race, by infanti-
cide, is *the equivalent* of the genocidal 'sterilisation', directed by
the North Americans, which is practised in Latin America
under the innocent name of 'family planning'.

'The liberation from Egypt, linked to ... creation, adds an

element of capital importance: the need and the place for man's active participation in the building of society.' It is at this point that Gutierrez most clearly dissociates himself from Moltmann's interpretation of the Exodus: 'We are far from the position of Jurgen Moltmann ... which would give the impression that he does not keep sufficiently in the mind man's participation in his own liberation'.[25]

The proliferation of the Hebrews, given as the excuse for their further repression (Exod. 1.9, 12–14), can be compared to today's population explosion amongst the Third World nations, in the sense that in both cases the security of the rich and privileged races is threatened.

These three examples are intended to show just how liberation theology's biblical hermeneutic may be applied in practice. In each case a specific attempt is being made to build an interpretative bridge from an ancient text to a modern social context of widely differing proportions.

Before leaving the subject of the Exodus, it is only fair to allow liberation theology itself to try to answer the two most common criticisms launched by those who challenge its hermeneutical methodology. Firstly, the Exodus is not chosen as an *a priori* biblical justification for the theme of liberation. As Ruiz says, 'we chose the Exodus as the focus-point of our reflection for its paradigmatic value and its importance for the history of Israel (and not precisely because we judge that it provides a biblical argument to prove the theology of liberation)'.[26] Indeed, the theology of liberation has always consistently repudiated the need for an *a priori* theological or biblical justification. Secondly, the Exodus is not chosen in place of other important Old Testament themes, such as the failure of the monarchy or the Exile, just because it happens to fit best a predetermined way of presenting present history (oppressor/oppressed; dominator/dominated; repression/revolution; cyclical/linear view of history; majority/minority; 'first' violence/counter-violence, etc.) but because it happens to be *the* archetypical event of Israel, which became converted into the foundation and motivation of all its laws and institutions, as well as its theological reflection.[27]

CHAPTER NINE

TOTAL AND UNIVERSAL LIBERATION

On various occasions we have noticed how the theology of liberation decidedly rejects any notion of a double historical process, such as might be derived, for example, from the division of history into 'salvation-history' and 'world-history'. We now propose to investigate briefly the biblical grounds given for this rejection.

The first ground relies on the argument that the decisive beginning point of God's revelation to mankind is the Exodus. Ruiz affirms, categorically, that 'the *first explicit revelation* of Yahweh, which is historically recorded, is contained in the Exodus, it is made to a group of men ... a group of slaves.' On the other hand, the religion of the patriarchs, in so far as this can be recovered, is for him, the religion of nomads, the veneration of the God of their fathers (Gen. 26.24; 31.42).

> The patriarchs are presented as the founders of sanctuaries, of places in which they erected an altar or invoked God's name. In fact these are the ancient Canaanite sanctuaries where the patriarchs found a cult going to the God 'El' ... In reality, these facts are already presented retrospectively from the experience of the Covenant.[1]

In a later discussion of the subject, when Ruiz is challenged – that it is 'a little hasty to state that God's first revelation took place at the Exodus ... there is a revelation to Abraham ... The revelation to the patriarchs ... is not just an adaptation to the Canaanite cults, but there is something that the patriarchs brought with them before this which has served as a vehicle of divine revelation'[2] – he modifies his position slightly. The new position is that 'it is the first explicit revelation with a community dimension ... It does not mean that it is the first time that God is known in history, but the first time he discloses himself explicitly in order to bring together a community.'[3]

The point at issue, which is quite fundamental for the interpretation, not only of the Exodus narrative but also of the entire
history of Israel, is: who is to be considered the father of the
people of Israel, Abraham or Moses? Did a people exist before
the Exodus with a clear understanding of a God who had
already manifested himself in history, spoken to the forefathers
and guaranteed, through the establishing of a first covenant
with Abraham, the fulfilment of a series of promises? At what
point did God's particular saving activity in history begin?

The theologians of liberation unanimously minimise Abraham's importance, seeing the entire history recorded in Genesis
as a kind of literary prolegomena to real history which begins
in Goshen. Strangely, however, they do not inquire after the
significance of this supposed prolegomena in Israel's subsequent
theological meditation in the light of the Exodus.

Several important consequences are drawn from this initial
premise that God first revealed himself in a historical and
definitive way to a group of slaves in Egypt.

I. GOD'S CREATIVE ACTIVITY CAN BE UNDERSTOOD ONLY IN THE LIGHT OF HIS SALVIFIC ACTIVITY

Expressed in a slightly more polemical way, the same statement
may read: creation is impossible without liberation. Three
reasons are given to substantiate this claim.

Firstly, the whole theme of creation is interpreted in the light
of what God revealed, through the Exodus, about man in the
world. 'The Exodus *kerygma*, with its demand for freedom, is
the most radical motivation in creation where God's "project"
concerning man is revealed.'[4] 'The creative act is linked, almost
identified with, the act which freed Israel from slavery in Egypt
... (Isa. 51.9–10).'[5] The creator God is the God who liberated
Israel, rather than the reverse. 'In the Bible, creation does not
appear as a prior step before the work of salvation or liberation,
but is the first liberating act. Israel's history is no more than
the prolongation of the creative act.'[6]

Secondly, as a consequence of the historically prior experience of God in the Exodus, creation is interpreted almost exclusively in terms of salvation. In this respect, Gutierrez is quite
categorical: 'Biblical faith is, above all, faith in a God who

reveals himself in historical events, in a God who saves within history. Creation is presented within the Bible not as a prior step to salvation, but as something already introduced in the salvific process.'[7] The proof text given to establish this claim is Ephesians 1.3–5. Gutierrez then gives a series of texts to establish this further claim that 'creation appears as the first salvific act': Isaiah 43.1; 42.5–6; 54.5; 44.24; Jeremiah 33.25ff.; 10.16; 27.5; 32.17; Malachi 2.10 and Psalms 74, 89, 93, 95, 135 and 136.

Thirdly, exactly the same point is made by the New Testament when it takes up the theme of the unity of creation and salvation in the work of Christ: 'The only christological meaning of creation and salvation (Col. 1.15–20) is summed up in the "creation of a new man".'[8]

> The redemptive action of Christ, the foundation of all that exists, is also conceived as a re-creation and presented in a context of creation (cf. Col. 1.15–20; 1 Cor. 8.6; Heb. 1.2; Eph. 1.1–22) ... The work of Christ is a new creation. In this sense, Paul speaks of a 'new creation' in Christ (2 Cor. 5.17; Gal. 6.15). Moreover, it is through this 'new creation', that is to say, through the salvation which Christ affords, that creation acquires its full meaning (cf. Rom. 8) ... Creation and salvation therefore have, in the first place, a Christological sense: all things have been created in Christ, all things ... saved in him (cf. Col. 1.15–20).[9]

2. GOD'S SALVATION EXTENDS TO THE WHOLE OF CREATION

From the viewpoint of a unitary concept of God's salvific acts in creation and in historical liberation, it is evident that salvation cannot remove a person from the world. Nor is there an interior space within man which, being somehow immune from contact with the world, can be the object of God's salvific activity. Moreover, God's salvific activity is collective; it starts on the political and social level and ends on that level. 'The liberation of the Israelites in Egypt was an event with political and social consequences. God did not begin by saving in the spiritual sphere, not even from sin. He saves the total man, whose human realisation he himself, or other men who abuse their power of social status, may hinder.'[10]

The salvation/liberation theme is taken up in the New Testament, especially by Paul, in the re-interpretation of the Exodus/Passover motif as the meaning of Christ's death and resurrection. This re-interpretation is the discovery of the 'reserve-of-meaning' in the Exodus, in the light of the Christ-event, which recapitulates, and extends the original liberating act.

> When we come to the Christ-event and to his Easter-mystery as a 'liberating act', we do not lose sight of those aspects of the Exodus which have already been manifested [i.e. political and social liberation]. These become subsumed in a decisive deepening of the theme ... The Old Testament was not able to develop a theology of the liberation of structures. But Paul does do so, because he interprets the Christ-event from the religious situation of oppression lived out by his people.[11]

The objective structures from which man is liberated are the law, sin and death, all of which estrange man from his original vocation and his possibilities of realisation.

The meaning of Christ's death and resurrection as a liberating act, involving the basic structures which hold man in slavery, unable himself to bring about his unique historical programme of humanisation, looks back to the Exodus as a first manifestation of liberation from oppression and forward to all subsequent acts in which 'every kind of action which has, as its goal, a fuller and more human life is within the sphere of love which springs from Christ's liberation.'[12] Salvation by Christ, then, 'is not a future event, but the final development, the ultimate consequence of a process already radically begun and on the way to success...'[13]

From the viewpoint of God's unitary salvation in creation and in historical liberation, it is also evident that salvation does not depend upon membership in the Church. Segundo argues this point, exegetically, from Paul's development of the Adam/Christ typology:

> It is well known how St Paul ... insisted on the typological opposition Adam/Christ. Adam communicates sin and death to everyone; Christ, *equally to everyone* ('even more', says

Paul), communicates righteousness and life ... Now it is strictly contradictory to affirm, simultaneously, Christ's total victory over Adam *in every man* even to the results respectively of righteousness and sin (Rom. 5), and a restrictive condition, totally absent in the diffusion of sin, namely, the need to be a member [of the Church], to respond with a personal act of conversion and faith. If Adam makes us, involuntarily, sinners, how can Christ's victory be so total that he wants us voluntarily to be believers?[14]

According to this argument, there must, therefore, be another way of being incorporated into Christ's universal and total salvation. 'Man is saved if he opens himself to God and to others, even if he is not clearly aware that he is doing so ...; men ... respond to [salvation offered in Christ] even when they do not know Jesus Christ explicitly; they do so when, under the influence of grace, [they] take on the task of constructing the world and ... enter into communion with their fellow men'.[15]

'The idea of universal salvation ... leads to the question of the intensity of the presence of the Lord and therefore of the religious significance of man's action in history.'[16] In other words, man is saved when he puts himself within the sphere of the continuation of Christ's saving work of liberating the oppressed.

7. CREATION AND MAN AS THE SUBJECT OF THE RECREATION OF HISTORY

Here we consider the way in which the universal extension of Christ's liberating work is applied to the free re-creation of man and how it is related to the biblical view of creation.

Man's creation in the Bible is portrayed only within the context of his first historical act of liberation and of his call to freedom and maturity. 'When the Yahwist and the Priestly document say that Yahweh created man free, they wish more to emphasise that man is free than that God created him.... In the Yahwistic narration (Gen. 2.4–4.26), the emphasis is on man's causality, not God's. 'The biblical description of the creation of man and woman (Gen. 1.26–4.16) is dedicated principally to emphasising [man's] autonomous human power.'[17]

In other words, the creation narratives were written precisely to emphasise the dignity, creativity and freedom of man with respect to a historical process for which he alone is responsible: 'The first chapters of Genesis offer us another kerygmatic "core" for the understanding of man's liberation. With one difference from the Book of Exodus. In this latter, an act of liberation is spelt out, whilst in Genesis we are given the image of "liberated" man who satisfies the Creator's plans.'[18]

Viewed from the perspective of a people who had experienced this act of liberation, and in contrast to the cosmogonic world views of other Near-Eastern peoples, the biblical narrative of creation brings out four aspects of man's charter for the conquest of time and space:

1. 'In the mythical world view man remains tied to the cosmos and the rite ... Thus, man does not construct a future – which is only possible by immersing oneself in time as a value – but continually projects his return to a primal and a historical time. In the Genesis "man-view", man is freed from the cosmos because God, the creator, is considered transcendent and distinct from the world ... The world is "profane" for free man. He has been placed in it to dominate it, to continue its creation (Gen. 1.28; 2.5–7).'[19]

2. 'In the biblical world-view creation is an *ephapax*. It is the starting-point for history and the *telos*. It does not repeat the cosmogony but anticipates eschatology.'[20]

3. 'There is a total denial of any dualism God/Chaos in Genesis 1. Chaos is "demythologised" ... The world, therefore, is intelligible because God orders it through his creative and efficacious word.'[21]

4. 'Each of the two creation traditions emphasises man's significance as the *telos* of creation. They are not concerned about man's component parts but about his purpose ... The subject of civilisation in Genesis 2 pictures man as created, in order to re-create the earth.'[22]

4. CONCLUSION

The close link made between creation and historical acts of liberation in a unitary, overall design of God for the world, gives to liberation theology its chief biblical/theological basis for considering man's history as an open-ended process for which he is fundamentally responsible: 'When man realises his potential, prolonging the work of creation through his labour ... he places himself inside the process of saving history.'[23]

Man's struggle to remove all barriers to genuine self-realisation, freedom and fraternity, is an integral part of God's continuing creative work seen in terms of liberation. 'To participate in the process of liberation is already, in a certain sense, a salvific work.'[24] This work is not the exclusive work of Christians, for every man, in so far as he is conscious of his place in creation and of the need to construct, within the society of men, a genuinely new creation, can participate in the process.

> If we look more deeply into the question of the value of salvation which emerges from our understanding of history – that is, a liberating praxis – we see that at issue is a question concerning *the very meaning of Christianity*. To be a Christian is to accept and to live – in solidarity, in faith, hope and charity – the meaning that the Word of the Lord and our encounter with him give to the historical becoming of mankind on the way toward total communion.[25]

In other words, to open oneself to the needs of one's neighbours (in today's reality of structural oppression this means the exploited), is to open oneself to God's continuing act of creation and salvation inaugurated in the death and resurrection of Christ. 'The human disposition to do "good works" or not do them ... is the only criterion for who is to be saved and who is to be condemned that we find in the New Testament.'[26] These works, one should add, spring from faith and obedience to God's call; they are not works of the law.

CHAPTER TEN

THE IMPORTANCE
AND REALITY OF MAN

I. MAN'S PLACE IN HISTORY

None of our writers has developed a full anthropology from the first chapters of Genesis. On the whole there has been a greater tendency to see man essentially as alienated man, primarily the object of a liberating process, rather than as man created free and responsible. Croatto, however, has dedicated several of his writings to the concept of man in the biblical narrative of creation. His conclusions contribute the background to a consideration of man as both alienated and restored to his manhood.

He begins by establishing the place of Genesis 1–2 in a study on liberation and freedom. 'The first book of the Bible, which interprets man's "meaning" in the world from the standpoint of his radical and ontological origin, does not speak of liberation; however, it clearly establishes the statute of *free* man.' This vocation of man for freedom has also to be viewed in the light of the Exodus experience. 'Man's vocation is understood in virtue of an historical experience of *liberation* ... The pages of Genesis ... are the interpretation of the latter, expressed in the language of origins, of man's ontological projection.'[1]

This 'vocation of man for freedom, to "be more", claimed for everyman in the ideological passage of Genesis' becomes the ideal for Israelite faith in all generations following that of the Exodus and can be taken up again as 'an interpreting Word ... [by] the prophet, to denounce false paths or to announce the blessing.'

Croatto emphasises certain aspects of the Genesis account of man, either because they have particular relevance to the subsequent themes of liberation, or because they give a profile of man from the standpoint of a liberation already effected:

a. *Man's essence and transcendence*

In contrast to the religious traditions of Egypt and Mesopotamia which speak only of the king (or high state functionaries) as possessing God's image, Genesis speaks of man as created in the image of God. Whereas the other religions speak of the king bearing God's image as from a particular, sacred moment of his life (e.g. his coronation), Genesis speaks of it as a reality as from his very creation. The 'royal ideology' of the whole ancient Middle East was broken, in principle, when Israel was liberated from the power of Pharaoh, considered to be God's viceroy on earth. The fact that the description of man occurs in a passage which emphasises that God is the creator, and that man bears God's image never wiped out by human sin, means that man possesses creative powers.

b. *Man's mission in the world*

'Man is the last of [God's] works, presented as unique. The most significant factor is that, once man is placed in the world, God ceases to create'. As the crowning part of the whole creation, man is not subject to creation but is placed over it to dominate it freely as an autonomous being. In Genesis 1.28ff., man is held responsible for the cultivation and domestication of the earth and the animals. In Genesis 4.17–22, 'technology' (metallurgy and architecture) which completes the cultural horizon of the ancient world, is added. Man is lord of the earth only as the unity, mankind. A man may not use his skills selfishly, in order to dominate other men, but solely for their benefit.

c. *Mythical man and biblical man*

According to the ancient cosmogonies, man lives in a world which, because it harbours the sacred life of the gods, must continually be 'consecrated' through elaborate 'rites of passage', according to the recurring rhythms of nature. Man is thus tied to a *kosmos* which has to be placated, in order that it may yield its life until the following year comes round: mythical man is not free, a creator in the sense of his vocational conscience; rather he is subjected to the *kosmos*. In this sense he ever searches for a non-creative security.

The Genesis account of creation, on the other hand, speaks of a creator God who exists prior to and independently of the *kosmos.* This concept of God first came to Israel in the Exodus experience of liberation when they were confronted with a personal God who acts in history, is independent of nature and superior to the gods of the other nations.

Man, therefore, created in the image of God, is man in history, responsible for his destiny. The world is not the abode of the gods, but of man. Man's relationship to God is not cosmic but dialogical: 'man is also called to account by the prophet or by the Gospel'; the promise imposes upon man a movement forwards. It possesses great significance for man's meaning in the world. Time is valued as a 'contribution to the future' which is 'fullness' and not 'an emptying'.

To sum up then, 'Man created in the image of God is free, both in his ontological radicality and in his projection in the world, in his essence and in his vocation ... Man is called to freedom both for himself and for others, as an ontological vocation and as one programmatically "liberated" by God in an Event of salvation history.'

2. MAN'S ALIENATION FROM HIS HISTORICAL DESTINY

a. *The old man*

Alienated man, in order to emphasise the contrast with the project of his re-creation in Christ, the 'new man', can conveniently and biblically be described as the 'old man': 'the old man is he who lives alienated from his essential vocation ... by losing his ontological and existential place.'[2] Man's vocation is, in Freire's phrase, 'to be more'. This vocation has been lost through injustice, exploitation, the violence of the oppressors and an unjust order. The result is man's dehumanisation, or 'being less', which is currently concealed by alienated man in the 'de-ontological illusion' of 'possessing more'.

This 'being less' is the result of a basic selfishness in which man closes himself off from God and from his fellow man. He is unable to fulfil his deepest calling: that of loving the other. The compensation of 'possessing more' leads, inevitably, to man's unfree domination of his neighbour. Moreoever the old man, man in the world since his original alienation, is now subject to alienating forces. Paul speaks of sin, law and death, which are manifested in a sense of bondage, in fear of oneself and in the corruption of the universe and of our own bodies. 'The evils from which we "are saved" are no more and no less than the shackles which hinder a creative existence.'

b. *The meaning of man's fall*

Those authors who have concerned themselves with the interpretation of the origin of man's alienation have not paid much attention either to the redactional or the philosophical problems of Genesis 3–11. They have been more interested in explaining the 'reserve of meaning' in these chapters for man's actual situation of alienation.

Once again, man's original sin can be fully understood only in the light of the Exodus experience. 'The sin of Genesis 3 is the breaking of a covenant, it is the reflection of a situation through which Israel lived many times. The biblical representation of sin presupposes a salvation-experience for man.'[3] 'Genesis was written completely under the inspiration of the Exodus and as a prologue to the irruption of Yahweh's justice, which, in saving a people from oppression, would determine history ... The Yahwist decided to write a pre-history of the Exodus in order to explain the origin of sin...'[4]

The fall of man is described as being due to man's own responsibility: 'Sin is foreign [to man], the work of his own freedom';[5] 'man ... cannot now attribute his ills to *destiny* but to selfishness and the lust for power over his brethren.'[6] Therefore, alienation may not be envisaged as an integral part of man's nature or essence. 'Sin is not deduced from the human essence nor from creation nor from contingency nor from finitude ... Sin and death *entered* into the world (Romans 5.12). They were not there at the beginning ... they entered because of one man.'[7] Theological fatalism conceives of original sin as an integral part of human nature.[8] We should not allow ourselves to be put off by it. This means, among other things, that capitalism is only one manifestation of a chain of aberrations which are caused by a fundamental and original distortion.[9]

However, the actual cause of man's fall is disputed by two different lines of interpretation: we may call one the *ontological* and the other the *moral* cause. Some writers (notably Croatto) look for the deepest significance of man's alienation in the Genesis 3 narrative, as this describes man's excessive ambition to appropriate for himself the attributes of divinity.[10] Others (notably Miranda) look for it in the Genesis 4 narrative, which describes the first actual act of injustice: namely, fratricide.[11] For some, then, the emphasis will be on the Pauline *asebeia*; for others, on *adikia* (Romans 1.18). The first, obviously, does not exclude the second; but the second has tended to exclude the first.

(*i*) *The ontological cause.* Man's basic problem, re-told in the story of Adam, is his supra-ontological desire to be as God. This desire is translated into the wish to 'possess' a knowledge which is both infinite and wholly autonomous but even more than this, the wish to be as God and not to die (Gen. 3.4). The result of the desire (sin) is pride which 'enters into the world' in the basic form of unbelief, selfishness, distrust and untruthfulness: 'selfism is the infinite *desire* for that which is beyond the limit (the divine); it loses sight of the infinite *demand* (of love) within finiteness.' Man is, thereby, wrenched from his true place in the world and lives a life of anxiety in the face of an existence without meaning and without trust.

Sin, according to the biblical *kerygma*, is opposed, in the first place, to faith rather than to love (the latter is the result of the former in the experience of salvation). 'If we remember the sweep of faith [faith as "recognition of God", as "confidence" in his Word, as "faithfulness" to the Covenant, as "acceptance" of the one sent, as "openness" to the gift and as the "power" of witness] ... we shall understand that the Bible offers us an inverse spectrum of sin as "ignorance" of God ... "denial" of his approaches, "inoculation" against his gift...'[12]

Man's real problem of alienation, then, is that he is no longer ontologically at home in the universe. Making himself 'as the gods', he has entered into the magic circle of sacredness and has lost his autonomy as a creature. All the sins described in Genesis 3–11 are but the outworkings, within civilisation, of man's lostness in the world.

In spite of his repeated emphasis on social and political injustice and the misery of man as the real concrete manifestations of sin, Gutierrez is in basic agreement with Croatto's analysis, in the sense that sin is more universal, radical and congenital than its particular manifestations in time and space might suppose.

In the Theology of Liberation, the term liberation is not reduced to the political level; even more, I would say, there is an insistence on liberation from sin and on communion with God, which is its immediate consequence and *raison d'être*. It is this liberation from sin which gives the process of liberation its unity ... The question which the Theology of Liberation asks is: what is the link between the liberation from sin, on the one hand, and political liberation and man's liberation on different levels, on the other?[13]

(*ii*) *The moral cause.* By classifying as the moral cause, a different interpretation given by other theologians of liberation to the question of the root problem of sin, we do not intend to imply that the ontological cause is not also profoundly moral. Rather, our intention is to point out one aspect of a particular exegetical study of the first chapters of Genesis. For in this case, those of our writers who have reflected seriously on the issue see Genesis 4, rather than Genesis 3, as the original account of man's fall. If Genesis 3 portrays sin in terms of rejection of confidence in the God who speaks, creates and saves, Genesis 4 portrays it in terms of an absolute rejection of concern and responsibility for my neighbour (i.e. the one who is nearest to me). 'Sin is to refuse to love, to reject communion and brotherhood, to reject even now the very meaning of human existence.'[14] Miranda has explored this thesis exegetically.

The difference in emphasis, if such it be, between Croatto and Miranda, cannot be discovered at the level of language, for Miranda also asserts that 'in Romans 1.18–32 Paul himself has described how the culpable ignorance of God by its own immanent recoil throws mankind into the growing power of injustice.'[15] Nor would Croatto necessarily disagree that the story of Cain and Abel is the original account of man's fall. Rather, the difference lies in the interpretation of the ultimate meaning of the break between man and God. For Miranda, knowledge of God is wholly to be conceived of in terms of inter-human justice. Sin, therefore, is also exclusively inter-human injustice. 'The biblical authors implacably insist that a god conceived of as existing outside the interpersonal summons to justice and love is not the God revealed to them, but rather some idol.'[16] 'The meaning of "sin" in Romans 3.9 is specified as inter-human injustice for the whole rest of the letter.'[17] Miranda's position can fairly be stated in the proposition 'The origin of evil is not in Adam's sin against God, but in Cain's sin against Abel.'

From the Exodus account of God intervening in response only to their *cry* of desperation (Exod. 3.7–9), to liberate a people from servitude, Miranda goes back to the Genesis account of Cain and Abel and finds in Genesis 4.10 ('the voice of your brother's blood is *crying* to me from the ground') an exact parallel to the Exodus passage. In other words, the clamour (Hebrew root *saʿak/zaʿak*) of the Israelites points to the basic human sin which is 'an arrogant disregard of elementary human rights, or cynical insensitivity to the suffering of others'.[18] And this sin, 'whose origin is being explained is the sin of Cain; it is not just any sin nor is it sin in general.'[19]

Miranda, then, lays an exegetical basis for various conclusions.[20]

1. That the true prologue to the Exodus narrative is only to be found in the anguished cry of the oppressed: that God's first liberating act was due to the 'pure' state of injustice which evoked 'the agonised plea of the victim for help in some great injustice' (cf. Exodus 22.21–3).
2. That God did not intervene on behalf of a people already constituted, nor because of some covenant or promise made beforehand. Rather, his intervention created a new people. Israel was created on the basis of God's just response to the cry of the oppressed.
3. That the origin of the clamour of the oppressed is traced back to Cain's voluntary act of murder which produced the first cry of anguish.
4. That the history of Adam, which demonstrates important parallels with that of Cain (e.g. 3.9 with 4.9; 3.17 with 4.11), is recounted only to emphasise that God did not create man a murderer from the beginning, but that his injustices are entirely his own responsibility.
5. That 'Cain is the first concrete man', and with Gen. 4.1–11 human history begins. 'The voice of your brother's blood is crying to me from the ground' is 'the essential

presentation of the God who intervenes in this history. And this was before there were covenants, patriarchs, promises, and commandments'.

The exact relationship, within the Scriptures, between *asebeia* and *adikia* will have to be explored later. As a preliminary statement we would agree with Dumas that 'the two fundamental sins of the Old Testament [and why not the New?] are injustice and idolatry'. We would also agree with Gutierrez that it is fruitless to speak, biblically, of a theology of liberation without having defined, exegetically, the relationship between various manifestations of sin and what he describes as sin, the fundamental alienation.

We believe that a careful study of this relationship will unlock unsuspected doors to a richer understanding of liberation and freedom, and at the same time, help to correct certain distortions within liberation theology's overall hermeneutical procedure.

c. *Sin structured into the kosmos*

Frequently our authors turn to the New Testament (and especially the Johannine) theme of the 'world' as the objective recipient of a super-personal concentration of evil – what Pironio calls the 'mystery of iniquity'.

This is the world in the sense of humanity as a whole, the third and only non-neutral meaning given to *kosmos* in the Johannine literature. In this sense the world is both 'impersonal, diabolical, the incarnation of Satan' and the object of salvation, the object of the removal of sin.

The nature of the world in the Johannine literature is described by Segundo as:

1. inherently impotent. 'The world cannot...' (John 7.7; 8.21–3; 14.17) see, know, give peace, hear (John 14.19; 14.27; 1 John 3.1; 4.5; 5.19).
2. ahistorical. Everything repeats itself. Its logic is the logic of what used to be new but is now custom, the logic of those unable to discern Christ's *hour*, his opportunity (John 7.4).
3. closed within its own circle, opposed to everything new, essentially conservative (1 John 4.5–6). 'Everything is

already fixed: both desire, love, and knowledge . . .' (John 15.19; 17.14; 1 John 2.15).

4. the sphere in which salvation has been consummated (John 3.16–17; 12.47; 4.42; 1.29; 6.33; 6.51; 1 John 2.2).

Segundo concludes that 'the fundamental sin, to which the Gospel refers, is not, then, individual breaking of the law, but the political denial of history. Jesus overcomes this in order to deliver men from being subject to the destructive lie.'[21]

3. THE NEW MAN

In accord with the theology of liberation's reiterated emphasis on the need for liberation to extend beyond the mere structures of society, in order that the permanent transformation of the latter may be guaranteed as a continuing reality, there has grown up in the theological literature of the continent (e.g. the Medellín Documents: 'We will not have a new continent without new and renewed structures; above all there will be no new continent without new men who, in the light of the Gospel, can be truly free and responsible') a discussion of the basis and characteristics of the new man.

As would be expected, the new man is firstly to be understood in terms of the resurrected Christ. Christ is the new man, definitively liberated, and the truth about man has been revealed by God in Christ. Christ is the new man because he has passed from death to life; from the sphere of Adam, the old man – the sphere of sin and death aggravated by the entrance of the law (Rom. 5.12–21) – to the sphere of freedom from these powers.

According to Croatto, it is supremely in Romans 6 that Paul throws light on the question, 'why Christ emerges into life *from death*, whose radical impulse is not the mortal condition of the body but *the deadly power of the law*'. The law 'kills' (Rom. 7.10) but Christ, 'born under the law' (Gal. 4.4), 'represents everyone subject to it, and takes upon himself its "curse" (Gal. 3.13) . . . The death of Christ is, therefore, the extreme and concentrated effect of the deadly efficacy of the law. But as he reaches death, he is raised by the Spirit and passes through to a new life (Rom. 8.11). In the Kingdom of the Spirit, of freedom and love, the law has no place.'[22]

This new life, naturally, is open to all those who are joined to Christ by baptism (Rom. 6.1ff.; and cf. the baptismal echoes in Gal. 2.19ff., 26ff.). They too have passed beyond the law's reach. 'The law of the Spirit of life in Christ has set me free from the law of sin and death' (Rom. 8.2).

> Everything that we noted about death as the liquidation of the law, sin and itself, is valid now for the Christian by means of and from the perspective of baptism. If sin led to death (Rom. 8.10; 6.13), in that very moment one dies *to* sin (Rom. 6.11) and one lives to God ... For this reason Paul can also point to the fact that the Christian *dies to the law* 'by the body of Christ' (Rom. 7.4), in a clear allusion to the resurrected body of Christ into which the former is 'incorporated' through baptism.[23]

The fundamental characteristic of the new man is that he is 'liberated from every alienation', but, more particularly, from the alienation of the law. Miranda develops this thought in the following argument. Man is delivered from this present aeon (a synonym for *kosmos*) through incorporation into Christ. The *kosmos*, or civilisation, is the institutional condensation of incarnated sin. The law, which generates this present civilisation (aeon) is the instrument of sin (Rom. 5.20; 7.11, 13; I Cor. 15.56; Gal. 3.19), or rather it is identified with sin as a supernatural reality. It is from this law 'as the normative quintessence of the entire cultural and social structure which we call human civilisation and Paul calls *aion* or *kosmos*,' that man is liberated (Gal. 1.4; 4.5).[24]

In other words, the passage from death to newness of life means, in Miranda's thought, the destruction of the whole of civilisation as it is presently organised under the law and the birth of a new world without law. 'Paul wants a world without law ... Neither Kropotkin nor Bakunin nor Marx nor Engels made assertions against the law more powerful and subversive than those which Paul makes. Paul is convinced not only that the law has failed in human history in its attempt to achieve justice, but that justice cannot be achieved in the world as long as law exists' (Rom. 5.20; 1 Cor. 15.56; Rom. 7.10–11).[25] 'At this moment [the moment of Christ's resurrection] God breaks all our schemata, whether moral, legal, cultural, social, religious, cultic, etc. According to these schemata, Christ is the impious one, the personification of sin. Therefore Paul says that God "sent him in the likeness of the flesh of sin and in the place of sin", and thus he was able "to destroy sin in the flesh" (Rom. 8.3). It is a question of believing in this God more than in human civilisation and law. Faith is an irreversible break: either ... or.'[26]

CHAPTER ELEVEN

CHRIST THE LIBERATOR

In the theology of liberation a re-interpretation of the Exodus is taken up in terms of the greater and deeper deliverance which Christ effects through his death and resurrection, forming a new creation, not now of one nation, but of the whole of mankind. Gutierrez, for example, pictures the activity of the Trinity as a series of concentric manifestations of the presence of God (Emmanuel) with his creation, culminating in the incarnation of the resurrected Christ, God's temple through his Spirit, in every man.[1]

For various reasons (e.g. insistence on concrete history as the sphere of God's activity; suspicion of any tendency to 'spiritualise' liberation; rejection of an existentialist Christology as ideologically conservative; and emphasis on a unitary history), the theology of liberation has placed less emphasis on a Christology of the 'Christ of Faith' and more on that of the 'Jesus of History'. Miranda, in the preface to *Being and the Messiah*, says for example that 'Christ died so that we might know that not everything is permitted. But not any Christ. The Christ who cannot be co-opted by accommodationists and opportunists is the historical Jesus.'

Nevertheless, even here, no kind of exhaustive study has been done. Miranda largely limits himself to the Johannine writings, and other writers to selected passages within the Synoptic Gospels. Assmann is absolutely accurate, then, when he says that Christology is one of the most dramatic of the gaps in the theology of liberation in Latin America.[2]

However, what has been done in the way of elaborating a New Testament Christology, using the hermeneutical key of oppressors/oppressed, although it is very limited, is not, thereby, less significant. We have been able to discover in the writings of the theology of liberation a certain typology in the use of the symbolic status of the historical Jesus. This typology has at least a three-fold dimension: the concept of grace in Jesus' teaching and attitudes; Jesus' attitude to the political reality of his time; and the Christology inherent in the 'parable' of the Last Judgment (Matt. 25.31–46).

I. THE CONCEPT OF GRACE IN JESUS' TEACHING AND ATTITUDES

From the point of view of a relevant hermeneutic for Latin America, it is important to discover the exact nature of the gratuitousness of Jesus' love, both in his life and in his self-offering death.[3] It is Segundo who has primarily tried to answer the question with an analysis of certain passages from the Synoptic Gospels.[4]

Starting from the question whether the Gospels presuppose a realisation of Christianity in 'mass' terms, or only in terms of individuals, Segundo refers to the use of the word *charis* in the teaching of Jesus. Although the word occurs only three times in a definite theological sense in Jesus' teaching (in Luke 6.32–4, in a threefold parallel rhetorical question) nevertheless, according to Segundo, the concept is central to his teaching, for it expresses his unique approach to ethics in the 'much more' which he demands of his disciples: 'but I say to you that hear, love your enemies ...' (Luke 6.27). This is Luke's summary of the ascending series of demands presented by Matthew and introduced with the formula: 'but I say to you ...' Its intention is to highlight the ethic of gratuitousness.

This ethic is a way of life which destroys the mechanistic and routine ethic of responding to others in the same way as they act towards you. 'Bless those who bless us, love those who love us, do good to those who do good to us, etc.', is a mechanism, says Segundo, 'which is both the simplest and most immediately satisfactory'. Jesus' ethic is not intended to be enforced with all the rigour of a new law, but is nevertheless to be a very definite guideline designed to distinguish his true followers. It is this ethic, or way of life, which is new, original and re-interpretative in the teaching of Jesus.

Jesus introduces the word *charis* (wrongly translated, according to Segundo, by 'merit' in some Bibles and, we would add, by 'credit' in others) at the precise point where he questions the mechanistic ethic of immediate results: 'if you love (do good, lend) those who love (do good, lend) you, *poia humin charis estin?*' The meaning of the word *charis* in this context is given by the Matthean equivalent, *ti perisson poieite* (Matt. 5.47) which Segundo translates, 'what extraordinary thing do you possess?' (cf. Arndt and Gingrich, *Lexicon*, pp. 885–6; the translation 'reward' of RSV and NEB seem too highly conventional). The *charis*, then, is synonymous with an extraordinary conduct, that is, 'whatever cannot be explained on the basis of mass-mechanisms, whatever cannot be expected from an automatic or mechanised response by man.'

Segundo concludes his initial study of Jesus' attitude, which is not unique to this passage (cf. Matt. 7.14; 9.37; 22.11; 6.24 5; Luke 12.32; 9.23–4), by saying that 'it would seem as if the only Christian ethic possible – the rest are not Christian according to our passage – is situated in that which is extraordinary (beyond the normal) . . . The Gospel is not destined for a mass-fulfilment.'

In the second part of his study on the concept of grace in the teaching and attitudes of Jesus, however, Segundo makes some very significant qualifications to this initial conclusion. This time his concern is hermeneutical rather than strictly exegetical; how is this Jesus (the Christ of the Gospels) who is listened to and understood from the perspective of a revolutionary commitment to the oppressed, to be presented? In other words, how do we forge a Christology for Latin America which is neither ideologically manipulated, nor vague, nor undifferentiated from the Christ who appears in the Gospel sources?[5] The problem for the revolutionary is that this Christ demands, not that kind of efficacious love whose fulfilment could be determined by the right kind of analysis in any given situation, but the kind of love which is not interested in 'success' as a criterion for its exercise.

In the light of the apparent contradiction between a revolutionary commitment and the ethical demands of Christ, many 'Christian' militants have abandoned the hermeneutical task. Not so Segundo, for he does not think that the problem lies in an inadequate exegesis, but rather in a too limited hermeneutic: 'Revolutionary commitment makes possible a new interpretation of the Jesus of History, hitherto unsuspected.'

The hermeneutical problem as posed in this way is insoluble

only if Christ's demands are universalised, if they are made the
only norm for any genuine transformation of society. However,
according to Segundo, this supposition is exegetically unsound
if we take into consideration three points. Firstly, the Gospels
do not present us only with a minority Jesus, i.e. one who
ignores the weight and necessity of mass-mechanisms. Without
giving in to these pressures, his love is honestly and humanly
exercised within an economy of energy. Secondly, 'Jesus ...
prudently but decisively, used mass-mechanisms for the preaching of his minority message.' Segundo gives as one example his
use of the term kingdom, 'charged with "mass" emotion ...
in the context of an Israel dominated by the Roman Empire
and in which the Zealots acted' and, as another, his works of
compassion. Both were evidently destined to awake expectations in the masses. Thirdly, 'Jesus was very careful ... not to
make his minority demands into a new ... "super-law" which
would replace the old one.' In other words, the ultimate ethical
norm in Jesus' teaching was what was made for man (i.e. for
man's future well-being). As a result, none of Christ's specific
demands can be said to be right in any and every circumstance.
There is a Christian liberty, which Paul made the touchstone
of what genuinely sprang from the New Covenant, and this can
manipulate the law in the interests of the creativity of love.

Segundo's approach to the understanding of one key passage
in the Gospels is significant for two interrelated reasons. Firstly,
it demonstrates succinctly how exegesis and hermeneutics may
be related together in the methodology of the theology of liberation; and secondly, it demonstrates how the theology of liberation rejects a chronological difference (or priority) between theological reflection (Christology) and ethical decision. We shall
discuss some of the implications of this approach in the final
part of this book.

2. JESUS' ATTITUDE TO THE POLITICAL REALITY
OF HIS TIMES

The theology of liberation takes advantage of the recent
renewed interest, in New Testament studies, in the political
consciousness of Jesus, represented by the studies of Cullmann,
Hengel, Brandon, Trocmé, Yoder and others. Although it

theoretically admits the correctness of a *redaktionsgeschichtlich* approach to the exegesis of the Gospels (the editorial process of the Gospels is hermeneutical), it tends to accept the text at its present face value, again without much attempt at a detailed exegetical study: 'We can recognise clearly this august figure which was Christ the Liberator, from his prophetic consecration in his baptism in Jordan to the drama of his death for the cause of man's liberation'.[6]

Gutierrez mentions three specific contexts in which Jesus' political attitude becomes sufficiently clear for us to be able to deduce a Christological hermeneutic from the Gospels: Jesus' relationship to the Zealot movement; his attitude to the religious and political leaders of the people; and his death at the hands of Pilate.[7]

a. *Jesus and the Zealots*

Gutierrez maintains that there were a number of points in which 'we find a coincidence between the Zealots and the attitudes and teachings of Jesus' and yet, that 'Jesus kept his distance from the Zealot movement'. He finds the coincidences in Jesus' preaching of the kingdom's proximity and the role he plays in its coming in the affirmation that 'the kingdom suffers violence' and that 'the violent conquer it'; in his attitude towards the Jews in the service of the Romans; in the episode of the cleansing of the Temple, and in his influence over the people who want to make him king.

He finds the differences in Jesus' consciousness of the universality of his mission which could not be equated with the Zealot's narrow nationalism; in their respective attitudes to the law; in the fact that, for Jesus, the kingdom is essentially a gift, not the fruit of one's own efforts; that he saw that oppression and injustice are not limited to one particular historical situation, and cannot be eliminated without going to their root causes; and that he resisted every kind of political/religious messianism because it fails to respect either the depth of religious sentiment or the consistency of political action.[8]

In general terms, when the theologians of liberation speak of Jesus' relationship to the Zealot movement they are careful to resist the temptation to find immediate parallels between one political situation and another (what Assmann would call 'fundamentalism of the left, short cuts which try to transplant paradigms and situations from the biblical world to ours without being aware of the historical mediations'.) They believe that Jesus was tempted by the Zealot movement (following Cullmann, *The State in the New Testament*) because of the people's expectations, but was never really sympathetic towards it as a concrete, historical answer to suffering.

b. *The political and religious leaders*

Jesus' relationship to the leaders of the people is governed by his belief that the chief benefactors of the kingdom which he proclaims are the poor: 'In a most remarkable way, Jesus seeks out the ill, the humble, sinners, children, foreigners. Each one "lacks" something; health, opportunity in life, prestige (in comparison with the "just"), abilities, acceptance with the Jews. They are all cast on one side. If they possess values, they cannot express them; neither the very poor, because no one is concerned to bring them justice, nor the rest because religious society scrupulously excludes them'.[9]

This action on the part of Jesus brings him into direct conflict with three groups of people: the Herodians, who are the internal oligarchy of a dependent nation; the Sadducees, who are the religious hierarchy who hide their religious scepticisms behind a façade of religious legality and gain for themselves privileges at the expense of the people; and the Pharisees who, although they reject in theory the sacrilegious presence of the Romans in the land of their fathers, console their consciences by 'a complex world of religious precepts and norms of behaviour which allowed them to live on the margin of that domination.'[10]

The conflict arose because Jesus, with authority, offered the kingdom of God to precisely those whom the Pharisees had excluded because they did not know the law: the Pharisees 'are the "just", those who know God's will and its faithful observers. Their praxis is that of the Law, not of love. Their certainty does not come from their commitment to God's Event, but from the "gnosis" which comes from their knowledge of the law'.[11]

c. *Jesus' death*

The theology of liberation follows the various indications in the Gospels that Jesus died as if he were a seditious political leader: for example, the title on the Cross, his connection with Barabbas, and the actual accusations made by the religious authorities (Luke 23.1–2; John 11.47–50). Gutierrez accepts the verdict of G. Crespy that 'the trial of Jesus was a political trial, he was condemned for Zealotism, although the accusation was not solidly established.'[12] He does not deny, of course, that the final act of judicial condemnation by Pilate was more the effect of a long process than the original cause of the crucifixion: 'The Sanhedrin had religious reasons for condemning a man who claimed to be the Son of God, but it also had political reasons: the teaching of Jesus and his influence over the people challenged the privilege and power of the Jewish leaders.'[13]

The religious reasons for wanting Jesus removed were in some cases the same as those experienced by Jeremiah (cf. Jer. 18.18ff.; 20.1ff.; and the passage 26.7ff. which possesses remarkable parallels to the trial of Jesus): his denunciation of the dehumanising sin of legalism; his promise that the religious institutions would be destroyed; and his circumspect claim to possess the unique authority of the Messiah. They were not, however, necessarily the most decisive. In fact, the theology of liberation inclines to the view, although it has never elaborated the point, that excessive emphasis on the religious reasons for Jesus' death may spring from a false hermeneutic of the Gospels which presents Jesus' ministry in individualistic, internal, apocalyptic and apolitical terms. For this hermeneutic does not see that religious and political motivations are, in fact, intimately linked just at that point where religion is reduced to the keeping of precepts and used as an instrument to bolster the privilege of power.

The theology of liberation does not go into the intricate exegetical and historical problems surrounding the trial of Jesus, though some authors show they have studied the relevant literature. Nevertheless, one interesting point made by Gutierrez underlines the characteristic procedure of its hermeneutic.

A good number of authors undertake to demonstrate that Jesus was innocent of the charges that were imputed to him (see Blinzer, Léon-Dufour, Benoit). It is not clear what the object of these attempts is. Innocent before what justice? Before the justice of the power groups of the Jewish people and the Roman oppressors, Jesus was guilty precisely because he challenged their legitimacy, in the name not of some partisan option, but of a message of love, peace, freedom, and justice. This message undermined the very bases of religious formalism, unjust privileges, and social injustice which supported the order of the power groups...[14]

In other words, Jesus *was* guilty according to a justice which the powerful administered in their own interests. As such he *had* to die.

3. THE LIBERATION THAT JESUS BROUGHT

Mesters dedicates a long section of his book, *La palabra de Dios en la historia de los hombres*, to answering a question which undoubtedly disturbs many in Latin America today: 'Why when Jesus defined his mission in terms of the liberation of the oppressed did he leave an entire people still in slavery?'[15] He begins his answer by arguing that it is wrong to try, without qualification, to identify Jesus' situation with ours. The very way in which the question is phrased shows that the real intention is to obtain Christ's authorisation for our praxis. This procedure, because it tends to start from ideological positions already well entrenched, leads to a sterile and artificial debate of Jesus' ministry. Rather, we should try to discover how the Gospel narratives, questioned from our perspective, can help us to understand our situation better. In this context, the first thing to realise is that whoever proposes to liberate man acts according to criteria which he has deduced from a particular vision of man. We have to ask ourselves, therefore, whether Christ had the same vision of man as we do, and whether we should not endeavour to discover this vision and allow it to criticise our own.

In doing this, we discover, secondly, that Jesus' activity and preaching was conditioned by his interpretation of the reality of the situation he lived in. The Jewish people's slavery was not so much due to Roman domination as to pharisaical religion. This was a far more dangerous slavery, because it was imposed by man upon man in the name of God. 'The "Sabbath" was the touchstone of the legalistic sensibility of the

Pharisees. And it is exactly the "Sabbath" – the day of remembrance of liberation – which is treated lightly by Christ. Because paradoxically, it had become a source of alienation and oppression of consciences.'[16]

Jesus eliminated the easy distinction between the good and the bad. He attacked the easily satisfied conscience of the man who thinks he has fulfilled all his duty towards God. He forbade any approach to man which reduced him to the status of a mere object to be analysed in the name of an abstract law. He especially defended all those who were criticised on account of their reception of the Gospel which he preached.

In other words, he rejected the Pharisees' interpretation of the kingdom as the time of the perfect observance of the law and taught a new version of the kingdom as God's gift of liberation, belonging essentially to the poor and downtrodden of the earth. Croatto understands the beatitudes as Jesus' essential message. They are placed in Matthew at the beginning of Jesus' ministry, in order to underline their 'programmatic' meaning. They are not a call to resignation, as they have often been interpreted, but a call to that liberation which Jesus had already inaugurated in fulfilment of the messianic prophecies which describe the future king as the establisher of justice and the liberator of the poor (Isa. 9.5–7; 11.1–9; Jer. 23.3–8; Ezek. 34.23–7).

Gutierrez, in a lengthy and well-documented discussion of the meaning of poverty in the Bible,[17] concludes that the Matthean version of the beatitude, 'Blessed are the poor in spirit . . .' must be interpreted as meaning spiritual poverty as this was understood in the tradition, beginning with Zephaniah ('ānāwim in 2.3; 3.12–13; 'ebyônim in Jer. 20.13, cf. Ps. 9.11; 34.11; 37.40; 25.3–5; 149.1) – i.e. those who look for the liberating work of the Messiah, those who are totally open to God's word now and in the future.

With regard to the Lucan version, which is more difficult to understand, Gutierrez is convinced that we should neither try to take it literally – 'the poor are privileged . . . because of a socio-economic situation imposed upon them' – nor assimilate it to Matthew's version as if they meant the same thing, for this second line of interpretation minimises the Lucan text. Rather, we are to understand it to mean that the poor are blessed because God's kingdom brings with it necessarily the re-establishment of justice in the world, and the kingdom of God has already begun (Mark 1.15). In other words, 'the elimination of the exploitation and poverty that prevent the poor from being fully human has begun ... Situated in a prophetic perspective, the text in Luke uses the term *poor* in the tradition of ... poverty being an evil and therefore incompatible with the Kingdom of God, which has come in its fullness into history and embraces the totality of human existence.'[18]

In the next chapter we will examine further the meaning of Christ's announcement of the coming of the kingdom and its relevance to the poor and oppressed. At this point we return to Mesters' initial question, and his answer to it.

The fundamental cause of man's alienation, encountered by Jesus, was Pharisaic religion which, instead of interpreting the law as the means of man's progressive liberation ('The Sabbath was made for man'), converted it into an abstract absolute, accepted a very limited vision of man and cut itself off from any change brought by God's free grace. Jesus, in contrast, gave back to man the possiblity of being really free. He brought a creative and regenerative love which, by going to the root of man's oppression within himself, abolished the concept of life as the keeping of external precepts.

The liberation which Christ brought can according to Mesters be expressed thus: 'Christ does not lend himself to man's projects of liberation, giving them the covering of his authority, but he puts himself beside man, stimulating him to project himself towards the future.'

4. THE PARABLE OF THE LAST JUDGMENT (MATT. 25.31–46

In general terms, the theologians of liberation have been more interested in the Christological rather than the eschatological motifs of this well-quoted text of Matthew. Without exhausting all that has been said by the theology of liberation on the subject, we will try, in this brief section, to unfold this further example of their exegesis and hermeneutic. The most extensive and systematic study of the passage has been undertaken by Gutierrez with reference to recent exegetical studies. His primary interest is to shed light on the relationship between one's neighbour and God through the Incarnation of the Word. His study is headed 'Christ in the Neighbour'.[19]

Following J. C. Ingelaere,[20] Gutierrez distinguishes three possible interpretations of the parable. Either it speaks of a general judgment of Christians and non-Christians alike, according to love shown to one's neighbour, especially to those who are most needy; or it speaks only of a judgment of Christians, according to their attitudes to the least favoured members of the Christian community; or the judgment will be of non-Christians, according to their attitude towards the Christian community.

Most exegetes accept the first interpretation, basing themselves on the universality of the two phrases 'all the nations' (v. 32) and 'one of the least of these my brethren' (v. 40). Gutierrez also accepts this interpretation and from it draws three fundamental conclusions.

Firstly, emphasis is put on fellowship and brotherhood as the ultimate meaning of human existence. 'Matthew's text is demanding: "Anything you did not do for one of these, however humble, you did not do for me" (25.45). To abstain from serving is to refuse to love; to fail to act for another is as culpable as expressly refusing to do it.' For this reason, the Matthean text tells us that 'we will be definitively judged by our love for men, by our capacity to create brotherly conditions of life. From a prophetic viewpoint, the judgment ("crisis") will be based, according to Matthew, on the new ethic arising from this universal principle of love.'[21]

Secondly, love can only become real in concrete terms; 'doing' is exalted over simple 'knowing'. The text re-affirms the Old Testament prophetic teaching that knowledge of God is 'doing justice':there is no genuine love for Christ outside of an authentic and concrete service of one's fellow man. The concrete terms are giving food, drink, clothing, welcoming, visiting, etc. Christ in Matthew 25 gives us a picture of judgment, in which a cup of water leads to eternal life and another one, refused, to eternal death.[22]

Thirdly, communion with the Lord is reached only through human mediation. The parable underlines that there is no fellowship with Christ except *by way of brotherly love*. At this point,

Gutierrez returns to Ingelaere's study and examines the various ways in which the identification between Christ and one's neighbour has been explained. These are mystical (the Son of Man as the ideal man, archetype of a new humanity already present in each individual), substitutionary (the Son of Man as a collective reality), and identification as a mode of expression which highlights the 'Christological scope' of love for one's neighbours. Ingelaere rejects each one of these explanations in favour of the representative nature of Christ's ministry through his disciples: 'every act done on behalf of the disciples is done on behalf of the Son of Man, present in their midst: (the relationship) is one of "sympathy" in the strongest sense of the word.' Gutierrez, however, extends the object of the relationship to include the whole of mankind and changes the nature of the relationship from one of representation to one of identification. Jesus Christ, therefore, expresses his relationship to humanity in specific acts of solidarity with the poor and exploited amongst men. And what he teaches us by this identification is that humanity's salvation passes through the disinherited of the earth; they are the bearers of the meaning of history and the 'heirs of the kingdom' (Jas. 2.5).

Dumas, who takes the parable as the biblical foundation for the main thesis of his book, namely that the oppressed masses are the other (alienated) face of the Church, 'the sacrament of humanity', interprets the text from yet another angle.[23]

Firstly, given the fact that Christ is present in the one who suffers (understood universally), our service to suffering humanity reaches Christ: 'he is the goal of man's brotherly gesture towards those who are in need or crushed down'. Secondly, this service does not have to be explicitly done for Christ in order for it to be valid: 'the surprise manifested by those at the King's right and left hand – "Lord, when did we see you?" – is not a simple literary device designed to give the judgement scene more life. It manifests the hidden presence of the Son of Man in history, whose mystery will be fully revealed on the Day of Judgement.' Thirdly, salvation is fulfilled in the daily drama of human existence: 'the profane content of human actions are charged with transcendence because the Son of Man lives among men and desires to be served there.'

Thus Dumas sets out from what he considers to be objectively true, namely, that Jesus is present with those who suffer, independently of man's attitude to them: '*I* was hungry and you gave me no food' (v. 42). Comparing other texts, it is clear that Christ identifies himself also with his disciples and with children (Mark 10.39–45, Mark 9.41; Luke 10.16; John 13.20; Mark 9.37; Matt. 18.5, Luke 9.48), but his identification with his disciples does not go beyond the limits of the rabbinic principle, whereas, if Christ is 'hidden' in the poor and children, it is because they have a very special solidarity with his person, his mission and his kingdom which cannot be reduced to the details of a judicial substitution. Dumas, like Gutierrez, also speaks of 'a real and efficacious substitution which goes as far as identification'.

In the final part of his analysis of the parable, Dumas considers the meaning of Christ's identification with 'the least of his brethren' (understood as the trilogy: disciples, children and the poor of Yahweh). Clearly the identification is not ontological for, although humanity is assimilated to Christ, it does not lose its own constitution: man is not Christ but shares his person, action and goods (or poverty). It supposes and indicates a vision of reality in which there is an interplay between the autonomy of the person as an individual and his existence as a corporate personality in his relationship to Christ. 'Jesus Christ teaches us that infancy, and even more necessity and poverty, constitute a special reason for this presence.' But it is a *situational* assimilation to Christ which does not presuppose that one has to continue being poor or a child to know Christ's presence more perfectly, only that in these situations we recognise dispositions for receiving Christ.

Jesus' identification with man is multiform and organic: 'each one ... is unique with relation to the others ... but if the final judgment is normative, *par excellence*, the Church ought, according to Matthew 25, to venerate this particular presence of Christ who is the least among his brethren ... The poor are ... the visible and evident embodiment, manifestation and continuation, on the public and historical level, of the incarnate presence of the Word of God.'

CHAPTER TWELVE

THE KINGDOM WILL COME

It is perhaps surprising that the theology of liberation, which arose partly as a result of and in response to European political theology with its strong eschatological emphasis, has elaborated no eschatological viewpoint of its own. This reluctance is due to its distrust of an excessive futurising of the eschatological hope. When the emphasis falls on the 'not yet', the urgency of the present (the 'now' of fulfilment) praxis of justice and liberation tends to be removed or to become relative.

Perhaps for this very reason, Miranda has attempted to develop, exegetically, a consistently 'realised' eschatology, in response to the need to put theology and exegesis at the service of liberation. Miranda's eschatological thought also basically includes his Christological reflection.

He starts from the 'suspicion' that a future-orientated eschatology, though having the supposed advantage of judging the relative worth of every achievement, in reality conceals an inability to take seriously and to work for actual radical changes in man's present position. He then concludes that only a realised eschatology makes possible a practical obedience to God's transcendent word of challenge to bring into being a world-order of justice, peace and brotherhood.

To postpone the kingdom, to postpone the Messiah, is to prevent them from ever being real. This is the eternal stratagem employed to separate us from the only real otherness that summons us. It is to fall back again into the eternal return, into the self's grand deception that enables us to continue enclosed in our own immanence, whispering to ourselves assurances that there is nothing new.... If there is no *eschaton*, the word ceases to be transcendent; its summons is neutralised and ceases.[1]

The coming of the kingdom, therefore, is of absolute value if the new man ('in Teilhardian terms the qualitative mutation of the human genus') is to be a reality here and now. 'The evangelising word is creative only if it is eschatological, that is, only if it makes us *believe* that the *eschaton* has arrived. Only then are the death and the resurrection of Jesus Christ really, not imaginarily, present to us.'[2] The function of proclaiming the Gospel, then, is unequivocal. It is to bring about the *eschaton* now, in the present moment of history; it is, in Marxist terms, to live wholly in the new age. Any other vision of eschatology is a question not of biblical exegesis but of unfaithfulness.[3]

In the light of his methodological approach, it is hardly surprising that Miranda is convinced that 'the most primitive Christian eschatology of which we have any record holds that the *eschaton* is present and not future'.[4] However, he is equally certain that the earliest strands of the synoptic tradition point in the same direction as the Johannine:

> This Synoptic tradition is not exactly equivalent to the Johannine eschatology that identifies the *parousia* with 'the hour' of the death and resurrection of Christ. But the difference is insignificant, because both John and the Synoptics, along with the historical Jesus, assert that the *parousia* occurs during the 'present generation', and this assertion, however stated, prevents postponement of the *eschaton*.[5]

In his study of the eschatology of the synoptic Gospels, Miranda begins from a series of texts (Mark 13.30; Luke 21.32 and Matt. 24.34) which explicitly state that the *parousia* and complete installation of the kingdom will take place during 'this generation'.[6] 'This generation', according to certain texts (Mark 8.12, 38; 9.19; Luke 7.31; 11.29; 17.25; Matt. 11.16; 12.39; 17.17 and 23.36), must be understood in a literal sense and not in the sense of the whole Jewish race extending into the future. The context requires us to understand a particular point in time: 'this' generation, not generation generically understood.

According to a traditional type of exegesis, the so-called apocalyptic passages of the synoptic Gospels have been divided into two parts: one part (Mark 13.24–7, or 20–7, or 21–7, or 19–27) predicting the coming of the *parousia*, the other the destruction of Jerusalem. This interpretation appeals to a certain 'prophetic enthusiasm' which, apparently, telescoped together events very far apart in time. Miranda, basing himself on the earlier studies of Ferdinand Prat[7] and Lagrange,[8] rejects this arbitrary distinction as having no basis in literary types, and appeals to Mark 13.4 ('When will this be, and what will be the sign when these things are to be accomplished?') to prove that the apocalyptic discourses refer to only one event.

This one event is understood as happening at a series of chronological points which culminate in the destruction of Jerusalem (Mark 13.4, 7, 8, 10, 14, 24, 26, 27), described as 'that tribulation' (v. 24) or 'the tribulation of those days' (Matt. 24.29). The inauguration of the kingdom, according to the Matthean account, will take place '*immediately* after...' The verse, 'but of that day and of that hour no one knows...' (Mark 13.32), is intended as an adversative addition to Mark 13.30, which helps to underline the inevitability of the fulfilment of what is precisely and definitely predicted for a future moment. 'The *parousia* will occur during the present generation, but it is impossible to specify on what day or hour.'[9]

Next, Miranda deals with the supposed problem of Luke's modifications of the Marcan text, as these have been interpreted as meaning that Luke consciously postpones the *eschaton*. His own view is that Luke intended to prevent his readers from reaching just this conclusion. For example, the omission of the phrase 'this is but the beginning of the sufferings' (Mark 13.8; Matt. 24.8) is due to the fact that, when Luke wrote, these things had already taken place, and it is precisely for this reason that he warns, 'this must first take place, but the end will not be at once' (Luke 21.9). In other words, the wars, rebellions and persecutions (Luke 21.12–19) are not the sign of the absolutely immediate arrival of the *parousia*. Equally, the long siege of Jerusalem (Luke 21.20–24) means, for Luke, only that the destruction of Jerusalem is assured. He makes a distinction between these events and the *eschaton*, for the former had already taken place when he wrote. His intention was to stop his readers being taken in by the expectation of an immediate *parousia*, but the future tenses do not intend to convey the idea of an indefinite or prolonged time sequence. Sufficient proof that Luke did not intend to postpone the *parousia* is given by verse 21.23, and by the fact that he did not include the qualification, if such it be, of Mark 13.32.

Matthew is even more definite than Mark that the destruction of the Temple will lead to the coming of the kingdom. The disciples' initial question is: 'What will be the sign of *your* coming and the close of the age?' The phrase, *sunteleias tou aiōnos* means, according to the prophetic expectation, 'the establishment of God's kingdom'.

The synoptic Gospels did not invent the idea that when the Temple made of stone was destroyed it would at once be replaced in the world by the messianic kingdom. 'The Samaritan woman's question (John 4.20) and Jesus' reply (John 4.21–4) clearly indicate that when the messianic hour arrives ("the hour is coming and now is") the stone Temple will be replaced by the living reality of men, members of the kingdom (cf. Mark 14.58; Rev. 21.22 with 3.12).' 'When Jesus was accused before the Sanhedrin of wanting to destroy the Temple (Mark 14.58; Matt. 26.61), the high priest understood perfectly that the Temple's destruction was equivalent to the Messiah's arrival (Mark 14.61; Matt. 26.63).'[10]

From these textual arguments, Miranda concludes that in the coming of Jesus Christ history has come to its end. 'The biblical *eschaton* is in this world. It is not beyond history, but is rather the final and definitive stage of history.'[11] The precise arrival of the *eschaton*, according to the synoptic Gospels, is connected with the destruction of Jerusalem, and with Jesus' resurrection, and according to John, with the coming of the Paraclete at Pentecost.[12]

If this reflects a certain chronological imprecision, it is of minor importance in comparison with the fact that the messianic kingdom, which means the arrival of complete justice and knowledge of God, the resurrection of the dead, etc., has now arrived, because 'this generation' had now 'passed away'. And the arrival of the kingdom is the content of the good news; it is the definitive liberation which has been implanted in this world, and which each person, by faith, is called upon to bring into being.

Christ came to achieve justice, the hour awaited by all mankind has tolled. The subversion is limitless ... All human history has been awaiting this moment. *Idou nun hēmera sōtērias*, 'Now is the propitious moment; now is the day of salvation

(2 Cor. 6.2)' ... The word *euangelion*('the great news') makes absolutely no sense if we are not yearning, with all the hope of mankind, for the definitive liberation, the total realisation of justice...[13]

PART IV

A CRITICAL DIALOGUE
AND AN ALTERNATIVE
THEOLOGY OF LIBERATION

CHAPTER THIRTEEN

INTRODUCTION

The theology of liberation, though a recent theological movement within contemporary Christendom, is not wholly new, for it shares similar concerns with other present-day movements in theology. It is Latin American in its orientation, yet not wholly so, for it springs partly from a reaction to other theological and ideological positions.

The theology of liberation has overcome the consistent inability of the Latin American Church to relate to new ideas and movements. In this respect it is heir to those creole priests who joined the Independence movements at the beginning of the nineteenth century. Like them it has taken an independent line within the Church, going far beyond the Church's recent modernising programmes. In this respect it is also heir of all those in the nineteenth century who believed that Independence was an unfinished task: political independence had been formally achieved; economic, social and cultural independence had still to be won. Paradoxically, then, the Latin American peoples, 150 years after Independence, are still dependent. They must achieve liberation.

The theology of liberation has been able to commit itself to this urgent task for two main reasons: firstly, it has rejected the old Catholic theocratic ideal whereby society acts as the depository of the Church's social teaching, and by this break it has evolved a new hermeneutic; secondly, it has read correctly the 'signs of the times' in modern Latin America.

Some people have rather maliciously suggested that the theology of liberation, with its commitment to a wholly new political order, has arisen as a compensation for the Church's loss of political power and privilege. This is untrue for three reasons: it rejects the modern Church's exercise of political power as such; its commitment to social change has come more through secular humanisms (e.g. Marxism) than through 'evangelical motivations', and it is critical of all political/religious messianisms of whatever hue. Nevertheless, the ancient notion that 'the Church's activity goes beyond that of saving souls, and includes the legitimate function of creating the kingdom of divine justice on earth' lingers on in the forefront of its genuine concern. Although it has certainly rejected an old-style ecclesiastical 'Constantinianism', it is open to the suspicion of being unduly attracted to a contemporary secular counterpart.

Simultaneously with the arrival of more flexible methods of study in Roman Catholic biblical and theological exegesis, the theology of liberation discovered Marxism as a new tool for the socio-political analysis of contemporary society. Both these factors enabled it to read the 'signs of the times' from within a fresh theological-political framework.

Modern Latin America, through the influence of Marxism, has provided the theology of liberation with a new agenda for theology. But liberation theology is not simply the result of an urge to produce a new theology. Its theological reflection has followed in the wake of its commitment to a determined praxis: it is 'a critical reflection on historical practice in the light of the Faith'. Orthopraxis takes precedence over orthodoxy: i.e. the criterion for measuring the correctness and usefulness of any theological formula is commitment to a process which will change situations of gross injustice. Obedience precedes theological interpretation. The latter does not justify the former but contributes to its more effective realisation.

Thus, the theology of liberation sees itself as the outcome of a new theological methodology. Theology is a necessary mediator between political commitment (i.e. commitment to historical, rather than abstract, man) and faith. It is dedicated to serving the Church in its mission of forging the 'new man'.

In the perspective of this commitment, theology in Latin America has had to reflect from within a totally new subculture: the culture of the undernourished, the homeless, the unemployed, the illiterate, the sufferers from all manner of violence. The Church, with the exception perhaps of a short period at its beginning, has never before entered this forlorn world of human misery, defeat and degradation. When it does so, and begins to reflect upon the nature of its mission in the light of this overwhelming reality, it stumbles against questions which it has never had to face before in modern times: how, for example, should one read the biblical message of liberation through Jesus Christ from within a shanty town whose existence is directly caused by man's greed and violence? This is the context for a contemporary biblical hermeneutic which cannot exclude from its consideration the reality of a poverty which *can* be eradicated.

The theology of liberation is a 'political theology' of a kind, for it concerns itself with political change. This concern it shares with its European counterpart. Likewise, it shares with the European political theology an interest in synthesising the revelation of the biblical God (starting with the God of the Exodus) with Marx's insights into the norms ruling modern society. However, the claim of a different social context upon its way of thinking has caused it to adopt a different method of theological interpretation: abandoning a certain philosophical idealism, it employs instead that particular socio-political tool of analysis which speaks in radical terms of transforming the present sub-culture of depersonalised humanity. In other words, the theology of liberation begins from the thesis that the 'non-man' can be liberated. The problems of secularisation hardly enter its horizon.

The theology of liberation is also a 'political hermeneutic of the Gospel', i.e. it is a reflection on political praxis in the light of God's Word. Because it seeks to reflect theologically (however novel its methodology may be), it cannot avoid the hermeneutical questions which must be put to any systematic theological thought which takes seriously the Scriptures as one of the principal parameters of its understanding. Indeed, the abandoning of the hermeneutical task by some Christian militants because, for example, they believe they cannot square their revolutionary commitment with Christ's ethical demands, has made the search for an adequate biblical hermeneutic even more urgent.

The final chapters of this book will try to assess, in the widest context, the theology of liberation's hermeneutical approach to Scripture, asking the question: What is the significance of the phrase 'in the light of God's Word' for a theological movement which avowedly champions a particular historical praxis as the first reference point for theological reflection?

As a second step, we shall very tentatively outline a different biblical hermeneutic, which we believe enshrines the most important ethical concerns of the theology of liberation, whilst at the same time allowing for a more consistent and justifiable approach to the use of Scripture as the *norma Dei* in the conflicts and convulsions of today's world.

CHAPTER FOURTEEN

WHY THE EXODUS?
WHICH EXODUS?

The priority given to the Exodus event by the theology of liberation, in its attempt to establish a sound biblical base for its reflection on praxis, has been questioned. It has been suggested that the Exilic theme, for example, would have greater hermeneutical possibilities within the current Latin American situation.[1]

Probably the Exodus has received disproportionate treatment, to the detriment of other significant Old Testament events, such as, for example, the failure of the monarchy and the rise of the messianic expectation. Nevertheless there are important reasons why the Exodus should occupy a major place in any comprehensive scriptural hermeneutic.[2] The theology of liberation stresses three reasons in particular.

1. The Exodus is central within the Old Testament. It is the key to Israel's understanding of both God and itself. For example, the decalogue is significantly prefaced by, 'I am Yahweh your God who brought you out of the land of Egypt, out of the house of slavery.' A similar preface occurs numerous times in connection with Israel's responsibilities as a newly constituted nation (cf. Exod. 22.21; Lev. 11.45; Deut. 4.37ff.; 7.6–11; 11.1ff.; 15.12–15). God, the law-giver, is essentially the God of liberation.[3] Israel's entire life is to be regulated by this fact: 'The Exodus is a constant call to live out a wholly new present in the light of the past'.[4]

2. The Exodus is repeatedly re-interpreted throughout the Bible: 'The memory of the Exodus pervades the pages of the Bible and inspires many re-interpretations both in the Old and New Testaments'.[5] 'The Old Testament exodus tradition has been heard primarily through its eschatological appropriation in Ezekiel and Isaiah. The hymn of

Zechariah speaks of the anticipated redemption with reference to Isaiah 60.1–2 and 59.8.'[6] This re-interpretation affords both a model and a justification for the hermeneutical task of reconsidering the theme of liberation in the light of today's reality.

3. The hermeneutical possibilities of the Exodus are unique for Latin American theology. This is particularly true if we consider the actual content of the Exodus narrative. A small racial minority is exploited, oppressed, tortured, threatened by genocide; it becomes conscious of its situation and, believing that deliverance is possible, defies unjust commandments and finally is successfully liberated. Each of these themes, and others, is pregnant with hermeneutical possibilities for peoples who experience similar situations today. Likewise, the Exodus, being the biblical paradigm of a suffering people,[7] reveals its 'reserve of meaning' supremely to those who suffer in like manner.

The actual handling of the Exodus narrative by liberation theologians depends upon their assessment firstly of the reality of the original event and subsequent levels of interpretation, and secondly of the relevant Latin American factors which cause the Exodus to 'disclose' its full meaning.

In the first case, two basic assumptions are made, though with little attempt to justify them historically. First, it is assumed that Israel did not possess a consciousness of peoplehood before the great drama of deliverance from Egypt: i.e. both their history and their theological reflection begin from this act. Secondly, the actual Exodus narrative is assumed to be the result of an elaborate theological reflection, *ex eventu*, which has obscured an original, non-'mythical' account of an escape to freedom.[8] Important hermeneutical lessons for present-day liberation are deduced from each assumption. These need to be examined.

The first assumption has been challenged by J. H. Yoder in an article which criticises the fundamental hermeneutical presuppositions of all political theologies in their handling of the Exodus narrative.[9] Even granting that the combined experiences of the people's suffering, Moses' vocation and the plagues played a large part in the formation of Israel's consciousness of peoplehood, nevertheless a people group existed before oppression began. On the level of the surviving traditions, that of the people's relationship to the patriarchs is both ancient and strong;[10] on the level of historical probability, Israel would scarcely have accepted Moses' leadership except on the grounds that he represented the God they knew from their past. Even more important is the consideration that oppression was the result of their being a people prior to Moses.[11] In other words, whichever way one approaches the present accounts one is forced to acknowledge that the Hebrew people, at the time of their persecution, already had a real sense of their past history. Subsequent events become meaningful only in the light of this consciousness of the past. But the meaning of the events will differ from that attributed to them by the theology of liberation, which minimises or eliminates this factor. This meaning will then contribute to a different hermeneutical pattern being derived from the Exodus.

The second assumption considers that it is possible to recover a nucleus of history with all supernatural elements removed. This original nucleus emphasised Moses' initiative in forming a people's liberation movement which successfully struggled for liberation from oppression.[12] Even where this reconstruction is not openly advocated, stress is invariably put on the people's responsibility for their own deliverance.[13]

Now this assumption is made, not argued. Were it to be argued, it is hard to see on what methodological grounds it could be advocated. Even allowing for a multiplicity of sources behind the present text, it would be impossible, for two reasons, to isolate any one source which presented the narrative in the way described. In the first place, any hypothetical history of a group of slaves struggling for and gaining their own freedom has been entirely eliminated from the sources (hypothetical or real) which make up the present narrative. Secondly, the only way to isolate an inner core of history in this way would be on the unsound methodological principle that the results required were already contained in the initial premise of analysis. Nor is this second objection overruled by the argument that there are, in fact, later traditions which re-interpret the Exodus narrative. For, whether supposedly later or supposedly earlier, the traditions/text uniformly present Yahweh as the initiator and agent of Israel's liberation.[14]

In the light of this discussion we need to assess the hermeneutical status of the theology of liberation's use of the Exodus story. The first obvious question is whether the insistence that a text be read from a particular praxis makes any difference to its *sensus literalis* (i.e. its intention). For example, the theology of liberation, under the influence initially of Moltmann and later of Alves, has insisted that *'ehyeh 'ᵃser 'ehyeh* (Exod. 3.14) can be translated only in a future or processive sense, because only in this way can the historical and continuing nature of Yahweh's action be preserved and all ontologically static notions of his being be eliminated.

Now, one could argue that the eschatological interpretation best fits the need for a *kerygma* which proclaims a God who keeps open the future as the sphere of man's creative possibilities.[15] Nevertheless, there are no objective reasons why appropriateness should determine the original meaning. The phrase is much disputed by scholars; our intention, therefore, is not to debate its meaning but to raise the methodological questions surrounding its interpretation. The chief of these, from the side of the theology of liberation, is the ideological suspicion that the traditional rendering, 'I am who I am' (so RSV, Jerusalem Bible and NEB), is made in defence of a *kerygma* which presents a God who does not require change.[16]

However, alternative translations such as 'I am He who is' or 'I am (He who is) really there',[17] if they are based on an objective assessment of the text's meaning, cannot initially be dismissed as ideological, without begging the question.

In this particular case, the *sensus literalis* appears to escape any one definition. The divine name genuinely transcends limiting nuances of grammar. For this reason, whereas the full force of God's revelation of himself as the God of history, of the future and of praxis should not be diminished, the 'active' *being* of God is also an absolutely indispensable part of talking about God. God is neither 'pure' being in an ontological sense, nor pure action in a wholly praxiological sense. The suspicion that certain ideologies have influenced interpretation may well be true, and any exegesis certainly needs to be tested by this criterion. Alternatively, this kind of criticism may simply betray a different ideological slant, equally incapable of hearing the message of the text.

This discussion of the divine name has raised issues intimately connected with the complex relationship between theory and praxis, which we shall investigate later (cf. Chapter 16). Our present purpose has been to use it as an illustration of how the hermeneutical practice of the theology of liberation, far from releasing the text's 'reserve of meaning', may obscure some of its riches, because of a *too narrow* praxiological vantage point.

The second fundamental question still remains. Does contemporary Latin American reality afford the best starting point for understanding the Exodus *kerygma?* Four possible answers to the question suggest themselves:

1. It affords the only legitimate hermeneutical context.
2. It affords the best context.
3. It affords the best context to understand certain parts.
4. It obscures the real meaning of the Exodus.

The actual handling of the Exodus narrative by the theology of liberation, as already described in Chapter 8, leads us to conclude that the third and fourth answers are both correct in differing degrees.

The actual experience of oppression by external forces beyond the control of the oppressed, an objective reality in Latin America irrespective of any particular ideological analysis of the situation or identification with the oppressed, brings to life certain fundamental aspects of the Exodus story. We could mention the following, amongst others: Pharaoh's racist policy; his concern to use Israel as cheap labour (an economic motive for exploitation) with the dual ideological cover-up of Israel's demographic explosion and supposed alliance with Egypt's enemies; Israel's labour used as 'surplus value' to produce accumulated wealth; oppression leading to an increase in the fear-syndrome of the oppressors; the civil disobedience of the midwives, etc. The hermeneutical procedure acts as follows. We listen attentively to the cry of today's exploited (i.e. of those possessing a dominated consciousness) and from this perspective we discover elements in the Israelites' plight which are remarkably similar. Because we believe that exploitation is one of the world's greatest problems needing urgent eradication, we consider that the elements of the Exodus story listed above are fundamental to its *kerygma*, i.e. both to the original message and to *all* subsequent re-interpretations. However, this consideration springs not from an uncommitted analysis of present-day oppression, but from one which previously evaluates it as ethically unjust and capable of being changed. It springs from a conviction that the Exodus story of oppression and the Latin American reality of exploitation enter into a simultaneous syntonic relationship based on man's innate and universal drive for power.

On the other hand, certain premises adopted by the liberation theologians have caused them to interpret the Exodus in unilateral 'horizontalising' terms. This interpretation has obscured both the original *kerygma* and its subsequent re-interpretation, causing at the same time a certain degree of embarrassment with regard to the New Testament's handling of the liberation theme. The denial or minimising of God's intervention as the cause of Israel's liberation comes from two directions. Firstly, it comes from a rejection of the purely 'spiritualising' interpretation of liberation, which has been deeply ingrained in traditional Catholic teaching on salvation.[18] Secondly, it results from humanistic presuppositions of the analytical tools chosen as most adequate to interpret Latin America's state of oppression. The first position is afraid of a 'quietist' attitude to social change; the second overestimates man's unaided capability to effect real and lasting change in the direction of freedom and humanisation, and ends, not infrequently, in an illusory 'triumphalism'.

This discussion of the hermeneutical handling of the Exodus by the theology of liberation is inconclusive, because the Exodus narrative is likewise incomplete without the complementary reinterpretations within the context of the whole of Scripture. We leave to a later chapter a more complete analysis of the biblical hermeneutical presuppositions used by the theology of liberation. Before undertaking this, we shall consider its appreciation of the New Testament's interpretation of the Old in the person and work of Jesus Christ.

CHAPTER FIFTEEN

THE NEW TESTAMENT
IS CENTRAL

I. JESUS CHRIST FULFILS AND RE-INTERPRETS THE OLD TESTAMENT

The manner in which the New Testament authors use the Old Testament in the interpretation of the Christ-event is decisive for the development of a biblical hermeneutic in the theology of liberation. This development can be traced in the meaning given to the two words, 'fulfil' and 're-interpret'.

These two words, in practice, describe two distinct views of the relationship between the Testaments. The first emphasises the historical fulfilment of the Old Testament in the ministry of Christ. It envisages a one-to-one continuous relationship between the Testaments. The second view, while not underestimating historical fulfilment, emphasises the 'added' elements in the New Testament's interpretation of the Old, and tends to transpose the Old Testament themes on to a new plane.

The distinction can be compared to the debate surrounding the concept of *sensus plenior*: 'Does God only want to say what the author of a book or scriptural text can be proved historically to have had in mind? ... Or does the expressive intention of God go further, so that each generation is justified in interpreting Scripture according to its own situation – i.e. *interpreting it and not simply applying it*.'[1]

Miranda's position is that the New Testament saw Christ's historical fulfilment of the Old Testament Scriptures basically in terms of what these latter 'had in mind': 'A new message is not expected with the dawn of God's kingdom. What will be proclaimed has been known from the time of Deutero-Isaiah. The longing is that it should be proclaimed ... *The new feature is not the message but the eschatological act* ... All the emphasis is on the action, on the proclamation, on the utterance of the Word which ushers in the new age ...'[2] In synthesis, this means that the New Testament *novum* is wholly contained in the realisation, now, of the *eschaton*. The difference between the New and Old Testaments is that 'what the prophecies and promises of the Old Testament regarded as future, and rightly so, has become present.'[3] '[Jesus] is constituted Messiah by the arrival of the *eschaton* to human history.'[4]

Consequently, for Miranda, the New Testament's theological interpretation of the Old is no more, nor less, than a description of how the Christ-event literally fulfills the Old Testament hope. For example, Miranda attempts to show, exegetically, that Paul understands the *dikaiosunē Theou* entirely in Old Testament categories and, that he adds nothing new to the Old Testament's description of Abraham's justifying faith. So he virtually denies that the New Testament produces a new synthesis, a new content, or a fresh insight into the intention of God's Word to Israel.[5]

Croatto, however, takes a different attitude to the New Testament's interpretation of Christ's fulfilment of Scripture. He does not emphasise any less the significance of the *factum* in Christ's appearing. Indeed he sees the Christ-*event* as the central stimulus to the New Testament's hermeneutic. But this hermeneutic transcends the strictly *literal* categories of the Old Testament, presupposing an event which caused a creative reinterpretation of the text to discover what was really 'hidden' there.[6]

Croatto develops this idea by showing the divorce between the New Testament's interpretation of the Old and what he calls the 'Pharisaic hermeneutic'. This latter does not spring from commitment to God's event but from the '*gnōsis*' of their knowledge of the law. 'The new Event cannot be enclosed in received schemes because it loses all its "meaning". Herod does not understand Jesus (Luke 9.7ff.), because he tries to classify him according to figures recognised by the tradition. Thus he could never "recognise" the historic Christ (who went beyond every messianic prophecy). In the same line is the Jews' embarrassment in John 9 . . . As they did not accept the "event" which could have liberated them from their own spiritual torture, they were caught in absurdity or in ridicule.'[7]

In other words, the manner of Christ's fulfilment of the Old Testament contains, as Negré suggests, an element of surprise: 'the fulfilment is different from what was announced and awaited.' The future was announced in images from the present (*sensus literalis*) in order that it might be recognised, although it was new (*sensus plenior*).

The debate between the two positions is not merely academic. It reflects profound differences of opinion amongst exegetes, and between these and what Grillmeier calls 'scriptural theologians'. It may well point to one of the greatest divides within contemporary theology, cutting right across confessional boundaries and the more serious for never having been clearly formulated and considered.[8] Here we will make one or two preliminary observations on the two positions, leaving till later a lengthier discussion of the issues.

Miranda's position is based on what he considers to be a scientific approach to biblical exegesis. He castigates modern exegetes not so much for their methodology as for the fact that they do not apply it with sufficient rigour. Modern exegetical studies often fail to acknowledge, because of false philosophical and ethical presuppositions, the fundamental concern of the text.[9] Nevertheless, Miranda is not always aware how much of his own exegesis is ideologically determined. Starting from the idea of a God who is 'pure demand', for example, he is predisposed to find in the New Testament only the command to make the kingdom present once and for all. Thus, he defends the absolute priority of praxis, of 'doing justice' and ignores the fact that the New Testament has transposed, though certainly not eliminated, the question of the command's fulfilment.[10]

As a result of his predisposition to set aside the possibility that the Christ-event has added new dimensions to both faith and praxis, not encountered in the Old Testament, Miranda often fails to do justice to the *sensus literalis* of the New Testament text (the New Testament *sensus literalis* is extrapolated from the Old Testament *sensus plenior*). One example of this would be his interpretation of John 1.17.[11] Here Miranda, with many modern exegetes, understands *charis kai alētheia* in terms of the Old Testament hendiadys, *ḥeseḏ weʿemeṯ* and translates it as: 'compassion and goodness', quoting the LXX translation of *ḥeseḏ* as *eleos*. From there, in line with his presuppositions, Miranda understands its meaning as 'good works: works of mercy, of solidarity, of compassion and goodness'. In other words, Miranda allows no new dimension to colour the original

Hebrew hendiadys. But why, then, did John not use *eleos*? Why that most significant of all words, *charis*? *Charis* is much more than *eleos*; it is God's global response to injustice, necessary just because man's compassion is insufficient. To understand the phrase in purely Old Testament terms makes the contrast with Moses trivial.[12]

Croatto's method highlights the central practice of New Testament interpretation: namely, the discovery of new meaning in the Jewish Scriptures in the light of the Christ-event (e.g. Luke 24.27, 32, 44–5; John 2.22; 5.39; 12.16; 14.26; Matt. 26.31ff.; Rom. 1.2ff.; 16.25–6 etc.). Nevertheless, by overstressing the aspect of newness in the Christ-event and the contrast with the Pharisaic hermeneutic, he does less than justice to the continuity of the two Testaments. This, in turn, means that he underestimates the ambiguity of 'pure' event. The Christ-event does more than just 're-take' and 'extend' the Exodus *kerygma*, i.e. incorporate the Exodus *kerygma* into the Easter mystery. It re-interprets it. And the re-interpretation is more than a Christological linguistic re-translation of the Exodus vocabulary; it is a new and definitive *kerygma*, an unfolding of the true meaning of the event.

Gutierrez, in one important passage, takes a mediating position which promises a better understanding of today's hermeneutical re-interpretations in the light of the New Testament's own hermeneutical practice. 'The proper way to pose the question does not seem to us to be in terms of "temporal promise or spiritual promise." Rather it is a matter of partial fulfilments through liberating historical events ... Christ does not "spiritualise" the eschatological promises; he gives them meaning and fulfilment today (cf. Luke 4:21); but at the same time he opens new perspectives by catapulting history ... towards total reconciliation. The hidden sense is not the "spiritual"; ... rather it is the sense of a fullness which takes on and transforms historical reality.'[13]

2. THE EARLY CHURCH AND THE ON-GOING TRADITION OF INTERPRETATION

Before passing from a mainly descriptive to a mainly evaluative study, we should try, by drawing together some of the threads left open at earlier stages, to delineate the main hermeneutical principle on which the theology of liberation bases its study of Scripture.

The Vatican II document *Dei Verbum*, which spells out the modern Catholic teaching on revelation, raises the tricky problem of the relationship between Scripture (God's Word written) and tradition (God's Word handed on). It shows how this was settled in such a way that neither seemed pre-eminent but together they formed a characteristically Catholic hermeneutical circle, i.e. that Catholic theology arises out of a *total* context which includes on-going tradition as a primary source for the hermeneutical task.

Now, it would seem that liberation theology uses a methodology akin to that underlying the rather imprecise theory of *sensus plenior*. The theory is built on the undeniable fact of re-interpretation within the Scriptures themselves (for example, the New Testament typological exegesis and the biblical authors' creative interpretation of secondary sources in the final editing of their works). The theology of liberation does not refer to *sensus plenior* as such, but uses such terms as 're-interpretation'; 'reserve-of-meaning'; 'donation-of-meaning'; 'word-significance'; 'word-in-suspense'.

It should not be thought that the theology of liberation wishes to undermine the importance of those technical methods which seek to arrive at the *sensus literalis*. However, this meaning is seen as relevant *only* in a hermeneutical continuum which stretches to our day, and therefore, if it is made normative for the Church's contemporary mission, it becomes bibliolatry or biblical fundamentalism.

The biblical text, because it incorporates the living word of Emmanuel – God with his people – has a consequent meaning, valid for other epochs, which is deducible with the help of a rational pre-understanding. It is this deductive process, as it is used in conjunction with the praxis of liberation as pre-understanding, which makes the biblical hermeneutic of the theology of liberation unique within contemporary theology.

The theology of liberation seeks to insert itself into a process of re-interpretation, already started within the Bible, which extends to the Church's contemporary situation. 'This manner of situating liberation in a specific [the Jewish and Pharisaical world] and at the same time open [liberation from sin and death] cultural context and with the backing of the Exodus "memory", allows us to "explore" it hermeneutically in its existential and prophetic present'.[14] In other words, just as the early Church embarked on a creative typological exegesis of the Old Testament in the light of the overwhelming experience of the Christ-event, so the contemporary Church, observing the 'signs of the times', may extend this typological interpretation into the present.

Justification for this task is deduced from the general theological principle that God's will is best captured through the Event and that he continues to manifest himself, in each succeeding epoch, through Events which extend the continuum of his salvific Event-disclosure in the history of Israel and the Church. The hermeneutical task, therefore, comprises the creative translation of the prophetic word spoken within the 'history of salvation' into the contemporary movement towards the 'salvation of history'.

It might be objected that since the Scriptures themselves know nothing of a general salvation history as this term is employed by the theology of liberation, the hermeneutical task is based on a false deduction from a general theological principle inimical to Scriptural revelation. Liberation theology would rejoin, as Catholic theology has always been prone to do, that revelation has not ceased with the apostolic age. Yesterday's revelation becomes a revelation of equal value today when the God-of-the-Event is captured by a 'faith-recognition' in today's 'signs of the times'. In this way the continuum of Event, Interpretation and Re-interpretation is completed, and the hermeneutical circle is closed. Rafael Avila explains the process thus:

> What is historical stands in a dialectical relationship between the objective (the historical situation) and the subjective (the prophetic word) ... The word is like a memorial which, accumulating meaning from the past, opens it up to a better and fuller expression. The event belongs to the past and the only possibility for its survival is through the 'subjectivisation' of the written word. The past is unrepeatable. However, it forms part of our antecedents and our gestatory process.

The past includes man's historical project in which the concrete signs of a divine (salvific) project, translated empirically
into historical immanence and, consequently, legible to the
prophetic community, become ever more clearly evident.
What has already been expressed has not been fully
expressed. It will not be expressed except through contact
with a new situation ... The word generates the situation
and the situation the word. The prophetic activity is not only
an interpretation of the event from the word, but also a re-
interpretation of the word from the event. The Apostles re-
interpreted the prophetic word from the Christ-event. This
spoken word remains in 'suspense' with respect to our existence. The New Testament, a point of arrival, is, for us, a
point of departure. The first contains the memorial of the
early Church, the second permits the prophetic activity of
the Church today. The prophetic role of the New Testament
allows us to interpret our history.[15]

In this whole concept of the extension to our days of the New
Testament's typological re-interpretation of the Old, in which
liberation theology suggests that the role of the Church's *magisterium* should be replaced by the awakened conscience of
oppressed humanity, the question remains as to how faith may
recognize the prophetic word in today's signs of the times; or,
by what criteria do we discern the manifestation of the liberating God-of-the-Event in today's realities? Avila gives a partial
answer to a crucial and yet obscure part of the theology of
liberation's hermeneutical circle:

The prophetic word reveals man's self-understanding in a
particular prophetic situation ... That anthropology which
possesses the greatest understanding of man becomes atheist
when it collides with a theology which demonstrates a lesser
understanding. In this way, it becomes converted into a theological instrument able to force theology to accede to a new
image of God.[16]

In other words, the criteria will be those instruments of analysis
best able to uncover and transform the causes of modern man's
alienation and oppression.

We shall now scrutinise further the legitimacy of this hermeneutical methodology.

CHAPTER SIXTEEN

REVELATION IN CONTEMPORARY EVENTS

I. THE CHOICE OF SOCIO-POLITICAL TOOLS OF ANALYSIS AND THEIR METHODOLOGICAL STATUS

Just as certain theological trends in Latin America, in advance of their times, were influenced shortly after Independence by European secular studies, so the theology of liberation has been shaped by certain socio-political and economic studies which began to dominate in Latin America at the beginning of the 1960s. These studies were developed from a basically Marxist interpretation of society and have been increasingly refined in their application since that time. Marxism, in fact, has acted in an analagous way to Positivism in the nineteenth century, as a new educating and humanising 'religion' of the new order which must be created, if necessary by force, out of the rubble of the old.

Why did the theology of liberation choose this particular instrument of socio-political exegesis? In answering this, we must bear in mind that, as Assmann and others have stressed, the choice was initially an ethical one.

Firstly, Marxism seemed to speak most cogently to the stark economic contrasts and deplorable social conditions encountered by young priests and laymen in their contact with the poor areas of the continent. The conditions were such that these people began to shed the Roman Catholic's long-standing fear of Communism. It is argued, for example, that justice for the oppressed is the overriding priority for Latin America and, that therefore, if certain civil liberities are threatened in the execution of justice, it should be remembered that the majority of humanity in Latin America is experiencing loss of liberty through exploitation. A so-called 'open society' for the few is a hollow mockery of democracy if maintained at the expense of the underprivileged majority.

Secondly, Marxism seemed to offer the only complete alternative programme to the ideology of development, which had clearly failed to solve the basic problem of exploitation. Moreover, Marxism appealed to a certain Christian 'idealism' because its theories seemed to rest on an ethical absolutism not found in the political and economic pragmatism that underlies the development theory.

Thirdly, certain Marxist themes, notably that of the class struggle, appeared to supply an effective method for producing liberation in a situation which hitherto had managed to neutralise all progressive forces for change. In this context, the Marxist belief in the proletariat as the harbinger of the values of the new age and history's designated agent for bringing it to birth was transferred from the industrial worker of the developed West to the poor of the Third World.[1]

Fourthly, Marxism claimed to give a scientific foundation to an ideological stance which could effectively deprive empirical Christianity in Latin America of its own idealism which minimised the class conflict in society. This idealism was based on the theory, abhorrent to most of the theologians of liberation, that Christianity has an independent message which can be used as a point of comparison with scientifically grounded analyses of man in society.

Finally, Marxism offered a complete interpretation of the Latin American scene. This trend towards the claim of absolute comprehension gave rise to the idea, more easily received, perhaps, by thinkers who felt the vacuum left by their abandonment of the absolutism of the earlier Catholic political synthesis, that the Latin American historical process is unitary, and that its one (Marxist) interpretation is self-evidently valid.[2]

Clearly, the choice of Marxism has had a profound effect on the theology of liberation in its actual hermeneutical procedure. At one level, reality interpreted by means of basically Marxist categories has dictated the agenda for the research of some biblical scholars – as indicated, for example, in the themes chosen by SAPSE (Argentine Society of Biblical Scholars) for their annual conferences since 1968. This research, however, is affected not only in its content (i.e. that preference is given to certain biblical themes), but in its hermeneutical procedure; for at another level, it is claimed that the biblical message can only be genuinely understood from the vantage-point of a praxis which is decisively influenced by the Marxist interpretation of liberation.

This latter hermeneutical claim has two strong points. Firstly, the Marxist interpretation provides an ideological mechanism capable of exposing the intentions of any exegesis which seeks, through the employment of pre-understandings tied to conservative philosophical systems, to use the biblical text either in whole or in part to defend the *status quo* of a pre-revolutionary situation. Secondly, Marxism provides a contemporary hermeneutical key which enables the biblical scholar to identify the Bible's central self-understanding. This key is found in the conflict between oppressor and oppressed and the Bible's self-understanding is given in its witness to God as the defender of the violated, the exactor of absolute justice and the executor of the Kingdom.

Perhaps one of the most important contributions of Marxist theory to biblical hermeneutics is its emphasis on the structural dimensions of liberation. Its ability to discern the fundamental play of economic forces, often deliberately hidden by sundry ideological apologetics for a free-enterprise system, provides an insight into one aspect of man's present alienation not fully considered by the biblical writers.[3] The corresponding liberation of man in this sense is also included in Christ's cosmic work of liberation effected by his death and resurrection.

Now, this Marxist insight may be considered as a species of 'hermeneutical plus' which clearly syntonises with the biblical revelation of the liberating God. At the same time it provides, as Miranda especially has sought to demonstrate, a feed-back into a fuller comprehension of the Pauline emphasis on structural evil in his concepts of *hamartia, ptocha, stoicheīa, archai, exousiai, kuriotes* etc.

In brief, Marxism, by providing a seemingly efficacious praxis for implementing structural liberation, enables the biblical student to enter into a hermeneutical circle in which not only is the message of Scripture heard in its fundamental dimension – that of a relationship-changing love – but obedience to it is also made possible. At this point, it is clear that the theology of liberation has taken over Marxist epistemology with its cardinal argument that knowledge comes through revolutionary action.[4]

Although an acceptance of the Marxist analysis has considerably affected liberation theology's interpretation of the Scripture, the hermeneutical procedure is not all one way: new understanding of certain biblical themes has influenced the way in which Marxism is handled and evaluated in the continuing process of biblical interpretation in Latin America. Were this not so, the theology of liberation could easily be accused of importing an alien philosophical 'totality' (to use Dussel's phrase) into the task of serious biblical exegesis, thereby making an exterior criterion into the chief biblical pre-understanding. The majority of the liberation theologians want to avoid this danger, because each of them considers Marxism to be limited in its understanding of total liberation and how this is to be achieved. Nevertheless, in general terms, the theology of liberation has not given much attention to the way in which the biblical message of liberation, as it is allowed to enter critically into the hermeneutical process, will, in fact, modify the function which Marxism is made to serve, in order, as Gutierrez's succinctly phrases it, to press for the transformation of the non-man into the new man.

The use of Marxism as a pre-understanding for the hermeneutical task creates a dilemma. If Marxist analysis is really as purely 'scientific' as its advocates make out, then its use as a tool should provide a theoretical, wholly objective base for the pre-understanding; but if Marxism is limited, for example in its understanding of loss of liberty as the basic situation of man in Latin America, then its usefulness as a pre-understanding is also limited.[5] These alternatives are not necessarily exclusive but they do highlight the fact that the theology of liberation has not yet given sufficient consideration to the methodological status of Marxism (for example, how far one can make allowance for its theoretical and practical limitation before its use as a hermeneutical tool becomes more ambiguous than helpful).

The theology of liberation has a double attitude towards the value of Marxism for the present situation. On the one hand, it is attracted by its claim to be a scientifically objective analysis of certain economic laws inherent in the capitalist system, especially as these are manifested in its expansion into Third World markets (e.g. the inability to curb the upward spiral of poverty, or to break dependence caused both by the always favourable trade agreements achieved by the industralised nations and by an ever-increasing national debt). On the other hand, it is also attracted by the Marxist global response to the deep-seated problems inherent in any radical change from the position of chronic economic dependence, and by its mobilisation for effective action.

In this double attitude there lies a certain tension for liberation theology between the 'scientific' status of its analytical methodology and the criteria it adduces to provide the motivation for man's total liberation. The tension is seen in matters to do with the relationship between how problems are described and how choices relating to those problems are to be made. The questions that follow on from this tension also raise the issue of the nature of Marxism. Is it an economic theory? a political science? a philosophical anthropology? or a secular eschatology? Obviously, we cannot resolve this question here. We can try to contribute some brief points which might help to establish guidelines for the place of Marxism as a pre-understanding for biblical interpretation. There appear to be three basic issues.

1. To accord Marxism the status of a science can be done only with certain strong reservations. In the first place, the field of economic studies has never, in fact, been equated methodologically with that of the exact sciences. Secondly, to be called scientific any theory must submit itself to the rigorous control of *generally* accepted criteria by which any theory is either verified as fitting the evidence or else rejected.[6] Thirdly, neither Marxism nor any other economic analysis has displayed much zeal for this type of critique. The main reason is clear. Economic theory, as Marx never tired of repeating, is concerned with man's position in society – and this, as later Marxists have more clearly demonstrated, cannot be reduced to an easy theory of cause and effect as implied in Marx's concept of infrastructure and superstructure. This means that man, as a total being, becomes personally involved in his own economic theory in a way in which he does not in the exact sciences. This fact inevitably makes his theories less objective and, therefore, less scientific.

2. Marxism is clearly not just an economic theory, for Marx

also devoted much of his writing to philosophical and political questions. These, which together form part of an integrated 'system', must also be judged according to the criteria which pertain in these disciplines. Were Marxism purely an economic theory, limited to describing the fundamental workings of a particular (capitalist) economic practice, it could not at the same time be a revolutionary theory; for whoever proposes to liberate man acts according to criteria deduced from a particular vision of man. The relationship, therefore, between Marxist socio-economic analysis and Marxist anthropology is highly complex. In its use of Marxism, the theology of liberation has attempted a quick methodological short-cut without careful exploration of this relationship.

3. Neither of these two basic reservations concerning Marxism should prevent us from acknowledging that it has provided certain insights into man's economic relations within the complexity of modern society, and this fact should challenge us to look afresh at the methods used to uncover the central biblical message for our time. In this connection, Marxism used as an ideological 'suspicion' has a positive role to play in helping to overcome the identification between empirical Christianity and biblical faith; thus helping to deter the former from being able to suppress the subversive nature of the latter. At the same time, Marxism clearly has added a wealth of knowledge about the nature and processes of modern society which, stripped of all ontological mystification, forms part of the reality which acts as one pole in the hermeneutical task.

Our conclusion is that the claim of Marxism to be an objective socio-political tool of analysis is valid within a limited field of competence; as a contribution towards a more faithful understanding of the biblical message about God, man and history it is ambiguous. The greatest area of confusion still surrounds the relationship between theory and practice; there is a certain ambiguity in the fact that revolutionary practice is ultimately derived from an ethical choice which only *partially* springs from an analysis of man in society.

The dilemma of Marxism, and consequently of its use in

biblical hermeneutics, is captured in this inevitable alternative: either Marxism offers a totally scientific analysis of modern society, in which case it belongs to the sphere of a positivistic economic treatment of reality; or else it is a revolutionary theory about how and why to change this reality, in which case it must derive its ethical choice from factors that transcend its positivism. How does the theology of liberation see this interplay of theory and practice?

2. REVOLUTIONARY THEORY AND REVOLUTIONARY PRACTICE

If our assessment of the methodological status of Marxism is basically correct then one conclusion, absolutely fundamental to our discussion, will logically follow. The notion that praxis can, by carrying its own internal self-evident justification, precede all theoretical reflection, is an illusion. Segundo has pointed this out with irresistible logic.[7] We, for our part, shall now try to clarify the situation further with reference to liberation theology's claim to provide a methodological reversal in theological thinking.

Assmann asserts that theology as critical reflection (critical of its own premises and content) upon action comes after and from within praxis. He is critical, therefore, of the classical theological procedure, which elaborates theoretical criteria before putting them into practice, because it reveals a positivist rather than a dialectical methodology.

It is true that theology in general has sought to move from the particular nature of its sources to the general nature of the world, thus bringing about a circular process. It is also true that the theology of liberation first arose from a practical commitment within a very particular situation, only later becoming a more general theological reflection (although one might ask whether this is not more of a historical accident than a methodological necessity). What is not true, however, is that this commitment was not preceded by a minimum amount of theoretical reflection.

Assmann seems to ignore a fundamental fact of man's ethical existence, namely, that both the grounds of the appeal to liberate man and the methods to be employed, have to be justified *a priori* according to values which are in themselves justifiable or not, open to question or not. If this were not so, how, for example, could the word 'more', which he himself uses in the phrase 'more human', have any meaning? Indeed Assmann recognises the inevitability of this fact in his discussion of what he calls the 'indicating-criteria' of quality which are a necessary defence against a utilitarian approach to man's liberation. What he does not justify is the wholesale rejection of theological criteria and their substitution by Marxist criteria as providing the *a priori* grounds for commitment to liberating praxis. Assmann's methodology basically assumes two things: that the reason for a particular praxis becomes clear in its execution and that Marxist analysis provides an unambiguous assessment of the situation.

In the light of this discussion, Marx's eleventh thesis on Feuerbach, which has greatly influenced liberation theology's methodology, would appear to contain only a half-truth, for the point is not only to change the world (or rather, not leave the world unchanged) but to discover a hermeneutical key which will reveal *every* dimension of the world which needs changing. Marxist polemic should be vented less against theological methodology *per se* than against those theologies which, by taking into their hermeneutical circle extraneous philosophical or cultural systems, have suppressed the Bible's critical and prophetic message.[8]

Marxist epistemology cannot therefore be used to deny the legitimacy of an *a priori* critical reflection; it can only be used to purge theology of those elements which act as a barrier to effective praxis. In this way, it can be used in establishing a critical circle for the hermeneutical task. The Christian faith will thus be cleansed of all false cultural accretions and, in its turn, will demythologise the pretensions of all socio-political analyses to constitute in themselves an exclusive approach to man and his liberation.[9]

So revolutionary praxis is dependent on revolutionary theory. This is true both for Marxism and for Christian faith, even if the former does not claim a new theory of knowledge. Moltmann's criticism of the exclusive priority of praxis, on the basis that transformation depends upon those representations which go beyond experience and the success of praxis (for example, Marx's representation of non-empirical 'total' man) is, therefore, correct. Consequently, in the choice of instruments of analysis, there is no real choice, as Assmann wants to pretend, between humanity and inhumanity, only actual humanity and *theoretical* humanity.

If we are correct in concluding that right praxis ultimately depends upon right theory, then the Bible will occupy a different place in a hermeneutic of liberation from that allowed it by the theology of liberation in general. Its particularly crucial contribution will be in analysing present reality on the human level and feeding back this analysis, including the biblical contribution, into the hermeneutical circle. We must therefore consider the place of the Bible in a possible hermeneutic of liberation, and particularly how the different cultural horizons may be brought together in order that the Bible may liberate its unique forces for the transformation of man on every level of alienation. In attempting this hermeneutical task, we hope to demonstrate how the theology of liberation can benefit from a more biblical (and, therefore, more radical) hermeneutic of liberation in relation to the demands of revolutionary praxis.

CHAPTER SEVENTEEN

THE TOUCHSTONE
OF REVELATION

I. SCRIPTURE AS THE MEDIATOR OF TOTAL
AND UNIVERSAL LIBERATION

In discussing the status of the biblical text in the hermeneutical circle of liberation, one could perfectly well begin by trying to establish the nature of the Bible's authority for the Christian's contemporary praxis of liberation. This would involve a debate within the context of what modern theology is actually saying about biblical authority. Once the nature of the Bible's authority had been established, then, according to the result obtained, the hermeneutical interpretation of Scripture could proceed.[1]

Such an approach, however, has two disadvantages. Firstly, it would be inordinately long and rather tedious, certainly outside the scope of this present study, though not necessarily outside its interests; secondly, it would not grapple with the hermeneutical problems raised by the theology of liberation, for this latter rejects a contemplation of the status or use of the Bible outside of its mediation in concrete contemporary events. This being so, we shall set the discussion within the context of what the theology of liberation considers to be modern theology's task namely, the liberating of forces for the construction of a more *human* society, i.e. putting the biblical testimony at the service of the Christian Church in its task of confronting the world with the demands of freedom.

The theology of liberation is basically concerned with the subject of universal salvation. This topic is also central to the whole biblical *kerygma*, not only in particular words whose occurrence may be limited, but in a cumulative sense. Man is enmeshed in a complex predicament from which he needs to be saved, redeemed or liberated.

The theology of liberation, therefore (at least on the level of the language it uses), is concerned with the central theme of the whole Bible. Liberation is not some newly-arrived concept but the very centre of the biblical *kerygma*. Consequently it would seem necessary in the interests of the theology of liberation, as a theology of salvation, to get a clear picture of the significance which the biblical writers attribute to the idea of salvation. In this task of clarification, which is always marked by the pressing challenge actually to practise liberation, the Bible will impress its authority, not in any general or abstract way, but by the power of its own analysis and the solutions it offers. The practical importance conceded to these solutions will then be measured by the influence allowed them in today's hermeneutical task.

The theology of liberation, rightly in our judgment, considers that the kind of oppression experienced by the Third World peoples is a unique position from which to hear and understand the biblical doctrine of salvation. There can be little doubt, for example, that insights into the nature and causes of this oppression, derived from socio-analytical tools such as Marxism, have shed new light on key biblical passages and concepts. However, this is not the same as saying that the origin and nature of oppression as the Bible portrays it can be determined by a particular modern interpretation of historical man; unless, of course, this interpretation is erected into a new *magisterium*, the ultimate authority for the meaning of Christian faith today. There is a tendency in liberation theology to do just this, especially in the writings of Assmann. Others, however, reject it on the grounds that if such a procedure were allowed, the ability of the Bible to contribute to the discussion and practice of liberation would be foreclosed.

The theology of liberation, therefore, needs to grapple more rigorously with the entire biblical notion of sin (or alienation) in order, at this point, to reduce the vagueness of its own language. Only when it does this can the status of the biblical text in a hermeneutic of liberation be fairly judged. Here we offer some comments on the status of the discussion within the theology of liberation.

Firstly we would say that Miranda is right to seek to discover the origin of oppression exegetically. By doing this, he already shows his dissatisfaction with the Marxist analysis of alienation and by implication, therefore, with its limitation as a tool for understanding the dynamics of liberation.[2]

Secondly, the basic exegetical clarification needed by the theology of liberation concerns the origin (and, therefore, the nature) of alienation. Here, the apparent difference of emphasis between Miranda and Croatto (cf. Chapter 7) seems crucial; other authors have not discussed the subject in such depth.

There are two interrelated questions, however, which need to be treated separately: they are the questions of the root-nature of alienation and its consequences or extension. On the answers to these questions will largely depend our evaluation of every project for liberation.

As to the nature of alienation, Croatto discovers in the Bible an ontological expression whose final and absolute consequence is death, and which is absolutely irreducible to other categories. It is not, therefore, a projection from or interjection into the infrastructure of economic alienation, but a fundamental reality of man which defies phenomenological analysis, yet without which such analysis can be shown by circumstances to be wholly inadequate.

Ontological alienation is described in the Bible in such terms as wilful disobedience, idolatry, unfaithfulness, abuse of freedom, etc. We have chosen to focus on the word *asebeia* (Rom. 1.18), partly because Miranda has used Paul's argument in Romans as a central platform for his concept of man's liberation through God's justice (Rom. 1.16–17), partly because it stands at the head of a Pauline meditation on man's fall (Rom. 1.18–25),[3] and partly because Miranda unaccountably ignores *asebeia*, giving precedence to the second element of the hendiadys, *adikia*.

In contrast to Foerster,[4] we judge that the meaning of *asebeia* cannot be reduced to that of *adikia*. Firstly, the context of the passage demands that we understand a progression from the one to the other; this is later confirmed by the transition from verse 23 to verse 24: 'Exchanging the glory of the immortal God ...' is *asebeia*; 'filthy enjoyments and practices ...', followed in verses 29–31 with a further catalogue of sins, is *adikia*. The progression from *asebeia* is recapitulated in verse 25: 'since they have given up divine truth for a lie ...' and verse 28, 'since they refuse to see it was rational to acknowledge God ...'

Secondly, verse 18b ('who keep truth imprisoned in their wicked-
ness') is an elaboration and clarification of the hendiadys,
by means of a chiastic structure, in which *asebeia* is linked to
truth. *Asebeia*, then, is the fundamental meaning of man's ontological alienation; it is the *action* whereby man deliberately and
unilaterally changes the reality of his relationship to the Creator
as a creature into one in which he demands the status of God.[5]

This interpretation is not meant to deny the fundamental
importance of *adikia* in Paul's discussion, simply to argue that
this passage which, as most exegetes suggest, reproduces a
midrashic-style commentary on the meaning of man's fall
(perhaps in the style of the Wisdom literature), requires us to
establish the correct link between sin and sins, alienation and
alienations, before we can speak of a biblical theology of
liberation.

Methodologically, the biblical concept of man's ontological
self-alienation stands as an hypothesis which (like Marx's
overall view of alienation) cannot be verified 'scientifically' but
which nevertheless most adequately accounts for the evidence
of man's incapacity to liberate himself. The evidence of human
resistance to the transformation of the 'non-man' into the 'new
man' should have important repercussions on the current discussion of liberation. Firstly, the notion that oppressed man is
ultimately free to throw off his shackles and transform his
fundamental social relationships will need to be re-examined.
Secondly, the relationship between the various levels of man's
liberation and the attempts to steer a path between all monisms
and dualisms will have to be re-elaborated.

The biblical teaching on alienation urges that man is structurally unfree to change the structures of his social relationships
to the point where they express real freedom for all. By placing
the nature of alienation within the context of man's *desire* to
alter the structure of the universe, the Bible constantly demonstrates why man has *altered* his relationship to his neighbour.
Because he does not acknowledge God as Lord, he sets himself
up as 'Lord' to his fellowman. Thus, he loses the capacity for
a relationship of brotherly equality. Hence the biblical writer
is right to preface Cain's destruction of his brother (*adikia*) with
Adam's sin against God (*asebeia*). For the same reasons,
exhortation to restore the horizontal relationship, or to bring

in the kingdom, is by itself an inadequate response to alienation. This is shown clearly by Israel's history subsequent to the Exodus – a history of social exploitation – and by the fact that the prophetic message, simultaneously with its denunciation of specific *adikia*, announces a coming Saviour who will deal with the basic problem of *asebeia* (man's self-assertion cf. Isa. 53.9; 42.2–3).[6] No amount of hermeneutical juggling can ever remove this basic understanding of liberation from the Old and New Testaments. In other words, modern man's unaided attempt to transcend a structural fault in present being, however he may clothe this in contemporary ideological language, only contributes further testimony to the biblical evidence of his ontological alienation.

The second task stated above is more difficult. To say that liberation must go beyond mere structures of society is a vague statement. The basic questions must be faced: where is the focal point of liberation and what are its priorities? Answers will depend upon how the hermeneutical task is conceived. Indeed, perhaps these questions have constituted themselves, within the theology of liberation's continuing reflection, into the touchstone of the hermeneutical circle. Croatto, for example, affirms that the liberation of the Israelites from Egypt was basically a political and social act. God did not begin by saving in a spiritual realm, not even from sin.

> He saves the whole man, whose human realisation may be hindered not only by himself [sin] but also by other men who abuse their power or social 'status'. This affirmation has serious hermeneutical consequences for a Latin American or Third World re-interpretation of the Exodus message. Have we ever considered that the first, exemplary, liberating Event which 'reveals' the God of Salvation, was political and social?[7]

This passage, indeed the whole of Croatto's treatment of the Exodus, raises some further questions: for example, what is the status of the Exodus as a witness to liberation? Is it repeatable? If not, does it not have to be primarily considered in the context of its subsequent re-interpretations? Does not the Exodus narrative, in fact, already witness to liberation on levels other than that of political freedom (for example, even that of liberation from the temptation to doubt the political liberation (Exod. 6.19–23; 14.10–12; 16.2–3; 17.2–3)? What kind of liberation is going to be necessary for those who abuse their power and their social 'status'? Will the crushing or extermination of them by revolutionary forces automatically syntonise with God's action in Egypt? Finally, does not the New Testament (as Croatto proposes to show in his exegesis of Romans 5–8) deepen the concept of salvation in the light of the Cross-Resurrection Event? For even on a political level, the Cross is portrayed as the result of forces which transcend the political.[8] It was not caused by the forces of political oppression (the Roman occupation) but by those of religious fanaticism behind which Paul saw 'the masters of our age' (1 Cor. 2.6).

Summarising, it would seem that the New Testament understanding of liberation recognises not so much different levels of liberation – political, psychological, spiritual (*pace* Gutierrez) – which would cause a pseudo-dilemma, as different moments and modes of liberation. Liberation is past, present and future; it is liberation from *asebeia* and, subsequently, from *adikia*. These moments and modes must then be operative on all the levels simultaneously, in order to do justice to the global reality of biblical salvation.

At the same time, this way of viewing the relationships reflects the characteristic New Testament eschatological tension between 'already now' and 'not yet',[9] a tension which avoids the contemporary polarisation between cynical escapism (not yet) and ingenuous illusion (already now) but marks the political divide between real change (already now) and change that is wholly real (not yet). This eschatological tension, in so far as it is based on biblical realism regarding the meaning of alienation and liberation, should influence a theological interpretation of all political projects and utopias.

We have sought to show that the biblical analysis of liberation from sin, because the Bible is the only source which discerns a fundamental ontological dimension, is unique. This uniqueness, at the least, constitutes the authority of the Bible for the Christian's contemporary praxis of liberation and, as such, on the sheer weight of the evidence of its content, it must be allowed a privileged position in the hermeneutical circle. When we speak of Scripture as the mediator of total and universal liberation, we mean that this text alone points to a liberation which is total, in the sense of producing the new man, free from every alienation; and universal, in the sense of producing the new creation.[10]

2. THE QUESTION OF THE HERMENEUTICAL KEY

Assmann has criticised classical biblical hermeneutics as a procedure lacking a key to unlock its possibilities. Croatto has confidently affirmed that 'scientific' exegesis is only instrumental, never profound, for it never uncovers the meaning of the text at the level at which contact with today's reality is possible. So, beyond the *sensus literalis* there is further meaning which may be disclosed when the right hermeneutical tools are applied to the text.

There are good reasons for liberation theology's insistence on the inadequacy of a purely technical investigation of the meaning of the text. For example:

1. There already exists a hermeneutical circle within the Bible.
2. The modern emphasis on the *redaktionsgeschichtliche Methode*, uncovered in part by technical exegesis, shows that wider theological concerns are a legitimate part of a comprehensive understanding of the text.
3. No technical investigation is absolutely objective. Some of the most far-reaching techniques for interpreting Scripture (source, literary and form criticism) have been based initially on hypotheses not ultimately verifiable on the basis of objective data.[11]
4. Even so-called technical interpretation is an art which involves such hermeneutical proceedings as translation, commentary, and application, into the horizon of the exegete's world.

Thus, unless technical exegesis recognises the wider meaning and context of what it is doing, the biblical message will remain isolated and fossilised within a purely speculative academic discipline.[12]

The *sensus literalis*, then, must be placed as one parameter within a hermeneutical circle which also takes account of today's salvific concerns. In order for the circle to be valid it must be able to respond to certain basic questions, of which the most important is, 'What tools (and why these tools) are going to be used in the task of actualising the meaning discovered by technical methods?' In other words, by what criteria do we establish which hermeneutical keys should be used to interpret Scripture, in the light of today's fundamental reality, and with the least margin of error?

We have already referred to certain facets of this question. First, we see that political theology at large works from a distinction between Greek and Hebrew thought.[13] This is one possible hermeneutical guideline which may set a perspective for the whole biblical message. Secondly, the categories of oppressed and oppressors have been advocated as containing the key to understanding both the biblical meaning of interpersonal sin and man's economic relationships today. If this can be established, then the categories enter into a trans-cultural syntonisation to produce a valid, conflictual hermeneutic. Finally, ideology has its use as a weapon of 'suspicion' which, from the vantage-point of identification with the oppressed, uncovers certain politically-motivated interpretations of the Scriptures.[14]

Each of these points is intended not so much to advocate a particular hermeneutical key, as to point to the kind of criterion which must be operated in its ultimate selection. There is a different class of criteria which also need to be weighed before any final choice is made.

Firstly, the key must be seen to be central to the Bible's understanding of itself. Experience shows that pre-understandings imported from non-biblical, contemporary thought-systems often obscure rather than release the meaning of Scripture.[15]

Secondly, the key must be verifiable objectively. A hermeneutic which, for example, establishes a priority of the real as word over the real as written (the former being more valid because it supplies the supplementary meaning which interpolates me in my given situation) is inevitably subjective, arbitrary and tends to allegory. Objectivity is given on the one hand by the establishment of the *sensus literalis* of the biblical text, and on the other hand by a sound interpretation of today's reality.[16]

Thirdly, the key must syntonise with the objectively established interpretation of contemporary man, wherever this goes outside the proper concern of the biblical text.

Finally, man's individual experience is generally an unsure guide to establishing an adequate hermeneutical key, because of his natural bias against the call for a liberating praxis.

Several biblical concepts might fulfil these requirements and thus qualify as the chief hermeneutical keys. Salvation/liberation, as we have tried to outline it above (pp. 170–5) is an obvious candidate. However, the concept of the *malkuth Yahweh*[17] would seem to be an even stronger contender, for it encompasses a wider range of biblical concerns: creation; redemption as liberation from alienation and for love and service; the cosmic lordship of Christ over the powers; the new man and the new creation; to mention the most important.[18] At the same time this concept includes the contemporary concerns of the theology of liberation for structural change, a new order, continuity between every level of liberation and a conflictual hermeneutic.[19]

3. BRINGING TOGETHER THE HORIZONS

Even if we can decide which hermeneutical key is most applicable today to the task of biblical interpretation, we do not automatically know how it should be used in order that Scripture may be more completely understood from within the contemporary situation. A practical conclusion to this problem will involve a discussion of the way in which the various parameters may be syntonised and the horizons brought together.

The theology of liberation has sought to do both these things through its insistence on the unitary nature of salvific history as world history and, within this, on the God who consistently goes on bringing about man's complete liberation. It advocates a continuing revelation of God, a fundamental interest in history as the *locus revelationis*, and a stress on the present as the time of salvation. Nevertheless this view suffers from certain serious difficulties, which we shall examine by reference to the views of Croatto and Segundo.

Croatto's position assumes that the present-day horizon, or reality, is unequivocal, and that God's present salvific, liberating act can be read off from today's events without ambiguity or doubt.

> To recognise the signs of the times or to read God's presence in world events means, at least, that there must be a very deep syntony between these and the Christian message, but this syntony occurs because God is first discovered *in the event*, from which one goes back to the archetypal message ... the opposite procedure ... may only effect a situational accommodation of the message to the actual event....
>
> The profoundest type of Christian faith demands two itineraries: to 'read' the events [and from them formulate the traditional message] and to listen to the Word of God already transmitted [in order to be more open to salvific events in the world].[20]

These passages manifest just how decisive for Croatto's thinking is today's reality as the revealer of God's salvific actions. Nevertheless, some questions need to be examined before this method can be said to have produced a satisfactory hermeneutical procedure.

Firstly, today's events, in so far as they concern man, can rarely be interpreted unequivocally. Here again, we need to reiterate that the human sciences, with their respective hypotheses concerning human behaviour, cannot claim the same precision and clarity as the exact sciences.

Secondly, even if a particular interpretation of today's events did manage to command either universal agreement or a very large amount of circumstantial support, the status of these events as revealers of God's salvific action in history would be difficult to establish.[21]

Thirdly, it is hard to see, logically, how God can be meaningfully discovered in today's event without an *a priori* commitment to the fact that he has acted in the archetypal Event. Without this commitment it would seem less ambiguous to interpret today's reality in purely secular terms. The question then is, What kind of commitment to the archetype is necessary? The theology of liberation, as a whole, evades the concrete challenge of this question.

Fourthly, the hermeneutical procedure proposed by Croatto, whereby the traditionally biblical message is reformulated from the perspective of present salvation-history, is not so much an open circulation as a closed circuit. This is because the possibility of syntonisation by which the reality of a present process of liberation, open to interpretation through biblical categories, is established, depends upon there being a core traditional message which remains objectively discoverable, apart from any reformulation.

Croatto's projected hermeneutic of liberation suffers, therefore, from the same failure as does Assmann's argument for the absolute perspicuity of today's reality, for the former depends upon the latter. However, the exercise is bound to be incoherent unless it is based upon a core biblical message which is comprehensible within its own terms of reference.

Segundo employs what is perhaps a more straightforward hermeneutical method. He admits that the normal exegetical methods present us with a Jesus who, when interpreted against his response to his own political background, can be seen to have acted and spoken from a particular ideological slant (e.g. his emphasis on gratuitousness and non-violence).

Having admitted what is, in fact, the case, Segundo does not try to produce a hermeneutic which would syntonise with or reformulate this ideological slant. Rather, using the same de-ideologising process on the biblical authors, which hitherto has been practised on modern theologies which have used biblical exegesis, categories and language to defend pre-revolutionary systems, he hopes to remove from it elements which, he considers, hinder the efficacy of Christian love in the present.

This procedure also elevates into controlling hermeneutical keys a certain interpretation of today's reality and a certain praxis. As a result it falls victim to the same criticisms levelled against Croatto's method. It also suffers from two further criticisms.

Firstly, there is Miranda's criticism of the widely held and rather arrogant view that our own perspective gives us a knowledge and discernment of God's revelation unknown or unavailable to the biblical writers. This kind of claim automatically excludes the Bible's ability to be either a critical liberating force in its own right or to say anything new or different to our situation.

Segundo's approach also divorces ethics from the prime Christian source. This is not so much because he establishes a prior *dogmatic* system equally applicable to every situation, but because he relies upon a prior *ideological* system as the ultimate source of contemporary truth.

One also finds a certain exegetical superficiality in Segundo's hermeneutical method. He is right to state that the New Testament has a certain ideological slant (if one concedes the use of that terminology), but he does not stop to consider how this might be incorporated into a valid hermeneutical circle for today. He dismisses it as ideologically negative. In other words, he does not consider that certain elements may be there by design, precisely because they represent a correct view of the reality of man in society. He assumes they are there either by historical accident or by relative cultural accretion. He does not ask, for example, what could be the significance for political reflection today, in the light of the crucifixion, of Jewish political commitment at the time of Christ;[22] nor whether, for example, the political element in the New Testament might not constitute a universally valid reflection on the significance of power and of community, the means to bring change and, finally, political liberation itself; nor does he ask whether Marx's analysis of man's relations in society is so objective and original that it constitutes a genuine *novum* for the hermeneutical task.

The approach of both Croatto and Segundo is common amongst the theologians of liberation but it does not solve the problem of synthesising the horizons, for it is too unilateral and *a priori*. In attempting to advance the discussion a little we will now consider the status of the *sensus literalis* in the hermeneutical circle.

One of the most important questions in contemporary biblical hermeneutics is whether the *sensus literalis* should enjoy an autonomy of its own or whether, in fact, it is impossible to establish its meaning outside of a particular hermeneutical stance. The question is a complex one, though vital to a study of a biblical theology of liberation. The following observations in the light of the preceding discussion may help to clarify both this issue and, as a result, some of the central issues being thrown up by the theology of liberation's novel methodology.

1. There are no absolutely objective and wholly reliable methods for establishing the meaning of any text. The exegetical tools currently used in the historical-critical method may approximate to methodological objectivity if the hypotheses advanced are open to dispute on grounds universally recognised as valid. By this test, linguistic and text-critical studies come closest to an objective method. Other studies, such as form-criticism, appear to be much more speculative and based, at times, on a near-circular argument.[23]

2. We have already observed a distinction in the levels of meaning of the *sensus literalis*. The encyclical, *Divino Afflante* (1943), has defined it as what the author *intended*, but at the same time has given the impression that it is the intention which the historical-critical method is able to establish. However, the definition raises certain questions: Is it intrinsically possible to discover what the author intended? Would it not require a degree of insight and knowledge which the modern exegete, so far removed in time, cannot be expected to possess? Or, conversely, would it not require a syntony between the respective situations of exegete and biblical writer, the necessity of which is already assumed in the search for a valid hermeneutical key? Perhaps, therefore, it would be better to define the *sensus literalis* as what the writer *said*, as this can be reasonably established by the criteria of linguistic and other studies. However, even this is not wholly satisfactory, for what the writer *said* is really a euphemism for what the writer *communicates* and this again presupposes the hermeneutical circle.[24]

3. The task of establishing the *sensus literalis* would, therefore, seem to involve the acknowledgement and use of evidence which comes from the two horizons about which we are speaking. Firstly, there is the knowledge to be obtained from a careful consideration of the text: its language, structure, history and the light shed upon it from other near-contemporary sources. All this has been worked, perhaps over-worked, by the historical-critical method with its genuine insights and also its substantial defects. Then there is the knowledge contributed consciously or

unconsciously, according to the vantage-point selected as the most relevant by the exegete.

This latter has often been referred to as the 'pre-understanding'. However, in the light of liberation theology's challenge to much contemporary hermeneutical methodology, the idea should be widened, for the input is not simply intellectual, as pre-*understanding* implies, but also profoundly practical. We are not concerned simply with my interpretation of the world, but also with my action to transform it; not simply with the input which comes by contemplating the challenge of the non-believer, but also the challenge of the non-man.

Clearly, liberation theology's contribution to the discussion of synthesising the horizons is the challenge to hear what the text communicates when studied from a praxis of solidarity with the oppressed, the despised and the heavy-laden. The importance of this perspective to the establishing of the *sensus universus Scripturae* has hardly been investigated at all. Indeed some exegetes might wrongly suppose that this perspective, if they are aware of its existence, would be bound to cloud rather than clarify Scripture's meaning.

Can a solution be found to this problem? Unexpectedly, perhaps, the answer may come through a reconsideration of the place and the role of the Church in the hermeneutical quest.

The Church is, in fact, already a way of relating horizons, for on the one hand, the existence of the text presupposes the people of God and the Bible is already part of God's liberating acts in history; and, on the other hand, the contemporary Church recognises her true identity only as she continually consults the original text about the meaning of her mission in the world. In between the two horizons the Church acknowledges a long tradition of biblical interpretation and hermeneutical practice which may act as either a guide, or a warning, to her own task.

However, there is a further complication to be faced, for one of the questions most insistently raised by the theology of liberation concerns the criteria by which the Church may be recognised today. The question may be put in terms of a new-style ecumenism which would include all revolutionary forces, or in terms of a reformulation of the old adage: *extra ecclesiam nulla salus*. The question should be, in our opinion, not about where the Church *is* (i.e. about certain formal or structural characteristics of the empirical Church, like ministerial order) but about how we may know which groups show the authentic signs of belonging to God's people. Only in this way may we safeguard the priority of obedience (orthopraxis) in our definition of the Church.

Clearly the Church, to be identifiable today, must stand in some definite continuity with the original people of God. This latter, in turn, if it is to be recognised as such, must stand in a unique relationship to God's original saving acts expressed in the reality of the kingdom. This relationship may be summed up by saying that the Church is recognisable as such when it manifests clear characteristics of the new order which God is creating.[25] Now this new order is clearly discernible in the New Testament (and the theology of liberation has elaborated particular aspects of this) in the polarity of the operation of grace and works: i.e. wherever God's grace is a reality through faith in the salvation of Jesus Christ and wherever this grace has clearly established a totally new set of relations and a new action in the face of the mind-set of this world (or this age) (Rom. 12.1–2). The criteria, then, include both grace and works interpreted in the light of the presence of the kingdom. They remain valid today in these ways:

1. God's grace in effecting man's liberation from *asebeia* by Jesus Christ alone remains a fixed reference-point.
2. God's grace in effecting liberation from, and new action within, the mind-set of this world (liberation from *adikia*) will be both constant and variable. The mind-set of the first-century world included in differing degrees legalistic religion, idealistic philosophy, gnostic syncretism and idolatrous politics. All remain to some degree, and require a particular response on the part of the Church. But the mind-set most affecting the Third World nations is the world structure of economic injustice and exploitation based on greed and the desire for power.
3. Consequently, the theology of liberation is right when it insists that today's empirical Church demonstrates itself to

belong to the people of God if, and when, it takes relevant
action against this particular manifestation of the *kosmos*.
4. The criteria of recognition cannot be given by the empirical Church (which is not the kingdom), only by the signs
of the new age manifested as the contradiction of the
kosmos, in the double expression of *asebeia* and *adikia*.

The horizons may be brought together, therefore, when this
particular people of God listens to the message of the text by
means of both the hermeneutical key of the kingdom and the
challenge of particular empirical manifestations of the rebellious *kosmos* today.

CHAPTER EIGHTEEN

SOLA SCRIPTURA: AN ALTERNATIVE HERMENEUTIC

In the final chapters we shall attempt to do two things: to show why it is necessary to reverse the methodological procedure of the theology of liberation, so that theology becomes a critical reflection on the message of revelation in the light of praxis and the challenge of actual historical reality; and to show how it is possible to do this without returning again to theology's classical methodology. In this way we hope to draw together into a different kind of theological synthesis some of the main concerns which have arisen out of this critical dialogue with the theology of liberation.

In every kind of modern biblical interpretation the Scriptures are used as both a point of departure and a point of arrival. Only thus can the biblical message be released to be an effective instrument for the Church's actual mission. At the same time, however, it raises a critical question: where should the common terminus be located?

The theology of liberation, with its characteristic emphasis on revelation as an Event-continuum, stresses the modern situation as the terminus, and the Scriptures, in consequence, as one departure-point. From this perspective, the most important aspect of biblical hermeneutics is that interpretation should syntonise with the demands of modern reality to produce a transforming praxis. The premise that modern reality most clearly discloses the truth about interhuman relationships in society has been made the foundation for all interpretation. Scripture, however, is not considered to have an equal perspicuity: therefore a new 'source of revelation' is necessary in order that it may speak its hidden reserve-of-meaning.

A process of re-interpretation leading from the New Testament to our own days is justified by the theology of liberation on the analogy of the New Testament's interpretation of the Old; new events warrant a new process of interpretation which will avoid modern legalistic, intellectualist or gnostic approaches to Scripture.[1] It is the Event, or praxis, rather than academic analysis without prior commitment, which will lead to a true grasp of Scripture's *sensus plenior*. If the classical way of doing biblical exegesis has been to move from the biblical texts to the writer's theological intentions and then to external referents, then the theology of liberation reverses the order, moving from the external referents to the biblical text.[2]

This procedure has a certain analogy with the Catholic understanding of the relationship between Scripture and tradition. In the latter case, the terminus is the Word of God in the living voice of the Church, which is concretely and formally announced through the Church's office of teaching. In the former case, the terminus is the Word of God speaking through God's present liberating Event. In answer to the doubt raised that the relationship may imply an unwarranted hermeneutical leap, inimical to the content of biblical revelation, Catholic theology has always replied that revelation did not cease with the apostles, nor has the modern Church direct access to the text, only an access 'filtered through the screen of a tradition in which they have been read'.[3] As a result, the Church has the obligation, in the interests of clarity and consistency in Christian doctrine, to monitor the various traditions of interpretation. The theology of liberation would vary this procedure, firstly by substituting a dialectical ideology for the institutional Church in the monitoring task, and secondly by performing it in the interests of the clarity and consistency of orthopraxis, rather than orthodoxy.

Although this procedure, as the theology of liberation states it, may be partly correct, it raises fundamental theological issues concerning the Christian source of truth. By discussing them at this point, we hope to be able to sketch the outline of another theology of liberation, showing that neither the content of the gospel nor the procedure of theology are limited to the choice between radical and traditional theologies.

The Reformers' appeal to *Sola Scriptura* as a *theological methodology* obviously has many facets, one of the most important being the intuition that Scripture remains the only legitimate terminus for the Christian understanding of reality. The reason for this is that no other source of Christian truth may ever claim an absolute value for its findings here and now. For, if we are right to see Scripture's testimony to the kingdom of God as the central hermeneutical key (or 'material centre'[4]) for its own understanding then, because neither the Church nor any particular ideological framework can be identified with the kingdom (which is God's ultimate design for the world's fulfilment), the autonomy claimed by either Church or current ideology, particularly as an ultimate authority in the interpretation of Scripture, is called into question.

This argument leads us to consider other reasons why the notion of *Sola Scripture*, in spite of (or maybe because of) a certain crisis in the principle of biblical authority noted amongst Western academic theologians, is still our most relevant hermeneutical guide today.

(*i*) *The Bible's contribution to the praxis of liberation needs to be kept open.* We have already discussed the Bible's unique contribution both to an analysis of human alienation and to human liberation. To this discussion we might add its equally unique testimony concerning the related problem of human and extra-human power-structures. Although it is true, for example, that Marxism, by emphasising the dialectic oppressor/oppressed, provides a valuable hermeneutical key to the Bible's own understanding of itself, it is equally true, as Miranda admits, that the New Testament goes beyond all Marxist descriptions of structural oppression in its understanding of human existence as 'life-before-death': 'the last of the enemies to be destroyed is death' (1 Cor. 15.26). How, then, should we consider today those so-called mythological elements of the New Testament which speak of externally structured, personal oppression?

We could ignore them, or demythologise them, though this latter course, as Gollwitzer has shown, amounts basically to the same thing.[5] We could also try to remythologise them, understanding the powers and potencies in terms of supra-individual structures of injustice (e.g. bureaucracy) or death as the untimely death of the oppressed brought about by undernourishment and exposure, or even by torture and brutality, which has robbed large sections of mankind of the opportunity of being man. Without denying for a moment that these structures of injustice and oppression are real and evil, the question remains whether by this particular hermeneutical process we have, in fact, rid ourselves not only of the *sensus literalis* (of the 'myth') but of the *sensus plenior* as well; whether the substance is not tied so intimately to its linguistic representation that this 'definite thing' (Gollwitzer), in which the New Testament authors passionately believe, is not so much explained as explained away.

This leads us to ask the liberation theologians a serious question: Does not any theory of oppression that banishes from its horizon the objective reality of the 'powers' (the active presence of all demonic alternatives to the kingdom) inevitably lead to a certain romanticism concerning the possibility of structural change? It is true that structural alienation, in Marxist terms, may be akin to the biblical concept of the 'powers', which also work against humanity, but there is also a clear distinction: whereas structural alienation as such can be concretely identified in society, the 'powers' can only be 'suspected' on the grounds that structural alienation is not an adequate way of accounting for man's resistance to liberating change. We conclude, then, that if liberation means only structural change (i.e. changes in the way society is at present organised) then the Christian view of liberation is less 'revolutionary' than the Marxist, but at the same time it is less romantic.

However, we are not suggesting that the theology of liberation has completely banished the concept of the 'powers' from its horizon. We do suggest that its hermeneutical procedure may foreclose the issue of the New Testament's contribution to the praxis of liberation, assuming that the concept of the 'powers' be allowed to stand and disclose its message. For example, Miranda, instead of allowing the biblical *kerygma* to correct the unilateral Marxist interpretation of structural alienation, attempts to incorporate into the Marxist dialectic a remythologised understanding of the 'powers'. However, by this procedure he is in danger of obscuring the absolute, ethically negative, aspect of the hostile forces. This, in turn, will affect our praxis, for it will determine both our whole attitude to evil and, on the analogy of obedience to Yahweh as absolute demand, on what level we place our resistance to the powers as forces to be absolutely rejected. In other words, biblical hermeneutics has no obligation to defend the Marxist analysis, though it is obliged, by the content of the message it discovers, to expound and defend the absolute ethic to love one's neighbour in a *particular way*. The concluding discussion of Miranda's book, *Marx and the Bible*, therefore, really negates his own claim that he is not interested in discovering parallels between Marx and the Bible.

Another way of stating this first point is by saying that hermeneutical objectivity can be guaranteed only if the text is allowed to question modern man, without being suppressed. Likewise, it must be allowed to scrutinise and question any selection of biblical material on the (extra biblical) grounds that it is relevant to modern praxis. So then, although the theology of liberation's acceptance of Marxist categories has led it to ask of the text (for the first time?) some highly relevant questions, it has also led to much superficial exegesis, for the same acceptance has inhibited it from asking other questions which might also be relevant.

In short, if the Bible makes no original contribution to the praxis of liberation, then it should be made clear that the hermeneutic of liberation is using the Bible in an 'inspirational' rather than 'objective' sense – i.e. as a means to further ends over which the Bible has had no decisive say. Subsequently, it may be asked whether, in fact, such a hermeneutic is not really dishonest.

(*ii*) *The hermeneutical key to interpret Scripture must be recognised as a central theme of Scripture.* Biblical theology, as a methodology for scriptural interpretation, needs to disengage one or more theological frameworks which appear absolutely central to the Bible. The choices it makes are then open to the scrutiny of the committed community and to the test of time and circumstances. Unfortunately, the choice has often been made uncritically, according to unquestioned ecclesiastical confessions or philosphical systems. There is also the danger of valuing the chosen elements too highly, regarding them as beyond criticism.

However, these dangers do not negate the necessary procedure. We have selected the kingdom-theme as central (without, of course, foreclosing the interpretation of its meaning, which is still vigorously debated) for two complementary reasons. In the Bible the theme is both sufficiently universal in its scope to be able to organise coherently other fundamental themes and sufficiently specific to be able to offer a definite *kerygma*; in the contemporary situation it both points to and demands a radical transformation of human relationships.

From the point of view of the theology of liberation's hermeneutic, the Scriptures, if they are going to be applied in a relevant way to contemporary praxis, must contain a basic message which expresses what Segundo calls their ideological slant. This message must be understandable in its own terms, otherwise the hermeneutical circle is not real, but simply reflects its own biases. It is unfortunate therefore that Segundo, for example, is not concerned to ask himself whether the ideological slant is there by chance or by design. This question also has enormous hermeneutical consequences (e.g. the indispensability, or otherwise, of the function and role of apocalyptic in the biblical concept of the kingdom).

Here it is important to recall Gutierrez' second hermeneutical principle (cf. chapter 6) which proceeds from the universal principles of the text to the particularities of a given praxis. At the heart of the biblical message – Jesus' preaching of the kingdom as an eternally subversive order – there is a content which Gutierrez considers has the power and authority to criticise and relativise every human political alternative.

The concept of *Sola Scriptura*, then, maintains that a hermeneutical understanding of the text is first derived from the text's own hermeneutical procedure, i.e. the discovery of the centre of God's self-revelation of himself in Christ. A difference must then be drawn between this discovery and the larger and changing hermeneutical context to which it must permanently speak.

(*iii*) *Modern pre-understandings need to be identified and analysed.* Modern biblical exegesis has often been much more sharply aware of the cultural climate of the original text of Scripture than it has of the particular cultural context and influence which it imports into its own interpretative procedure. Because of both these factors, technical exegesis, if not supplemented by a consciously assumed theological exegesis, falls into the error of positivist historiography which believes that texts from the past can be reconstructed from zero.

Any history of modern biblical exegesis can quickly identify the way in which 'particular ontologies' (Gollwitzer) have profoundly influenced deductive interpretations of the text.[6] From the point of view of a 'political' reading of the New Testament, for example, many contradictory attempts have been made to interpret Jesus' mission, teaching, trial and death in political terms.[7] Likewise, Gollwitzer identified the ideological bias underlying an attempt by Conzelmann to restrict the sociopolitical implications of the Church as God's new order.[8] Other examples could be given of how every pre-understanding brought to the biblical text, even when it is not overtly political in intention, nevertheless has profound ideological overtones.

Of course, it would be hard to imagine an interpretation of the biblical message which was totally exempt from prior cultural conditioning; such an interpretation, in any case, would be aseptic. There can be no question, therefore, of a 'neutral' reading of Scripture; but there is every reason why particular pre-understandings should be clearly identified and *justified*.

Any valid hermeneutical circle presupposes, then, a method for identifying and justifying particular pre-understandings. In the case of the theology of liberation, Marxism has been used effectively to detect interpretations which are ideologically motivated or influenced. However, Marxism as a means of identifying and criticising false pre-understandings is limited by two factors.

1. It is not, in spite of claims to the contrary, wholly rational, autonomous and objective. Because Marx also participated in a culturally relative situation, the epistemological use of the system which bears his name needs to be defended on the basis of a further, trans-historical ethic.
2. Although Marxism can be effectively used to establish a critical circle for biblical hermeneutics in that it exposes the traditional identification of empirical Christianity with the forces of stability and security, a further, more fundamentally critical stance will be needed to expose the identification of Christianity with those forces which, having overthrown the forces of stability and security, take their place. In other words, Marxism, though it acts as a vital polemic against those theologies which have

suppressed or muted the Bible's critical and prophetic message by taking extraneous ontologies into their hermeneutical circles, is not subversive enough, by itself, either in theory or practice, for a continuous prophetic task.

The theology of liberation, then, has not fully considered the Bible's profound questioning of every pre-understanding. Gollwitzer maintains that the hermeneutical relationship of theology to any ontology must be eclectic;[9] however, given the domesticating effect on the biblical message of almost every pre-understanding, it should rather be critical and conflictive.

Almost every modern hermeneutical pre-understanding has been influenced by the Enlightenment notion of the historical autonomy of modern man. The use of Marxism is no exception. It is equally a child of the modern rationalistic dichotomy. It is but one example of the modern tendency towards philosophical monism. Biblical anthropology, however, not only establishes a theoretical contradiction of this idea but, more importantly, places the centre of man's alienation precisely in his desire to be autonomous with regard to his Creator (autonomy being understood in the context of his world-view rather than, for example, of his scientific task). Conversely, the biblical view of liberation sees man's freedom only in terms of the recognition that he is a creature, absolutely held to account by God for the way he pursues his relationships. Likewise, the Son 'makes free' (John 8.34–6) when he is recognised as the only one sent by God to take away the sin of the world (John 1.29) (i.e. its rebellious 'mind-set' or *asebeia*).

So, both Marxism, because of its inadequate analysis of evil, and modern ontologies, because they uniformly re-interpret the biblical view of a space/time fall in terms of an existential encounter with present sin, are inadequate and, if pressed, ultimately confusing tools to be used as pre-understandings for the hermeneutical task.

Thus, in synthesis, it is a basic hermeneutical premise that only by immersing ourselves in the biblical world and being prepared to accept biblical thought-forms shall we ever be able to hear fully the biblical message.

(iv) All interpretation needs to be conducted with the greatest possible

objectivity. Biblical hermeneutics should not be regarded as an end in itself, nor its discussion merely a refined academic exercise; it is designed to help the people of God criticise and redefine their mission in the light both of present reality and of the promised fulfilment of God's kingdom. This being so, biblical hermeneutics should be conducted between two objective and separate poles. There is the pole of man's contemporary situation, scientifically analysed (assuming the control of a true scientific methodology) and the pole of the biblical message, interpreted according to its own criteria.

However, man's propensity to interpose either his own subjective and idealistic feelings or limited human context and understanding between the two objective poles of the hermeneutical task has proved a tenacious obstacle to an adequate biblical hermeneutic. The theology of liberation has clearly identified this tendency in Western theology, giving us an example of its silence concerning the objective need for an alternative social order to that of capitalism. However, the hidden motives which have tended to neutralise the prophetic impact of the Bible's central message of the kingdom have not yet been so clearly identified.[10]

The principle of *Sola Scriptura* should lead to a vindication of the truism that only as man ceases to look for his identity within his own subjectivity, apart from these two poles, will he ever face the demand for radical renewal and transformation.

The theology of liberation has opted for a contemporary historical pre-understanding before approaching the text. By doing this, it believes that theology's perennial ideological problem will be solved and its contribution to man's liberation consequently maximised. This is not so, however, for the text questions and confronts man much more radically than does that particular ideology from which the option has been made. For this reason, we insist that the task of modern theology should be a consciously critical reflection on God's Word in the light of a contemporary praxis of liberation. If this is not the order of our methodology then the phrase (in Gutierrez' definition), 'in the light of God's Word', ultimately becomes emptied of content.

Our hermeneutical methodology therefore, cannot be that of the theology of liberation. Even less does it agree with that of traditional theology, for it is clearly done from a practical commitment to a demand made by both poles of our hermeneutical circle.

This exposition of a contemporary understanding of *Sola Scriptura* as the only adequate terminus for a hermeneutic of liberation has attempted to suggest a different way of looking at the resources for liberation contained in the biblical revelation of God, and to solve satisfactorily the tension between biblical authority and modern pre-understandings from the perspective of contemporary praxis. One final task remains: namely, to discuss the relationship between the finality of God's revelation in the Christ-event as an alternative source of revolutionary theory and contemporary praxis for the Christian Church.

CHAPTER NINETEEN

THE FINALITY OF CHRIST, PRAXIS AND THE PILGRIM'S PROGRESS

Throughout this evaluation of the theology of liberation's approach to the Bible we have been assuming that a Christian acknowledges an ultimate point of reference for the hermeneutical task, i.e. a final ground on which he can simultaneously justify both the notion of *Sola Scriptura* and any particular praxis (or means of obedience). This ultimate point is the revelation of Jesus Christ as the new man whom God has given to the world as his complete 'wisdom, righteousness, holiness and liberation' (1 Cor. 1.30).

The meaning of Christ as a final reference-point must be related both to the idea of a continuum of revelation, which we personally question, and to the praxis of liberation, which we accept.

The formal statement of Christ's finality would not be disputed by any of the theologians of liberation. However, the content given to the phrase would vary according to the way in which biblical hermeneutics has been operated in practice. Thus, Croatto's hermeneutic of the Event which assumes a consistent revelation-continuum stretching from the New Testament to our days, parallel to that stretching from the Old Testament to the New, establishes a basis which allows our contemporary re-interpretation of the New Testament a certain precedence over the text itself. Segundo's hermeneutical procedure allows him to sit relatively loosely to the actual content of Jesus' teaching (none of Christ's specific demands can be right in any and every circumstance), although he admits that Jesus' ethic of gratuitousness is original and orientative. Both authors, therefore, have effectively contributed, by means of their respective hermeneutical circles, to a relativisation of Christ's finality as the ultimate source of God's truth.[1]

For the sake of clarifying the hypothesis we are presenting, we shall state several objections to these relativising hermeneutical procedures.

1. The finality of Christ is based on both inductive scriptural exegesis and deduction from the premise that the concept of promise and fulfilment is the most adequate way of expressing the reality of God's activity in history. Upon both these scores it can be maintained that, whereas the Old Testament does not claim to present a final revelation of Yahweh, for it consistently points to a fuller and more direct manifestation of his presence with his people, the New Testament does claim that Christ was such a final revelation. *Prima facie*, then, our freedom to re-interpret the New Testament is of a wholly different order from that which Christ and his apostles exercised in their interpretation of the Old Testament.

2. This argument does not directly contradict Croatto's hermeneutical procedure, which stresses that the Christ-event must be interpreted from the reality of God's present fulfilment of the kingdom, always assuming that this latter syntonises with the former. It does, however, question the mystique surrounding the idea that the present event belongs to the same continuum of revelation as the Christ-event itself. Croatto argues that God's new present event authorises me to question, transmute or add to the revelation given in the Christ-event as recorded in the New Testament. He argues that this procedure is legitimate because, as we are immersed in the continuum of the same Body of Christ as the early Church, so we may continue the same interpretative process begun by Christ and the apostles in their handling of the Old Testament. However, the New Testament points to the fact that the apostles, as witnesses of the actual inauguration of the new era in the resurrection, lived a totally unique, and therefore unrepeatable, moment in which to receive God's definitive revelation of himself in Christ. This revelation is consciously stated to be the Word of God (e.g. 1 Thess. 2.13; 1 Cor. 2.7–10, 12–13; Eph. 3.3–11). It is final in the sense of being the divinely commissioned clarification of this one

final (or end) event. Naturally, this revelation must be unfolded afresh by every new generation of Christians who, as in the present case, may well benefit from a reading of the 'signs of the times' in a new theological/political framework. But it is not outmoded and cannot be changed without implying a rejection of the definitive nature of the inauguration of the new age.

3. One of the presuppositions underlying the belief that the present event reveals God as explicitly as did the Christ-event is the ingenuous idea that praxis can spontaneously generate new revelation and new unambiguous interpretations of that revelation. However, this view of praxis comes close to baptising all of history in the name of a particular revelation none the less esoteric for being contemporary and, as a consequence, is easily manipulated in the interests of privilege and oppression. Miranda shows that he sees this issue clearly when he states that 'the Christ who cannot be co-opted by accommodationists and opportunists [is] the historical Jesus.' Taking into account a full New Testament Christology, one could go further and state that without the reality of God *speaking* and *acting* (Acts 1.1) in the history of his Son, who is the New Man, by whose resurrection the new era has once for all been inaugurated, nothing remains of praxis except a great historical vacuum which man will compulsively fill with his own alienated ideas and symbols.

4. If God's revelation in Jesus Christ is not unique and final, then he may be passed over for subsequent Christ-symbols, like Camilo Torres or Che Guevara, which could be considered authentic receptacles of God's wholly contemporary revelation in the new Event. However, such a process would contradict, not syntonise with, the New Testament data, for the New Testament demands that we recognise and submit to Jesus Christ as the *deuteros anthrōpos* (the second man) 1 Cor. 15.47). Indeed the parallel between Christ and Adam is drawn in such a way that the possibility of a 'third man' is excluded: 'the first man Adam ...; the last Adam' (1 Cor. 15.45). This second man is also 'the Lord from heaven', the judge of all human pretensions to define the new man apart from him.

5. If the biblical Christ is the only Christ capable of defining the contours of the new humanity and incapable of being manipulated by the forces of reaction, then it is difficult to see how we can fail to take seriously his specific demands. This is what Miranda alone among our five principal protagonists tries to do. Especially in his book *Being and the Messiah*, he seeks to establish the only sufficient basis for both a hermeneutical interpretation of the Christian message and a call to obedience. This aspect of biblical hermeneutics needs to be spelled out in more detail.

The definitive inauguration of the kingdom in Jesus Christ is the determining factor of all hermeneutics which seeks to be contemporary. In other words, the finality of Christ is a call not only to deduce a Christological hermeneutic from the Gospels, but also to practice all theological interpretation in the context of obedience to God's will disclosed in the coming of the kingdom.

Right praxis ultimately depends on right theory. This means that the biblical revelation of Christ will determine the *means* of being obedient rather than just freeing us for obedience, leaving the means dependent upon human ingenuity within the relative nature of any given situation. But right theory, unless it is consummated in the praxis which it demands, soon becomes either distorted, 'spiritualised' or manipulated in the interests of minimising those demands. The history of the Church can be written as a series of tragic attempts to justify the toning down of the absolute demands of radical discipleship in the kingdom.

The theology of liberation has, therefore, done a great service to theology in general by insisting on the priority of praxis as the *locus praecipuus* of the theological task: this is the meaning of the call to a new method in theology; i.e. to move theology from a discussion about faith to the obedience of faith (Rom. 1.5).[2] The biblical message is not ultimately disclosed to the idly curious, however technically correct their exegesis may be, but only to those who are practically committed to the realisation of the kingdom. Further disclosure of meaning is always based on a further practice of obedience. This is the meaning of pre-

understanding as a concrete praxis rather than as an intellectual system.

What the theology of liberation has done, at this point, is
to relearn from Marx what was always true for biblical epistemology: namely, that knowledge is not gained speculatively
but obtained through obedience in concrete historical action.
Biblical exegesis, therefore, should work from the constant
supposition that its task is to serve a revelatory truth which
automatically demands to be realised. Technical exegesis,
which seeks to 'hear' the Word, must be complemented by
a hermeneutical circle which seeks to 'do' it *here and now*, for *what
we hear depends upon what we are prepared* to put into
practice.

The theology of liberation issues a prophetic call today to
the universal Christian Church to consider the sub-culture of
poverty and inhumanity suffered by the people of the Third
World as the pre-eminent context for today's hermeneutical
task.

From this discussion of praxis as an indispensable pole of the
hermeneutical task arise two questions which take us to the final
stage of our discussion of the theology of liberation and its
approach to Scripture. Acknowledging that the complementary themes of *Sola Scriptura* and the finality of Christ force us
to recognise that the biblical revelation of God and man produces a unique contribution to the praxis of liberation, how
should this contribution, as a means of obedience to God's absolute demands, be worked out in concrete detail? Is the struggle
to eliminate oppression and forge a more human society the
only relevant praxis for the hermeneutical task?

Firstly, how should present-day commitment to the kingdom
be fulfilled? 'To be Christian is to believe that one man of history
loved us by loving his contemporaries as far as giving his life
for them, who loved the poor by preference and for them confronted the great and powerful of his times, and who was put
to death as subversive. He is God. The great principle hermeneutic of the faith and, therefore, the foundation of all theological discourse, is Jesus Christ.'[3] The means of commitment
to the kingdom in present-day praxis is controlled by Jesus' attitude and action. Jesus is he who, in the words of Gutierrez

quoted above, has shown the only true liberating praxis in history.

It is unfortunate that the theology of liberation has not followed its epoch-making insistence on a new theological method by a new method in praxis. Its analysis of reality is precise and clear, its call to base praxis on this analysis is also unequivocal; but its defining of concrete praxis is often vague, unreal and tending to romanticism. There are many reasons for this.

1. Though liberation theology has accepted the Marxist analysis of the sub-structure of inter-personal relation-ships in society in terms of economic exploitation, it has not totally endorsed what Gutierrez and Segundo call the deterministic, or mechanistic, presuppositions of certain views of the classless society. This has meant a search for a more total transformation of man than that en-visaged by any Marxist theory. However, the contours of this transformation in a new social order are, as yet, indistinct.

2. It manifestly repudiates the concrete tendencies of several communist states to absolutise and freeze a revolutionary process. It prefers to speak, therefore, of a Latin Ameri-can-style socialism, which will simultaneously end capi-talist exploitation and guard against rigidity in the new structures. Nevertheless, this socialism is still an abstrac-tion, for no such society yet exists.

3. It does not allow the Christ-event to make a *unique* con-tribution to political praxis. The reason for this is bound up with its rejection of the kind of methodology which led to the 'theocentric humanism' ideology of certain Latin-American Christian Democrat parties. However, such a total rejection of a particular methodology has caused the theology of liberation to lose a unique source of creative thinking on liberating praxis. It has, uncon-sciously perhaps, confused content with methodology. The result is a stultification of the search for a new future seen in a repetition of its own language, the tendency to with-draw into a misunderstood ghetto,[4] and a failure to take its own exegesis seriously.[5]

Following on from this, then, the new theological method of the theology of liberation, when corrected by what we should consider the more consistent hermeneutical methodology outlined in these pages, will issue in a new method of praxis.

This new method will take seriously the way in which Christ identified himself with the poor; his own specific definition of the poor as *all* outcasts of society (i.e. those who challenge the stability and security of society by being different: lepers, demon-possessed, harlots, Samaritans, women in general, the economically poor, those whose religious sentiments are easily exploited for gain, widows etc.); his attitude to the abrogation of the law; his teaching on fundamental alienation as self-righteousness; above all his attitude to political power and violence and the creation of a new non-hierarchical, and therefore non-exploitative, community, where no one will be called Master (since there is only one Lord) where all are brothers, and the most servant-like will be accounted the greatest and the arrogant will be abased (Matt. 23.8–12).

What is needed by the Church both in Latin America and elsewhere is a praxis based on a Christological hermeneutic of the Gospel which seeks to implement the kingdom (not derived from this world) in the light of both the Cross and the concrete reality of oppression, analysed dialectically. From this new praxis, dedicated to the creation of Christian communities in which the private owners of the goods of this world cease to be the owners of the Gospel, and in which the alienating reality of both old and potentially new identifications of the Gospel with human ideologies have been eliminated, and dedicated to the struggle for the implementation of justice for the exploited, there will hopefully arise an open-ended, prophetic, constantly relevant, biblical reflection able to contribute to the renovation of the Christian Church in whatever circumstances it finds itself.

Neither modern Catholicism, even in its more radical form, nor modern Protestantism will be able to achieve this until each one has reflected much more carefully on its conscious or unconscious hermeneutical practice. Hopefully, such an unscripted reflection would bring them together in different parts of the world to fulfil more obediently that mission which is demanded by both the kingdom and present reality.

Why should the struggle for social justice and external liberation be given pride of place in the hermeneutical circle? In fact,
some of the theologians of liberation, notably Gutierrez and
Segundo, include evangelisation as part of the Christian's contemporary call to obedience. However, they tend to restrict
evangelisation in a way that does not syntonise with the
declaration of Jesus Christ's finality, and therefore they limit
the scope of the contribution of obedient praxis to the hermeneutical circle.

Segundo, for example, misapplying the Adam/Christ typology, minimises the concrete need for both a personal act of
conversion and faith in the Gospel together with membership
in the Church.[6] He defines evangelisation in terms of making
a superficial Christian aware of the total liberating dimensions
of the Gospel as good news today. Gutierrez, likewise, emphasises the conscientisation aspect of evangelism: the *communication*
of joy which springs from an appreciation of God's gratuitous
gift, and of the good news of the love of God who has changed
our lives; the *announcing* of the mystery of sonship and fraternity;
the *becoming aware* that the situation of exploitation is contrary
to the Gospel and based on human-created injustices.[7] He does,
however, emphasise that evangelisation necessarily involves the
convoking of a community. However, both of them, because
of a refusal to recognise the personal call to radical discipleship
and conversion from self-righteousness as these are embodied
in Christ's Great Commission, lapse into an ingenuous universalism.[8] But universalism, paradoxically for the theology of
liberation, is non-dialectical (i.e. it leads to an evasion of conflict) for it does not take seriously either internally-structured
alienation or the divisive nature of Christ's messiahship (John
6.59–66; Mark 6.14–16). By trying to adopt a dual ecclesiology,
Segundo is really seeking to do the impossible. On the one hand
he calls the Church to be a minority community and, on the
other, he extends salvation to cover those who reject this
minority call.

The Church's contemporary understanding of the Gospel
and its praxis of evangelisation also need to be reconsidered.
If the theology of liberation has narrowed evangelisation by
repressing the individual dimension of repentence and conversion, by faith, to new life in Christ, other theologies in the

world-wide Church have narrowed it by neglecting both the social aspects of man's alienation, from which the individual has to turn in order to find foregiveness, and the call to a relevant liberating praxis. It is certainly doubtful whether an authentic gospel of the kingdom is being consciously proclaimed by more than a small minority of the Church in any part of the world. Hopefully, the debate surrounding the theology of liberation will lead to a new appreciation of the full measure of the gospel committed by Jesus to his Church.

Errors and deficiencies have led to one-sided commitments, out of which it is impossible to construct a faithful biblical hermeneutic. Only as the full dimensions of the radical meaning of the kingdom in today's reality become apparent will an authentic theology of liberation arise.

CHAPTER TWENTY

CONCLUSIONS

It is not an exaggeration to declare that the theology of liberation marks a watershed for the continuing theological task of
the Universal Church.

Firstly, it is probably the first non-imitative theology to have
sprung from the Third World nations; indeed, the first creative
theological thought to have arisen outside of Europe or North
America since the earliest years of the Church. For historical
and cultural reasons, Latin America, as the only 'christianised'
part of the Third World, has been able to produce the first systematic reflection from a Christian perspective on the common
situation of dependence and powerlessness which all Third
World nations experience. This theological movement is
already stimulating further reflection by Christians in analogous situations in other parts of the Third World, for there
is a growing sense of solidarity amongst the Churches of the
dependent nations.

Secondly, due to the origin and nature of the theology of
liberation, there may arise a certain cleavage between the Western tradition of theology and theology done from a liberating
praxis within the Third World. Part of the intention of this
study has been to try to avoid any unnecessary division which
may result from a lack of understanding of the theology of
liberation, by clarifying its fundamental context and aims. At
the same time it is necessary to exhort Christians in the West
to grant to theology done from a Third World perspective at
least as much universal claim as the idealistic theology of the
West. A certain amount of critical tension between two ways
of viewing theology could be a stimulus to creative reflection
on the function of theology in today's world, so long as hasty,
paternalistic or domesticating criticisms of Third World thinking is not allowed to prevail.

Thirdly, liberation theology raises wholly new questions for
theology in general and suggests a new methodology for biblical

hermeneutics in particular. 'The Theology of Liberation,' says Gutierrez, 'is a theology of salvation incarnated in the concrete historical and political conditions of today.' It is a theology, therefore, which deliberately starts from an identification with persons, with races and with social classes which suffer misery and exploitation, identifying itself with their concerns and struggles.

This starting point certainly appears to coincide with the bias of the Christian gospel itself ('good news to the poor . . . release to the captives . . . liberty to those who are oppressed', Luke 4.18). If this is true, then there can be no neutral or idealistic vantage point from which theological reflection may commence. There is no option; theology must be done from out of a commitment to a living God who defends the cause of 'the hungry' and who sends 'the rich empty away' (Luke 1.53).

We are still only at the beginning of the discussion concerning the overall implications which arise out of these new questions. For example, can, or should, the theology of liberation ever become intrinsically a universal theology, as the Western tradition of theology has aspired to be? What is the real relation between theoretical thought and practical action? Can this relation ever be defined theoretically, or must it be lived out in concrete practical experience? From out of this present debate with the theology of liberation certain conclusions can be drawn which may contribute to a clarification of the issues in order that the discussion may continue and be fruitful.

Clearly, Western theology is deemed to have failed the Third World Churches as a relevant theological methodology. This can be seen particularly in the stringent criticisms levelled against the 'political theology' movement in general, even though that movement has engaged most radically with political issues from the standpoint of the Western theological tradition. It is earnestly to be hoped that theological institutions in the Third World will in the future use Western theology more as a sounding-board and limited point of reference for their own creative thought, than as the main content of their academic curriculum.

In order for this to happen, the purpose and method of theological education in the Third World will still have to be drastically revised. Imitation of the Western academic ideal, with its over-emphasis on cognitive input in learning skill, threatens a really creative new approach to theology. The task of exploring, synthesising and continuing the first tentative beginnings of a new approach to the theological task in the Third World still needs to be undertaken.

The real novelty of the theology of liberation lies in its methodological approach. The content may change, indeed is changing, at least in part, for it is not a static, systematising reflection, but one which is willing to continue reflecting in the light of constructive criticism and new circumstances (*semper reformanda*). But its methodology, perhaps with the kind of modifications suggested in the final part of this study, is likely to remain. Now, a methodology may be universalised (indeed, this is what Western theology has already attempted), and therefore the question of its contextual relevance outside of the Third World can at least be raised.

In this context, Miguez asks a basic question about the character of theological methodology *vis-à-vis* the nature of the Bible. He suggests that the Western tradition of theology is basically conducted in a manner in which 'theology begets theology'. 'It is a process aimed at determining, explicating and possibly vindicating, the correct doctrine, on the basis of the study of the Scripture and Tradition, and sometimes with the use of philosophical categories. We go through this process in order to derive from it correct Christian action in all realms of the life of the Christian Community.' He then goes on to pose to Western theology the following issue:

If we see theology in this way, and if we follow this procedure, a fact that should make us pause is that in the Scriptures we find very few instances, if any, of such a process of theologising. We find in the Bible scarcely any kind of this theology which engenders theology. What we usually find there is the story of a particular situation of a people of God, and how the Word of God comes to comfort, to admonish, to command, to advise, to correct or to condemn God's people in such a situation. If I may put it in a simplistic way, the Bible is the collection of such visitations of God to his people in different conditions. Such a collection is the theological norm that we have, and we should pay attention to the character of this norm.'[1]

Although expressing it in different terms, Miguez reflects the distinction made by Gutierrez between theology as wisdom, as rational knowledge and as critical reflection on praxis. What is being questioned here is not the abandonment of one kind of theological reflection, but the order in which they are pursued. Running the risk of over-simplifying the issues, we would say that, for the Church in the midst of today's world, 'prophetic' theology must precede 'wisdom' theology.

Liberation theology's call for a new look at theological methodology has not yet provided a satisfactory hermeneutical procedure for interpreting Scripture. The stress on the priority of praxis, for example, has not offered us an indisputable technique for relating the Church's contemporary call to obedience to its use of the Scriptures. As Gutierrez rightly says, 'The Theology of Liberation ... demands the *deepening* of questions of biblical hermeneutic, conditioned by a *greater clarification* of its Old and New Testament foundations.'

Now, the use made of the Bible by the theology of liberation is naturally tentative and cautious. At times it is also, unfortunately, quite tendentious and its hermeneutical procedure, to say the least, is questionable. Nevertheless, it is certainly struggling with the right kind of questions and there are good reasons for suspecting that its methodology will become more refined. In particular, it needs to distinguish between and relate together more carefully the meaning of praxis for biblical interpretation, its own ideological concerns and the content of the biblical *kerygma* in order to escape from its present 'inspirational', programmatic, ephemeral and non-normative use of Scripture. To pay more careful attention to its biblical hermeneutic is not an invitation to abandon its concerns for liberation or for the liberation of theology, but to lay a more solid foundation for future reflection.

This study has attempted an inquiry into the premises and outworkings of the use of the Bible by the theology of liberation, with a subsequent discussion of the role of praxis (and the place of Marxism as a revolutionary theory related to praxis) in the hermeneutical circle of Bible, Church and the Third World reality of poverty and exploitation. As a complement to the whole discussion we have suggested a comprehensive, alternative approach to biblical interpretation; one which allows the distinctively biblical message of liberation through Jesus Christ free course within the necessities and challenges of the devastating human results of the evil of this present age: the Third World poor, the off-scourings of our modern, 'enlightened', civilisation. In this light, we gladly echo these words of Gutierrez.

[We need to be] conscious of the always critical and creative character of the liberating message of the gospel: a message that does not identify itself with any social form, no matter how just it may seem to us in a given moment, but which always speaks from the stance of the poor and which asks of us a very concrete solidarity in the present of our situation and our capacity to analyse it, even at the risk of being mistaken. The Word of the Lord interprets every situation and places it in the wider perspective of the radical liberation of Christ the Lord of History.[2]

NOTES

1. K. M. Schmitt et al., *The Roman Catholic Church in Modern Latin America*, p. 5. The fullest account of the conflict is still Lloyd B. Meecham, *Church and State in Latin America*; see also F. B. Pike et al., *The Conflict between Church and State in Latin America*.

2. See C. C. Griffin, 'The Enlightenment and Latin American Independence' in *Latin America and the Enlightenment*.

3. See G. Figuera, *La iglesia y su doctrina en la independencia de América*, pp. 26 7. He believes that the basic cause can be traced to the concept of popular sovereignty as developed by Vitoria, Soto and Suarez, an authentic, if minority, opinion within Spanish Catholicism.

4. The Bourbon administration was less rigid than the Hapsburg, allowing French liberal thought free flow to the colonies: A. Henriquez, *Historia de la cultura hispanoamericana*, pp. 59–67 and D. Herring, *A History of Latin America from the Beginnings to the Present*, pp. 243–8.

5. What priests there were came largely from the creole middle class. They represented, therefore, a small minority within the largely *mestizo* and Indian populations.

6. Pike, op. cit., pp. 5, 8.

7. E. Dussel, *Historia de la iglesia en América Latina*, p. 54.

8. The majority of the Brazilian clergy identified themselves with the cause of Independence from the beginning. This goes a long way to explaining the absence of anti-clericalism in Brazil during the first half of the nineteenth century.

9. A. Espinosa, 'Catholicism and the National Tradition', in Pike, op. cit., p. 104.

10. F. Navarette, 'Conflict in Mexico ...'. Defense of the Clergy', in Pike, op. cit., p. 132. The quote is from Mungría.

11. The principal factor in allowing freedom of religious assembly was economic, not ideological or religious. The opening of trade between Great Britain and the River Plate Republics brought with it the first small wave of non-Catholic immigration.

12. R. Pattel, *El catolicismo contemporaneo en Hispanoamérica*, pp. 11–12.

13. K. S. Latourette, *Christianity in a Revolutionary Age*, Vol. III, p. 293.

14. I. Vallier, *Catolicismo, control social y modernización en América Latina*, p. 136.

15. Quoted by W. R. Crawford in Pike, op. cit., p. 112.

16. E. Dussel, *Hipótesis para una historia de la iglesia en América Latina*, p. 136.

17. E. Portes, 'Conflict in Mexico ... 1854–1876: Defense of Civil Power', in Pike, op. cit., p. 127.

18. Not just that of A. Comte but, for example, that also of J. S. Mill and Spencer; see L. Zea, *The Latin American Mind*, pp. 223–32, 241–53.

19. Zea, op. cit., p. 50. For the history of the gradual separation of Church and State and the conquest of whole areas of civil life by legislation based on new ideas see Dussel, *Hipótesis* ..., pp. 126–37.

20. The struggle in Brazil dates from about 1870, a little later than in Spanish-speaking America.

21. Particularly in Colombia. Cf. the fairly typical reaction of Argentine bishops during the last months of the Peronist regime in 1955: 'Social reform requires a basic doctrinal foundation and Catholic moral teachings can ever supply such a foundation', quoted in Pike, op. cit., p. 192.

22. F. Houtart, 'The R. C. Church and Social Change in Latin America', in H. Landsberger, *The Church and Social Change in Latin America*, p. 119.

23. H. Landsberger, 'Time, Persons, Doctrine: the Modernisation of the Church in Chile', in Landsberger, op. cit., pp. 77–8. This author maintains that Catholic social action in Chile kept ahead of subsequent Encyclicals; see pp. 85–93.

24. H. Gnatt, *The Significance of Changes in Latin American Catholicism since Chimbote*, chaps. 2, 3, 7. See also W. J. Coleman, *Latin American Catholicism: A Self-Examination*, pp. iv–v.

25. F. Houtart, *La iglesia latinoamericana en la hora del concilio*, pp. 53–62.

26. See the extensive critique by J. L. Segundo, *Función de la iglesia en la realidad rioplatense*. This is one of the first pamphlets ever written specifically to introduce more radical ideas into the ferment of Catholicism. Cf. Vallier, op. cit., pp. 96–7, 196.

27. The Second General Conference of the Latin American Episcopate. It followed immediately after Pope Paul VI's visit to Latin America, and it addressed itself to basic and concrete issues in the underdeveloped world.

28. F. Houtart and E. Pin, *The Church and the Latin American Revolution*, p. 256.

29. The standard work on this subject is E. J. Williams, *Latin American Christian Democrat Parties*. See also W. V. D. Antonio and F. B. Pike, *Religion, Revolution and Reform in Latin America*, pp. 10ff., 14ff., and J. Castillo, *L'Expérience démocrate chrétienne au Chili*, pp. 55–68. Since these works were published dramatic changes in Chile have profoundly challenged the CDP development. For the moment Frei's 'Revolution in Liberty' is dead.

30. E.g. 'Catholic Social Justice, Democracy and Pluralism' in Pike, op. cit., pp. 209–17.

31. Essay in Landsberger, op, cit., p. 140.

32. Active participation in the parties does not depend on commitment to Catholicism. The Church, as such, has no official relationship to the parties.

33. M. McGrath, 'The Church and Social Revolution' in J. J. Considine, *Social Revolution and the New Latin America*, pp. 153–4.

34. Preface to C. Antoine, *Church and Power in Brazil*. Antoine notes the failure of the Church to live up to its own radical programme in the change that took place between 1963 and 1969. In the former year the Central Committee of the National Conference of Bishops took up a radical position on the urgency of basic reforms. In the latter year, the same Committee no longer

spoke of the liberation of the masses but condemned revolt and repression alike; p. 266ff. At the beginning of 1977 the Episcopal Conference meeting at Itaici produced a carefully worded but uncompromising rejection of the reactionary ideology of 'National Security' used by the military to justify its continuing exercise of an arbitary and uncontrolled authority. Cf. *Exigências cristãs de una orden politica.*

35. F. C. Turner, *Catholicism and Political Development in Latin America,* p. 3.

36. Cf. the opinions of H. de Lima Vaz cited in Turner, op. cit., pp. 21–2. J. Miguez Bonino states that the basic difference lies in the political-social assessment of Latin America reality. The CDP arose as an attempt to present an alternative to Marxist socialism. It is linked ideologically to utopian socialism. The NCL accepts the Marxist 'scientific' analysis whilst rejecting its determinism (Letter to author, May 1974).

37. This is done quite vehemently in the final document of the First Latin American Encounter of Christians for Socialism, *Los Cristianos y el Socialismo,* (Buenos Aires, 1973), pp. 255–74

38. The awareness brought by these studies in the field of economics was extended to the whole cultural field. The NCL became convinced that the fundamental reality of Latin America is that its people are 'dependent peoples responding to initiatives and forces from outside'. R. Shaull in Landsberger, op. cit., p. 135.

39. F. Houtart in Landsberger, op. cit., pp. 128–32. The comments in parentheses are mine. L. Gera y G. Melgarejo, 'Apuntes para una interpretación de la Iglesia Argentina', pp. 61–3, outline three different groups: (i) traditionalist, with a strong tendency towards a religious-political monism and against any kind of modernisation; (ii) progressive, insisting on the autonomy of the temporal, modernisation of ecclesiastical structures and on evolution in the socio-economic sphere; (iii) revolutionary, with a strong concern to apply the faith, starting from the situation of the oppressed masses.

CHAPTER TWO (pp. 23–8)

1. G. Gutierrez, *Teologia de la Liberación: perspectivas.* Quotations are from the English translation, *A Theology of Liberation,* pp. ix, 13.

2. This is why some writers speak of the liberation of theology: cf. Gutierrez, op. cit., p. 15; J. Miguez, 'Theology and Liberation'; H. Bojorge, 'Para una interpretación liberadora'; and especially J. L. Segundo, *La liberación de la teología,* which has now appeared in English as *The Liberation of Theology.*

3. Cf. *Populorum Progressio* (Cath. Inst. for Int. Relations, London, 1967), paras. 8, 9, 21, 33, 57.

4. H. Camera et al., '15 obispos hablan en pro del Tercer Mundo' in S. Galila, *Documentos sobre la pastoral,* pp. 284ff.

5. His most influential books are *Pedagogy of the Oppressed* and *Cultural Action for Freedom,* both published in 1972. More recent books include *Concientizacion: teoriá y practica de la liberación* (1974) and *Education, Liberation and the Church* (1973).

6. For an adequate bibliography see Gutierrez, op. cit., Part III, ch. vi, notes 6–31.

7. For an example of this distinction see E. Schillerbeeckx, *God and the Future of Man* (London, 1969), pp. 198–9.

8. It should be noted that the theology of liberation arose, not so much as theoretical debate on revolution, as a felt need to reflect from the Christian faith on ways of bringing it about.

9. *Documentos finales de Medellín* (Buenos Aires, 1972⁶), pp. 25–8, 73–7.

10. E. Dussel, *Caminos de liberacion latinoamericana*, I, 110–11.

CHAPTER THREE (pp. 29–34)

1. Segundo, 'The Possible Contribution of Protestant Theology to Latin American Christianity in the Future', p. 61 ; and *Iglesia latinoamericana: protesta o profecía*, p. 16.

2. Segundo, *Acción pastoral latinoamericana: sus motivos ocultos*, pp. 19–26. Also H. Assmann, *Teologia desde la praxis de la liberación*, pp. 132–3, ET *Practical Theology of Liberation* (the English translation does not contain the full text of the Spanish original) ; and B. A. Dumas, *Los dos rostros alienados de la iglesia una; ensayo de teología polítca*, pp. 236–40. The consumer society is a typical expression of the deep alienation produced by the capitalist system which, in words borrowed from Friere, covers up a 'loss of being' with an abundance of things (literally 'being less' and 'having more'). Cf. Croatto, 'La función del poder: salvífica u opresora?' p. 43.

3. Dumas, *Los dos rostros* ..., p. 190; Gutierrez, *Theology of Liberation*, p. 268.

4. H. Assmann, *Teologia desde la praxis* ... p. 132 and especially ch. 4.

5. Cf. Gutierrez, op. cit., pp. 272–7.

6. Althusser, quoted in Gutierrez, op. cit., p. 277.

7. H. Camera, *The Spiral of Violence*, pp. 30–4.

8. Ibid., p. 30.

9. J. Miguez, 'El nuevo catolicismo' in R. Padilla et. al., *Fe cristiana y Latinoamerica hoy*, pp. 109, 113; and *Revolutionary Theology Comes of Age*, ch. 7.

10. H. Assmann, *Opresión–liberación: desafió a los cristianos*, p. 151. Cf. Gutierrez, op. cit., pp. 153ff.

11. Gutierrez, op. cit., p. 167.

12. Ibid., pp. 54–6.

13. Ibid., p. 232.

14. Ibid., p. 237; also J. P. Miranda, *Marx and the Bible*, pp. 213, 219; Miranda, *Being and the Messiah*, pp. 56–7.

15. S. Galilea, 'La teología de la liberación como critica de la actividad de la iglesia en America Latina' in Comblin et al., *Fe y secularización*..., pp. 58–61.

16. J. L. Segundo, *Acción pastoral*..., pp. 29–34.

17. Ibid., pp. 102–11. Cf. Gutierrez, op. cit., pp. 269–71.

CHAPTER FOUR (pp. 35–41)

1. B. A. Dumas, *Los dos rostros*, p. 188.

2. H. Assmann, *Practical Theology*, pp. 30–1, 112.

3. E. Dussel, *Para una ética de la liberación latinoamericana*, I, pp. 97–156; II,

pp. 52–9. Also 'El momento negativo: el ateísmo de los profestas y de Marx: afirmación ética de la alteridad', in E. Karlic et al., *Fe y política*, pp. 68–88.

4. J. P. Miranda, *Being and the Messiah*. See ch. 12 below.

5. H. Assmann, *Opresión–liberación*, p. 141.

6. J. L. Segundo, 'Instrumentos de la teología lantinoamericana' in C. Moncada et. al., *Liberación en América Latina*, p. 41; Gutierrez, op. cit., p. 143.

7. J. L. Segundo, *Masas y minorías en la dialéctica divina de la liberación*, p. 78; J. P. Miranda, *Being*, ch. 1. Croatto, *Liberación ... pautas*, p. 146.

8. Segundo, *Masas y minorías*, p. 92.

9. P. Negré, 'Biblia y liberación', p. 70.

10. Segundo, *Masas y minorías*, p. 94.

11. Ibid., p. 94. For further discussion see below, ch. 6.

12. Miranda, *Being ...*, p. 80. Cf. J. C. Scannone, 'Teología y política' in *Fe cristiana y cambio social*, p. 257.

13. Scannone, op. cit., p. 251.

14. C. Moncada et al., *Liberación en America Latina*, p. 10. Cf. Scannone, op. cit., p. 251.

15. Assmann, *Reflexión teológica*, p. 76; *Practical Theology*, pp. 30–1; Miranda, *Being ...*, p. 79.

16. Gutierrez, op. cit., p. 97, n. 40.

CHAPTER FIVE (pp. 45–54)

1. J. Miguez, 'El nuevo catolicismo', pp. 98–113, produces an interesting typology of the different schools within the movement. The discussion by J. C. Scannone, 'Situación de la problemática', pp. 27–46, of the similarities and differences between the statements of the Peruvian Episcopate and of the Christians for Socialism is an excellent analysis of different theological perspectives, reflecting respectively the influence of Gutierrez and Assmann. The long and critical article by the general secretary of CELAM, Alfonso Lopez Trujillo, 'Las teologías de la liberación in America Latina' in *Liberación: dialogos en le CELAM*, also presents a useful typology, although he tends to caricature positions at certain points.

2. Subsequent changes in the political climate of Latin America have led to a shift in emphasis from the Exodus to the Captivity motif. Cf. L. Boff, *Teología desde el cautiverio* and E. Dussel et al., *Liberación y cautiverio* (Mexico, 1975).

3. He has, for example, co-edited a new selection in Spanish of the writings of Marx and Engels on Religion (Salamanca, 1974) to which he has contributed an introductory philosophical essay.

4. Assmann, *Opresión–liberación*, p. 24.

5. Ibid., p. 19.

6. Ibid., pp. 19, 174ff.

7. Assmann, *Practical Theology*, pp. 38–9.

8. Ibid., p. 112 (my italics).

9. Quoted by Segundo, *Masas y minorías*, p. 84, from Assmann, *Prólogo: habla Fidel Castro ...*

10. Assmann, *Practical Theology*, p. 85. 'There is a final culminating point

that love can reach in the process of liberation, the capacity for whole-heartedly laying down one's life for one's brothers which strikes at the centre of all human questions related to liberation and which finds both its symbol and its reality in the cross of Christ.'

11. Assmann, *Opresión–liberación*, pp. 164–5; *Practical Theology*, p. 69. In other words it is the Christian's eschatological commitment which keeps the dialectical process truly dialectical, and never finally synthesised.

12. Assmann, *Opresión–liberación*, p. 165. Among these criteria he mentions the 'dangerous memory of the subversive elements of the Bible', to which Metz refers; the kingdom of God as a utopic category which is simultaneously the presence and absence of liberation, and the concept of the 'new man' as a gift from outside given by the Lord; cf. *Practical Theology*, p. 31.

13. Assmann, *Practical Theology*, p. 60.

14. E.g., the studies of Cullman and Hengel on the 'revolutionary' Christ, to correct purely ideological Christologies which have arisen in Latin America as the result of a superficial reflection on the deaths of Camilo Torres and Che Guevara: *Practical Theology*, p. 104. In a later study, 'La actuación histórica del poder de Cristo' in J. Miguez Bonino et al. *Jesus ni vencido ni monarca celestial* (Buenos Aires, 1977), Assmann calls for a more intensive biblical reflection by biblical exegetes aware of the past ideological conditioning of all biblical studies.

15. *Opresión–liberación*, pp. 125–6.

16. Assmann, *Practical Theology*, p. 104. In a private conversation with the author he qualified this by saying that 'the hermeneutical key is not to be found so much in a revolutionary theory as in a capacity to love. If it were not for this I should be quite capable of manipulating others by means of any theory – Marxism, Functionalism, etc.'

17. Ibid., p. 64. Again in private conversation he qualified this by making a distinction between the 'semantic' and the 'semiological' meanings of the text; i.e. the message discoverable only by the use of the right hermeneutical key is not contained in what the text says (*sensus literalis*) but in what it represents (*sensus figurativus*).

18. Assmann, *Opresión–liberación*, pp. 103–5.

CHAPTER SIX (pp. 55–72)

1. Gutierrez, 'Praxis de liberación, teología y evangelización', in *Liberacion: diálogos en el CELAM*, p. 81.

2. Ibid., p. 87.

3. Gutierrez, *A Theology of Liberation*, p. 15.

4. Gutierrez, *Praxis de liberación*, p. 88.

5. Ibid., p. 71.

6. Ibid., pp. 72–3.

7. Ibid., pp. 78–9.

8. Ibid., p. 73 (my italics).

9. Ibid., p. 69. 'Subversive' is used in the etymological sense of 'from below'.

10. Ibid., pp. 79–80, and *A Theology of Liberation*, pp. 11–13.

11. Gutierrez, *A Theology of Liberation*, p. 307.

12. Ibid., p. 29.

13. Ibid., p. 175.

14. Ibid., pp. 176–7. The overwhelming emphasis on socio-political liberation is constant throughout the book, which was first published in 1971. Since
then certain events have occurred which caused Gutierrez (and Assmann) to
re-evaluate a certain 'triumphalism' in their handling of the entire subject
of liberation. Gutierrez still maintains the three levels of liberation but is inclined to emphasise the second. It is the level, he believes, which effectively
avoids a false dualism (spiritual or political liberation) or a false juxtaposition
(allowing any of the three levels an autonomy of its own). The unity is
achieved in the concept of the 'new man' who is brought into being both
by 'God's free gift of liberation from sin' and by historical efficaciousness.
(From notes taken during a personal conversation with the author.)

15. Ibid., pp. 28, 29, 46, 68 and 91

16. *Liberación: diálogos en el CELAM*, pp. 257–8.

17. Gutierrez, *A Theology of Liberation*, p. 173

18. Ibid., p. 113.

19. Ibid., p. 211, n. 36. This quotation is one of the conclusions of an extensive exegesis of Matthew 25.31–46.

20. Ibid., pp. 45–6.

21. Ibid., pp. 4–11.

22. Ibid., pp. 155–60.

23. Ibid., pp. 196–203.

24. Ibid., p. 226.

25. Ibid., p. 231.

26. Ibid., pp. 229–30.

27. Ibid., pp. 220–25.

28. Miguez, *El nuevo catolicismo*, p. 101.

29. Segundo, *Evolución y culpa*, ET *Evolution and Guilt*, p. 131.

30. Segundo, *Acción pastoral*, pp. 29–49.

31. Ibid., p. 20

32. Ibid., p. 67.

33. Ibid., pp. 22, 26.

34. Ibid., p. 100.

35. Miguez, *El nuevo catolicismo*, p. 99, says of him that he is 'perhaps the
most ecumenical of the new Latin American Catholic theologians because
of his deep roots in European theology, his interest in tradition and the ampli-
tude of his theological subject matter.'

36. Ibid., p. 100: 'Without any doubt Segundo's philosophy of history is
profoundly indebted to the thought of Teilhard de Chardin'.

37. In the final chapter of his book, *De la sociedad a la teología*, he defends
the propriety of translating the message of Christ into the modern language
of evolution. See pp. 155–73.

38. This had already begun in Europe in various writings: e.g. B. Towers
et al., *Evolution, Marxism and Christianity* (London, 1968) and in an African
perspective, L. Senghor, *On African Socialism* (London, 1968). The celebrated
Christian–Marxist dialogue was initiated in Paris by Catholic theologians in
the Teilhardian tradition; H. Cox, 'New Phase in the Marxist-Christian
Encounter' (*Christianity and Crisis* XXV, 1965, 18).

39. Segundo, *Evolution and Guilt*, pp. 13–14.

40. Ibid., p. 127.

41. Ibid., pp. 126–9.

42. Segundo, *Grace and the Human Condition*, pp. 182–3; *De la sociedad a la teología*, p. 90. He believes that the concept of salvation for another life is basically a pre-New Testament concept, which arose in the inter-testamental Wisdom literature, *De la sociedad*, pp. 84–6. Also he believes that this concept was abandoned by Christians in New Testament times for an integral this-worldly projection.

43. Segundo, *Evolution and Guilt*, pp. 104–10.

44. Segundo, *Our Idea of God*, p. 39.

45. Segundo, *Masas y minorías*, pp. 93–4.

46. Ibid., p. 108.

47. Segundo's fullest discussion of hermeneutics, *The Liberation of Theology*, was published after I completed the research for this book. I have discussed its arguments in my forthcoming *Theology Encounters Revolution*.

48. Segundo, *Our Idea of God*, p. 175.

49. Ibid., p. 37.

50. Segundo, *Evolution and Guilt*, pp. 120–1.

51. For this whole argument see *Masas y minorías*, pp. 78, 104–7. He develops his understanding of the hermeneutical circle still further in *The Liberation of Theology*; ch. 1.

CHAPTER SEVEN (pp. 73–92)

1. S. Croatto, 'El Dios en el acontecimiento', p. 53.

2. Ibid., p. 57.

3. Croatto, 'Liberación y libertad: reflexiones', p. 33.

4. Croatto, 'El Dios', p. 56.

5. P. Ricoeur, *Finitude et Culpabilité: la Symbolique du Mal*, pp. 153–6. Cf. also M. Eliade, *Aspects du mythe* and A. Asti Vera, 'Mito y semántica' in *Mito y hermeneútica*, pp. 57–81.

6. Croatto, 'El hombre en el mundo según Génesis', p. 50.

7. Croatto, 'El Dios', p. 55.

8. Croatto, 'Liberación ... reflexiones', p. 3.

9. Ibid., p. 3.

10. Croatto, 'El lenguaje: reinterpretación y reexpresión del evangelio', p. 360. He borrows the scheme from Lapointe, *Les trois dimensions de l'hermeneutique*, substituting Latin American reality in the third register.

11. Croatto, *Liberación ... pautas*, pp. 78–9.

12. Ibid., p. 142.

13. Croatto, 'El Dios', p. 59.

14. Ibid., p. 56.

15. By 'horizon' is understood a particular perspective or point of view. The word has been used in a specialised sense by H. G. Gadamer, *Warheit und Methode*.

16. Croatto, *Liberación ... pautas*, p. 20.

17. Miranda, *Marx and the Bible*, p. 265.

18. Ibid., p. 254.
19. Ibid., p. xvii.
20. Ibid., p. 250. Cf. *Being and the Messiah*, pp. 1–14, 20–1.
21. Ibid., p. 202. Cf. *Being*, pp. 36–9.
22. Ibid., p. 137. Cf. *Being*, p. 56.
23. Ibid., p. 21.
24. Ibid., p. 19.
25. Ibid., p. 30.
26. Ibid., pp. 44, 48. The key passages which Miranda adduces are Jer. 22.13–16; Hos. 4.1–2; 6.4–6.
27. Ibid., p. 59.
28. Ibid., p. 60. Cf. *Being*, pp. 20–1, 32–6, 127ff.
29. Ibid., p. 114.
30. Ibid., p. 123.
31. Ibid., p. 250.
32. Ibid., pp. 162–3.
33. Ibid., p. 163.
34. Ibid., pp. 176–218. It is important to note that Miranda understands the NT as if it were still repeating the OT, the only difference being that in Jesus Christ eschatological justice has arrived. He states, for example, that 'what is new is not contained in the content of the message but in the eschatological event.' In this he appears to adopt a different hermeneutical approach from that of Croatto who understands that the event incites a re-interpretation of the OT. Nevertheless, their contrasting hermeneutics bring them, by different paths, to substantially the same conclusion – as we shall see.
35. The corporate nature of *adikia* is based on the curious argument that if we were to interpret it in individual terms then Rom. 2.13–15 would contradict 3.19–20. Miranda concludes that 'the entire letter deals with the problem of society ... the collective slavery which has gained control of human history ... individuals can very well be just and fulfil ... the true will of God' (p. 178).
36. See ibid., pp. 186–8, for Miranda's discussion of the Pauline definition of *kosmos*.
37. For Miranda, faith is faith/hope that the world will be transformed by God's intervention through the Messiah and faith/action, synonymous with the changing of this world into a world of righteousness and love (ibid., pp. 225, 229–30).
38. Ibid., pp. 189–92.
39. Ibid., p. 227.
40. Ibid., p. 255.
41. Miranda, *Being*, pp. 137, 140.
42. Ibid., p. 174.
43. Cf. ibid., pp. 64, 73–5, 123–4.
44. Ibid., p. 189.
45. Ibid., p. 193–6.
46. Ibid., p. 73.
47. Miranda, *Marx*, pp. 57–9.
48. Ibid., p. 60.

49. Ibid., p. 19.
50. Miranda, *Being*, pp. 113, 177, 182.
51. Miranda, *Marx*, pp. 53, 43, 105, 123.

CHAPTER EIGHT (pp. 95–104)

1. Croatto, *Liberación* ... *pautas*, p. 38; S. Ruiz, 'Teología bíblica de la liberación', pp. 341–2.
2. Assmann, *Opresión–liberación*, p. 120; *Practical Theology*, p. 66; Croatto, *Liberación* ... *pautas*, pp. 33–4.
3. Gutierrez, *A Theology of Liberation*, p. 155; Dussel, *Caminos*, p. 146.
4. E.g. C. Mesters, *La palabra de Dios*, p. 10; B. Villegas, 'La liberación en la Biblia', p. 157.
5. Mesters, op. cit., pp. 9, 11; Villegas, op. cit., p. 159.
6. Miranda, *Being*, p. 31; Assmann, *Opresión–liberación*, p. 21.
7. Miranda, ibid., pp. 34–5.
8. The majority of interpretations understand Exod. 3.14 in a future sense – 'I will be what I will be' – Miranda, *Being*, pp. 42–3; Gutierrez, *A Theology of Liberation*, p. 165.
9. Croatto, 'Liberación ... reflexiones', p. 5.
10. H. Bojorge, 'Exodo y liberación', p. 35.
11. Dussel, *Caminos*, p. 146.
12. Croatto, op. cit., p. 4.
13. Segundo, *Grace*, p. 120; P. Negré, 'Biblia y liberación', p. 76.
14. Segundo, ibid., p. 120; Negré, ibid., p. 74.
15. Gutierrez, *A Theology of Liberation*, pp. 158–9.
16. Croatto, *Liberación* ... *pautas*, pp. 28–30, 55–9.
17. Assmann, *Practical Theology*, p. 66.
18. Bojorge, 'Exodo y liberación', p. 33.
19. Croatto, 'Liberacion ... reflexiones', pp. 4–5.
20. F. Rivera, 'La liberación en el éxodo', p. 18.
21. Croatto, 'El hombre nuevo', p. 45.
22. Croatto, *Liberación* ... *pautas*, p. 29.
23. Ibid., p. 32.
24. Ibid., p. 34.
25. Gutierrez, *A Theology of Liberation*, pp. 158–9, 182 n. 41.
26. S. Ruiz, 'Teología bíblica', p. 341.
27. Cf. the criticisms of Bojorge in this regard, 'Exodo y liberación', pp. 36–7 and 'Para una interpretación liberadora', pp. 70–1.

CHAPTER NINE (pp. 105–11)

1. Ruiz, op. cit., p. 342.
2. J. Mejia in CELAM, *Liberación: diálogos*, p. 371.
3. Ibid., p. 373.
4. Croatto, 'Liberación ... reflexiónes, p. 6; Miranda, *Being*, p. 37.
5. Gutierrez, op. cit., p. 155.
6. A. Morelli, *Libera a mi pueblo*, p. 43.
7. Ibid., p. 191.

8. Assmann, *Practical Theology*, pp. 67–8.
9. Gutierrez, op. cit., p. 158.
10. Croatto, *Liberación ... pautas*, pp. 38–9.
11. Croatto, 'Hombre nuevo', p. 44.
12. J. Casabó, 'La liberación en S. Juan', p. 238.
13. Segundo, *De la sociedad a la teología*, p. 90. Croatto develops the unitary process of salvation from first creation to final re-creation through Christ in greater detail in *Liberación ... pautas*, pp. 135–46.
14. Segundo, *Masas y minorías*, pp. 7–8. Gutierrez calls the concern for individual acts of conversion a preoccupation with quantity, whereas the real object of Christ's salvation is to be a gradual quality; op. cit., pp. 150–2.
15. Gutierrez, op. cit., pp. 151, 179 n. 8, quoting a preparatory document for the Medellín Conference.
16. Ibid., p. 152.
17. Miranda, *Being*, pp. 31, 32–3.
18. Croatto, 'Liberación ... reflexiónes', p. 6.
19. Ibid., p. 6; 'El hombre bíblico', p. 22.
20. Croatto, 'El lenguaje', p. 362.
21. Croatto, 'El hombre en el mundo', p. 45.
22. Ibid., pp. 46–9.
23. Gutierrez, quoted in Assmann, *Practical Theology*, p. 68.
24. Gutierrez, *A Theology of Liberation*, p. 72.
25. Ibid., p. 49.
26. Miranda, *Being*, p. 98.

CHAPTER TEN (pp. 112–22)

1. Croatto, *Liberación ... pautas*. For this whole section see pp. 63–70.
2. Croatto, 'El hombre nuevo', p. 42.
3. Croatto, 'El hombre in el mundo', p. 51.
4. Miranda, *Marx*, p. 89.
5. Croatto, *Liberación ... pautas*, p. 66.
6. Ibid., pp. 14–15.
7. Miranda, *Marx*, p. 226.
8. Miranda, *Being*, p. 14.
9. Ibid., pp. 18–20.
10. Croatto, *Liberación ... pautas*, p. 119.
11. Miranda, *Being*, p. 34.
12. Croatto, *Liberación ... pautas*, pp. 119–20.
13. Gutierrez, *Liberación, diálogos*, p. 379; cf. *A Theology of Liberation*, pp. 175–7.
14. Gutierrez, *A Theology of Liberation*, p. 198.
15. Miranda, *Marx*, p. 170.
16. Miranda, *Being*, p. 45.
17. Miranda, *Marx*, p. 281.
18. Miranda is following here the study of N. M. Sarna, *Understanding Genesis*, p. 145.
19. Miranda, *Marx*, pp. 89–90.
20. Ibid., pp. 88–94.

21. Segundo, *Masas*, pp. 40–5 and Casabó, 'La liberación en S. Juan', pp. 236, 239.

22. Croatto, *Liberación . . . pautas*, pp. 132–3.

23. Ibid., p. 134.

24. Miranda, *Marx*, p. 187.

25. Ibid., p. 187.

26. Ibid., p. 192.

CHAPTER ELEVEN (pp. 123–35)

1. Gutierrez, *A Theology of Liberation*, pp. 190–4.

2. Assmann, *Practical Theology*, p. 103. One full-length Christology written from within Latin America is L. Boff, *Jesus Cristo, Libertador*. In this the Brazilian theologian does not deal with liberation theology. However, in a later book, *Teología desde el cautiverio*, he expounds and defends the theology of liberation, reassessing its role in the changed situation of humanity now experiencing the pain of 'exile' within its own societies. The first full-length systematic 'Christology' to appear is J. Sobrino's *Christology at the Crossroads: a Latin American Approach*. This attempts an inductive Christology 'from below', relying heavily on the Synoptic Gospels.

3. Assmann, op. cit., pp. 77–80, poses the question but does not attempt an exegetical answer.

4. Segundo, *Masas*, pp. 32–7; 103–6.

5. Assmann, op. cit., p. 103, asks the same kind of question.

6. Croatto, *Liberación . . . pautas*, p. 93. See further J. Miguez et al., *Jesus: ni vencido ni monarca celestial*, pp. 129–201.

7. See also C. Mesters, *La palabra de Dios*, pp. 184–213.

8. Gutierrez, op. cit., pp. 227–8. 'Rather than simply advocating the complete abolition of the Zealot spirit, he proposes an alternative to Zealotism. Historically speaking, Jesus acted out of love and was for all human beings. But he was for them in different ways. Out of love for the poor, he took his stand *with* them; out of love for the rich, he took his stand *against* them. In both cases, however, he was interested in something more than retributive justice. He wanted renewal and re-creation.' Sobrino, *Christology*, p. 370.

9. Croatto, op. cit., p. 96.

10. Gutierrez, op. cit., 228.

11. Croatto, op. cit., pp. 96–7.

12. G. Crespy, 'Recherche sur la signification politique de la mort du Christ' (*Lumiere et Vie*, 101, 1971), pp. 89–109.

13. Gutierrez, op. cit., p. 229.

14. Ibid., p. 247, n. 94.

15. Mesters, op. cit., pp. 184–213.

16. Croatto, op. cit., pp. 113–15.

17. Gutierrez, op. cit., pp. 291–9.

18. Ibid., pp. 298–9.

19. Ibid., pp. 196–203.

20. J. C. Ingelaere, 'La parabole du jugement dernier' (Matt. 25.31–45)', (RHPR, i, 1970), pp. 23–60.

21. Gutierrez, op. cit., p. 199. Miranda finds a close parallel between this passage and the passage Rom. 2.5–12. He believes that both relate, point by point, to the OT idea of judgment as *mišpāṭ eleos* as this is taken up in the teaching of Jesus – Matt. 9.13; 12.7. See his *Marx*, pp. 117–18.

22. Segundo, *Grace*, p. 207.

23. B. A. Dumas, *Los dos rostros*, pp. 82ff.

CHAPTER TWELVE (pp. 136–40)

1. Miranda, *Being*, pp. 191–2.

2. Miranda, *Marx*, pp. 247.

3. Miranda, *Being*, pp. 198–200.

4. Ibid., p. 181.

5. Ibid., p. 220.

6. Ibid., p. 204, 214–19.

7. Ferdinand Prat, *Jésus-Christ* II (Paris, 1933).

8. Lagrange, *Évangile selon saint Marc* (Paris, 1929⁴).

9. Miranda, *Being*, p. 217.

10. Ibid., pp. 219–20.

11. Ibid., p. 60. This is based on the evidence of the sign of Jonah – Luke 11.29–30; Matt. 12.38–42; 16.1–4.

12. Ibid., pp. 219–20; 203–8.

13. Miranda, *Marx*, p. 246.

CHAPTER FOURTEEN (pp. 147–52)

1. So H. Bojorge, 'Goel: Dios libera a los suyos', pp. 9–10; 'Para una interpretación liberadora', p. 70; R. Sartor, 'Exodo-liberación: tema de actualidad , .', p. 75. It is true that L. Boff, *Teología desde el cautiverio*, has initiated a discussion of this important biblical theme, but as yet little systematic consideration has been given to it.

2. See D. Daube, *The Exodus Pattern in the Bible*; and W. Zimmerli, *Man and his Hope in the Old Testament*, pp. 52–5.

3. B. S. Childs, *Exodus, a Commentary*, pp. 401–2.

4. Daube, op. cit., p. 11. He writes: 'I soon discovered there was none [patterns of deliverance in the Bible] remotely comparable to the Exodus.' See also J. Muilenberg, *The Way of Israel* (London, 1962), pp. 48–54.

5. Gutierrez, *A Theology of Liberation*, p. 158. Here I have preferred my own translation.

6. Childs, op. cit., p. 233.

7. T. F. Glasson, *Moses in the Fourth Gospel*, pp. 9, 15.

8. The term 'myth' is used in the sense given to it by A. Asti Vera, 'Mito y semántica', in SAPSE *Mito y hermenéutica*, pp. 59–81; and Croatto, 'El mito-símbolo y el mito-relato', ibid., pp. 85–7. It is the symbolic or figurative representation of an archetypal truth about man in history.

9. J. H. Yoder, 'Exodus and Exile', pp. 29–41.

10. The section Exod. 3.1–12 which first mentions the relationship of the patriarchs to Israel, reflects a genuine tradition of a call to Moses as the precursor of the prophets (cf. Childs, op. cit., pp. 55–6): the Lord identifies

himself as the God 'who had always been worshipped by Israel's ancestors' (so R. E. Clements, *Exodus*, p. 21). Modern views of the origin of the name 'Yahweh' place it in the patriarchal period – e.g. J. P. Hyatt, *Exodus*, pp. 78–81. Cf. also G. Fohrer, *Introduction to the Old Testament*, pp. 124–5.

11. Yoder, op. cit., pp. 33, writes: 'Even before there could be a Moses and a people to hear him, there had to be an oppressed community affirming its identity by talking about the fathers and the God of the fathers.... The identity of the people, and even in a serious sense the identity of the liberating God himself were dependent upon the confessing community ... Peoplehood is the presupposition, not the product of Exodus.'

12. See Croatto, *Liberación ... pautas*, p. 44; Morelli, *Libera a mi pueblo*, pp. 54–6; Mesters, *La palabra de Dios*, pp. 9–12.

13. E.g. Gutierrez, op. cit., pp. 113–14.

14. Even as sceptical a scholar as M. Noth, *Exodus: A Commentary*, p. 41, emphasises that 'in both cases [those of E and J] the sole initiative in the events which now begin clearly remains with Yahweh himself.'

15. So W. Pannenberg, 'The God of Hope' in *Basic Questions in Theology* Vol. II, pp. 242–9.

16. Miranda, *Being*, pp. 42–5.

17. E. Schild, 'On Exodus iii.4', pp. 296–302; and Childs, op. cit., p. 69.

18. Segundo, *Función de la iglesia*, pp. 14–15; *De la sociedad*, pp. 65–76; *Acción pastoral*, pp. 34–5, 49.

CHAPTER FIFTEEN (pp. 153–59)

1. P. Grillmeier, 'The Divine Inspiration and Interpretation of Sacred Scripture', p. 238 (my italics).

2. Miranda, *Marx*, p. 213, quoting Friedrich, TWNT, II, p. 726 (my italics).

3. Miranda, *Being*, p. 174.

4. Ibid., p. 180.

5. Ibid., pp. 57–8. Cf. also p. 174: 'John did not write a history of salvation, neither in his Epistle nor in his Gospel; he affirms that history has arrived at its end and the end is already here.' Miranda sees his position as a direct contradiction to 'established theology'.

6. Croatto, 'El hombre nuevo', pp. 44–5; *Liberación ... pautas*, pp. 99–105.

7. Croatto, 'El Dios en el acontecimiento', p. 58.

8. The following have touched on the issues: J. Lindblom, *The Bible: a Modern Understanding*, pp. 91–6. H. Schlier, 'What is meant by the interpretation of Scripture?' in *The Relevance of the New Testament*; X. Leon-Dufour, *Resurrection and the Message of Easter*, pp. 195–201; and James Barr, *The Bible in the Modern World*.

9. Miranda, *Being*, pp. 73, 78–80, 182, 184, 198. The fundamental concern of the text is to present truth as moral imperative: ibid., pp. 78, 87–8, 188–9.

10. Of the four final considerations announced by V. P. Furnish, *The Love Command in the New Testament*, pp. 198–218, the first two fit Miranda's exegesis (the *command* to love and love as the sovereign command of a sovereign Lord); the last two, however (the calling into being of a *community* of love and love as simultaneously a call to repentance and a proffer of forgiveness) imply

in my opinion, a reinterpretation of the way in which the command should be implemeneted.

11. Miranda, *Being*, pp. 148–53.

12. According to Segundo, *Masas*, pp. 33–5, Jesus' ethic of gratuitousness (*charis*) is precisely what is new, added and original 'with regard to everything that has been said'. Not a few commentators in John's Gospel understand *charis* in terms of contrast rather than identity: e.g. B. Lindars, *The Gospel of John* (London, 1972), pp. 97–8.

13. Gutierrez, *A Theology of Liberation*, pp. 166–7.

14. Croatto, *Liberación ... pautas*, p. 143.

15. R. Avila, 'Profecía, interpretación y reinterpretación' in 'Moncada, *Liberación en América Latina*, pp. 121–4.

16. Ibid., pp. 124, 126.

CHAPTER SIXTEEN (pp. 160–68)

1. This was through the influence of F. Fanon, *The Wretched of the Earth* (Harmondsworth, 1970) and the Mao Tse Tung, who had already bent the term 'proletariat' to include the peasant class. See S. R. Schram, 'Introduction: the Cultural Revolution in historical perspective' in *Authority, Participation and Cultural Chance in China* (Cambridge, 1973) and J. Ch'en, *Mao* (Englewood Cliffs, 1969), pp. 22f., 88, 159, 164.

2. J. C. Scannone, 'Situación de la problemática', pp. 44–6; 'Christianos por el Socialismo', pp. 262–3. It is highly significant that many Latin American Christians have spoken of their 'conversion' to Marxism.

3. Croatto, *Liberación ... pautas*, pp. 139–40. Nevertheless it may be argued that the warning of judgment upon the rich in James 5.1–6 does not contain elements which prefigure Marx's theory of surplus value. See further my forthcoming *Theology encounters Revolution*.

4. Cf. J. Miguez, *Doing Theology in a Revolutionary Age*.

5. Segundo, *De la sociedad*, pp. 96–9.

6. K. Popper, *Conjectures and Refutations*, pp. 215–48.

7. Segundo, *Masas*, pp. 91–100.

8. Segundo elaborates this in his *The Liberation of Theology*.

9. Cf. Arias Reyer, 'Teología de la liberación o liberación de la teología?', p. 186. See my treatment of the values and limitations of Marxism in articles in *Missionalia* (1978).

CHAPTER SEVENTEEN (pp. 169–84)

1. See, e.g., J. Barr, *The Bible in the Modern World*, pp. 23–34.

2. More particularly in *Being*, pp. 12ff.

3. See M. Hooker, 'Adam in Romans 1', pp. 297ff.; G. Bornkamm, 'The Revelation of God's Wrath: Romans 1–3' in his *Early Christian Experience*; and C. K. Barrett, 'From First Adam to Last', pp. 17–20, 24–5.

4. Foerster, *TWNT* VII, p. 190.

5. See further my article 'La presencia y ausencia de Dios en la revelación de su ira según Rom. 1.18ss'; M. Black, *Romans*, pp. 51–2; and Barrett, op. cit., p. 19.

6. Dussel, *Teología de la liberación y ética*, II, pp. 167–9.

7. Croatto, *Liberación ... pautas*, p. 39.

8. Suggesting that, when isolated, there is no such thing as 'political liberation', just as there is no such thing as 'spiritual liberation'.

9. Cf. R. Padilla, 'El concepto bíblico del Reino de Dios' in *El Reino de Dios y Latinoamérica*.

10. The use of the word 'universal' does not imply 'unversalism'; we believe that the NT rejects the quantitative jump made, e.g. by Gutierrez, from the believer or believing community as the Temple of God to everyman – see *A Theology of Liberation* chap. 10.

11. Cf. R. de Vaux, 'Method in the study of early Hebrew history' in J. P. Hyatt et al., *The Bible in Modern Scholarship*, pp. 15–29.

12. Cf. B. S. Childs, *Biblical Theology in Crisis*, ch. 8.

13. J. Barr, 'Athens or Jerusalem? The question of distinctiveness' in *Old and New in Interpretation* is not very convinced by the arguments adduced for distinctiveness. However, he is basically concerned with the way in which the idea of distinctiveness has been abused by the 'biblical theology movement'. A weakness of his treatment is that he does not treat the epistemological question in any depth.

14. Cf. J. Yoder, *The Politics of Jesus*, pp. 56–7.

15. Cf. Dussel, *Teología de la liberación y ética*, pp. 149–58 with 173–5.

16. I.e. the first and third registers of Lapointe's hermeneutical procedure. See above, ch. 7.

17. So, e.g., J. A. Baird, *The Justice of God in the Teaching of Jesus*, pp. 122ff.; and J. Jeremias, *New Testament Theology*, vol. I (London, 1971), pp. 96, 103.

18. Cf. my 'El Reino de Dios en S. Pablo' in the *Festschrift* presented to R. Obermuller (Buenos Aires, 1979); and J. Yoder 'El significado del Reino como un método hermenéutico para la ética' in Padilla *El Reino de Dios y Latinoamérica*.

19. On the conflictual nature of the kingdom in Scripture see: Dan. 7.14–27; Isa. 9.2–7; Matt. 5.10; 8.12; 11.12; 13.41; 19.23–4; 21.43; 23.13; Luke 9.62; 13.23–30; Acts 14.22; 1 Cor. 6.9; 15.50; Gal. 5.21; Eph. 5.5; Jas. 2.5; Rev. 11.15.

20. Croatto, *Liberación ... pautas*, pp. 19–20. Cf. Avila, op. cit., p. 115.

21. On the ambiguity of the phrase 'God's salvific acts' see J. Barr, 'Event and Interpretation: the Bible as Information' in *The Bible in the Modern World*.

22. As does J. Moltmann, *The Crucified God* (London, 1974), pp. 136–53; 325–9.

23. For a good account of the method see A. R. C. Leaney, 'Form criticism and the historical Jesus', in *The Pelican Guide to Modern Theology*, vol. 3, pp. 252–65. See also K. Koch, *The Growth of the Biblical Tradition*.

24. See further the essay 'Method in the study of biblical theology' by K. Stendahl in Hyatt, *The Bible in Modern Scholarship*.

25. Cf. J. Miguez, 'The struggle of the poor and the Church', p. 42.

CHAPTER EIGHTEEN (pp. 185–94)

1. Within European and North American biblical circles there is a small but growing group of exegetes who are inclined to look for a distinctively

'class' interpretation of the Bible, e.g. Sergio Rostagno, 'Is an interclass reading of the Bible legitimate?' and F. Belo, *Lecture matérialiste de l'evangile de Marc.*

2. So J. Barr, *The Bible in the Modern World*, p. 175.

3. Ibid., p. 143.

4. The term is from Barr, op. cit., pp. 160–1.

5. H. Gollwitzer, *The Existence of God as confessed by Faith* (London, 1965), pp. 113–16.

6. See further A. C. Thiselton, 'The parables as language-event', pp. 437–68.

7. Moltmann discusses some of these in chapter 4 of his *The Crucified God*, and Yoder in his *The Politics of Jesus*, chapter 2.

8. Gollwitzer, 'Liberation in History' (*Int.* XXVIII, Oct. 1974, 4), pp. 414–6.

9. Gollwitzer, *The Existence of God*, p. 109.

10. Cf. J. Ellul, *Violence* (London, 1970), p. 172. The modern move away from traditional orthodox views of biblical inspiration and revelation has also undoubtedly been a prime factor in tilting contemporary theology towards further subjectivism.

CHAPTER NINETEEN (pp. 195–203)

1. Barr, *The Bible in the Modern World*, p. 142, unwittingly perhaps succeeds in relativising the Christ-event in a similar way when he states that the Bible is not a resource-book which can lead to specific decisions; it 'only bears upon the whole man, his total faith and life and that out of that total faith he takes his decisions as a free agent'. This kind of argument seems to me to be illogical since the bearing of the Bible on the whole man can only be in the context of specific decisions. J. H. Yoder, *The Politics of Jesus*, pp. 94ff., has some stringent comments about a hermeneutic which attempts to separate the 'spirit' of the teaching of Jesus from its concrete content. Miranda, too, objects to this methodology which he attributes to the Western feeling of superiority with regard to the biblical world-view, *Marx*, p. 19.

2. Limiting the task of the Church to declaring 'what the Church and Christians *believe* today' (Barr, op. cit., p. 10) is a typical example of the intellectualist approach to theology. J. M. Lochman, 'The importance of theology for Church and society', *SJT*, vol. 26, no. 3 (1973), p. 265, shows that he is prepared to listen to the challenge of the theology of liberation in order to adopt a new procedure in theology.

3. Gutierrez, *Praxis of Liberation and Christian Faith*, p. 40.

4. Gutierrez, ibid., p. 57, claims that 'the spirituality of the Exile is more important today in Latin America than that which is inspired by the paschal experience of the Exodus'. However, the Exile (=the removal of freedom and thus the antithesis of the Exodus) was the result of God's punishment on Israel's unfaithfulness and injustice. The situation of Christian minorities in Latin America is in no way analogous. Certainly 'the times do not permit an attitude of euphoria', but have they ever? The model of Christian spirituality is neither the Exodus nor the Exile but the inauguration of the new era through Christ's death and resurrection.

5. The supreme example is the treatment by Gutierrez of 'Jesus and the

political world'. He does not follow through the implications of his own insights into the meaning of Jesus' relationship to contemporary political power or of his second hermeneutical option: *A Theology of Liberation*, pp. 225–32. He rightly dismisses the charge that the life and death of Jesus are less evangelical because of their political connotations, but he does not explore the evangelical connotations of their political dimension.

6. Segundo, *Masas*, pp. 7–9.

7. Gutierrez, *Praxis of Liberation*, pp. 48–55.

8. Gutierrez, *A Theology of Liberation*, pp. 152–3, 193, 258ff.

CHAPTER TWENTY (pp. 204–8)

1. Miguez, 'The struggle of the poor and the Church'.

2. Gutierrez, *Praxis of Liberation*, pp. 52–3.

ABBREVIATIONS

Act. Past.	*Actualidad Pastoral*
Cat. Lat.	*Cataquesis Latinoamericana*
CBQ	*Catholic Biblical Quarterly*
CELAM	Consejo Episcopal Latinoamericano
CHR	*Catholic Historical Review*
CIAS	Centro de Investigación y Acción Social
Conc.	*Concilium*
Crist. y Soc.	*Cristianismo y Sociedad*
Cuad. de Teol.	*Cuadernos de Teología*
Eccl. Xav.	*Ecclesiastica Xaveriana*
Ec. Rvw.	*Ecumenical Review*
Ev. Rvw. Th.	*Evangelical Review of Theology*
Ep. Th. Lov.	*Ephemerides Theologicae Lovanienses*
Int.	*Interpretation*
IRM	*International Review of Missions*
J. Rel	*Journal of Religion*
LQ	*Lutheran Quarterly*
LTF	Latin American Theological Fraternity
Mens.	*Mensaje*
NTS	*New Testament Studies*
PT	*Perspectiva Theológica*
REB	*Revista Ecclesiastica Brasileira*
RGB	*Revue Generale Belge*
Rev. Bib.	*Revista Bíblica*
RHPR	*Revue d'Histoire et Philosophie du Religion*
Sel. Teol	*Selecciones de Teología*
Str.	*Stromata*
SJT	*Scottish Journal of Theology*
TV	*Teología y Vida*
Visp.	*Vispera*
VT	*Vetus Testamentum*
WSCF	World Student Christian Federation

SELECT BIBLIOGRAPHY

This bibliography does not pretend in any way to be an exhaustive list of books and articles written on the subject of liberation theology. Given the popularity of the subject in the last fifteen years, such a list would itself run to the size of a book. The studies which are included here are, for the most part, ones which I have used in my own study of liberation theology. I have also tried to include one or two of the most recent publications: those which appeared after my manuscript had been completed.

I should like to take this opportunity of thanking Eduardo Bierzychudek, editor of the journal *Bibliografía Teológica Comentada* (Buenos Aires, Argentina), and his team of collaborators, for allowing me to use their extensive files on theological publications in Spanish and Portuguese, and translations of these into English.

LATIN AMERICAN AUTHORS

Alves, R., *A Theology of Human Hope* (Cleveland, 1969)
Alves et al., *De la iglesia y la sociedad* (Montevideo, 1971)
Amuntegui, F. & Barros, Arana, *La iglesia frente a la emancipacion américana* (La Habana, 1967)
Arias Reyen, 'Teología de la liberación o liberación de la teología' (*TV*, XIII, 3, 1972)
Arroyo, G., 'Violencia institucionalizada en América Latina' (*Mens.* 17, 1968)
Assmann, H., *Opresión–Liberación: desafío a los cristianos* (Montevideo, 1971)
Assmann, H., *Teología desde la praxis de la liberación* (Salamanca, 1973)
Assmann, H., *Practical Theology of Liberation* (London, 1975)
Assmann, H., *Theology for a Nomad Church* (New York, 1976)
Assmann, H., 'Reflexión teológica a nivel estratégico-táctico' (in Moncada)
Assmann, H., 'La dinámica de un encuentro de teología (in Assmann et. al.)
Assmann, H., et al., *Pueblo oprimido, Señor de la historia* (Montevideo, 1972)
Asti Vera, A., 'Mito y semántica' (in SAPSE)
Auza, N. T., *Católicos y liberales en la generación del ochenta* (Cuernavaca, 1966)
Avila, R., 'Profecía, interpretación y reinterpretación' (in Moncada)
Boff, L., *Jesus Christo, Libertador* (Petropolis, 1973)
Boff, L., *Teología desde el cautiverio* (Bogota, 1975)
Boff, L., *A graça liberadora* (Petropolis, 1977)
Boff, L., *Teología e práctica: teología do político e suas mediações* (Petropolis, 1978)
Boff, L., 'Jesus Cristo libertador: una visão cristológica a partir da periferia' (*REB*, 37, 147, 1977, pp. 501–24)
Bojorge, H., 'Exodo y liberación' (*Visp.* 4, 19/20, 1970)
Bojorge, H., 'Goel: Dios libera a los suyos' (*Rev. Bib.* 32, 1, 1971)

Bojorge, H., 'Para una interpretación liberadora' (*Rev. Bib.* 32, 1, 1971)

Bojorge, H., 'Revelación, interpretación bíblica y teología de la liberación' (*Persp. Teol.* (Sao Leopoldo) X, 20, 1978)

Bravo, C., 'Notas marginales a la teología de la liberación' (*Eccl. Xav.*, XXIV, 1, 1974)

Broucker, J. de, *Dom Helder Camara* (New York, 1976)

Camara, H., *Evangelho e liberatação humano* (Porto, 1976)

Camara, H., *Church and Colonialism* (London, 1969)

Camara, H., * *The Spiral of Violence* (London, 1971)

Camara, H., * *The Desert is Fertile* (New York, 1976)

Cardenal, E., *La santidad de la revolución* (Salamanca, 1976)

Cardenal, E., * *The Gospel in Solentiname* (New York, 1976)

Casa, F., 'Pascua significa todavía una resurrección?' (*Rev. Bib.* 4, 1971)

Casabó, J., 'Violencia y revolución' (CIAS, XVIII, 181–2, 1969)

Casabó, J., 'La liberación en S. Juan' (*Rev. Bib.* 3, 34, 1972)

Casabó, J., 'Discernimiento cristiano y opciones políticas' (in Karlic)

Castro, E., 'La creciente presencia de criterios de interpretación histórica en las evoluciones de la hermenéutica bíblica' (in Assmann et al.)

CELAM (I), *Liberación: diálogos en el CELAM* (Bogotá, 1974)

CELAM (II), *Evangelización y pastoral* (Bogotá, 1976)

Comblin, Avellano y Galilea, S., *Fe y secularización en América Latina* (Quito, 1972)

Cristianos por el socialismo, Los, *Los Cristianos y el socialismo* (Buenos Aires, 1973)

Croatto, S., *La Historia de la Salvación* (Buenos Aires, 1966)

Croatto, S., *Liberación y libertad: pautas hermenéuticas* (Buenos Aires, 1973)

Croatto, S., 'El hombre bíblico no es un prometeo' (*Visp.* 2, 5, 1968)

Croatto, S., 'El mito-símbolo y el mito-relato' (in SAPSE)

Croatto, S., 'El lenguaje: reinterpretación y reexpresión del evangelio' (*Cat. Lat. 7, 1970*)

Croatto, S., 'Hermenéutica de las representaciones escatológicas' (*Str. 26, 1–3, 1970*)

Croatto, S., 'Liberación y libertad: reflexiones hermenéuticas en torno al Antiguo Testamento' (*Rev. Bib.* 1, 1971)

Croatto, S., 'El hombre en el mundo según Génesis' (*Rev. Bib.* 1, 1973)

Croatto, S., 'La función del poder: salvífica u opresora?' (*Rev. Bib.* 2, 1972)

Croatto, S., 'El Dios en el acontecimiento' (*Rev. Bib.* 1, 1973)

Croatto, S., 'El hombre nuevo y liberación en la carta a los romanos' (*Rev. Bib.* 1, 1974)

Cussianovich, A., *Desde los probres de la tierra* (Salamanca, 1977)

Cussianovich, A., *Nos ha liberado* (Salamanca, 1976)

Dumas, E. A., *Los dos rostros alienados de la iglesia una: ensayo de teología política* (Buenos Aires, 1971)

Dussel, E., *Hipótesis para una historia de la iglesia en América Latina* (Barcelona, 1972)

Dussel, E., *Historia de la iglesia en América Latina: Coloniaje y Liberación* (Barcelona, 1972)

Dussel, E., *Caminos de liberación latinoamericana* (Vol. I) (Buenos Aires, 1972)

Dussel, E., *Caminos de liberación latinoamericana* (Vol. II): *teología de la liberación y ética* (Buenos Aires, 1974)

Dussel, E., *Para una ética de la liberación latinoamericana* (Vols. I and II) (Buenos Aires, 1973)

Dussel, E., *El dualismo en la antropología de la critiandad: desde el origen del cristianismo hasta antes de la conquista de América* (Buenos Aires, 1974)

Dussel, E., *Método para una filosofía de la liberación: superación analéctica de la dialéctica hegeliana* (Salamanca, 1974)

Dussel, E., *History and the Theology of Liberation* (New York, 1976)

Dussel, E., 'El momento negativo: el ateismo de los profetas y de Marx, afirmación ética de la alteridad' (in Karlic)

Dussel, E., 'Coyuntura de la práxis cristiana en América Latina' (*SIC*, XLI, 403, 1978)

Escobar, S., *'Evangelization and man's search for freedom, justice and fulfillment' in J. D. Douglas, ed., *Let the Earth Hear his Voice* (Minneapolis, 1975)

Escobar, S., 'Identidad, Misión y Futuro del Protestantismo latinoamericano' (*Boletín Teológica* (LTF) 3/4, 1977)

Escoria (encuentro de), *Fe cristiana y cambio social en América Latina* (Salamanca, 1973)

Farré, L., *Dependencia y liberación en Latinoamérica* (provisional title) (Buenos Aires, 1979)

Figuera, G., *La iglesia y su doctrina en la independencia de América* (Caracas, 1960)

Frank, A. G., 'El desarrollo del subdesarrollo' (*Desarrollo*, 1, 1, 1966)

Frei, E., *'Catholic Social Justice, Democracy and Pluralism' (in Pike)

Freire, P., *Concientización: teoría y práctica de la liberación* (Buenos Aires, 1974)

Freire, P., *Cartas à Guiné-Bissau* (1977)

Freire, P., *Pedagogy of the Oppressed* (Harmondsworth, 1972)

Freire, P., *Cultural Action for Freedom* (Harmondsworth, 1972)

Freire, P., *Education, Liberation and the Church* (Geneva, 1973)

Galilea, S., *Documentos sobre la pastoral* (Cuernavaca, 1968)

Galilea, S., *Teología de la liberación: ensayo de síntesis* (Bogota, 1976)

Galilea, S., *A los pobres se les anuncia el evangelio?* (Bogota, 1972)

Galilea, S., 'Notas sobre las actuales teologías latinoamericanas' (*TV*, 12, 3, 1972)

Gera, L., 'Liberación del pecado y liberación histórico-secular' (*Servir*, 8, 12)

Gera, L. & Melgarejo, G., 'Apuntes para una interpretación de la iglesia argentina' (*Visp*. 4, 15, 1970)

Gibellini et al., *La nueva frontera de la teología en América Latina* (Salamanca, 1977)

Gnatt, E., * *The Significance of Changes in Latin American Catholicism since Chimbote* (Cuernavaca, 1969)

Gomez, I. A., *Viajeros pontificios al Rio de la Plata: 1823–5* (Cordoba, 1970)

Gutierrez, G., *Teología de la liberación: perspectivas* (Salamanca, 1972)

Gutierrez, G., *Teología desde el reverso de la historia* (Lima, 1977)

Gutierrez, G., *A Theology of Liberation* (New York, 1973; London, 1974)

Gutierrez, G., *Praxis of Liberation and Christian Faith* (San Antonio, 1974)

Gutierrez, G., 'De la iglesia colonial a Medellín' (*Visp*. IV, 1970)

Gutierrez, G., 'Praxis de liberación, teología y evangelización' (in CELAM (I))

Gutierrez, G., 'Revelación y anuncio de Dios en la historia' (*Páginas*, Sep. 1976, 2, 1)

Henriquez, L., *Historia de la cultura hispanoamericana* (Mexico, 1947)

Hernandez, J., *Esbozo para una teología de la liberación* (Bogota, 1971)

Jaguaribe, H., et al., *La dependencia político-económica de America Latina* (Mexico, 1970)

Karlic, E., 'Presentación' (in Karlic et. al.)

Karlic, E., et al., *Fe y Política* (Buenos Aires, 1973)

Kloppenburg, B., 'Las tentaciones de la teología de la liberación' (*Sel. Teol.* (Madrid), 15, 60, 1976)

Laje, E. J., 'Análisis marxista y teología de la praxis en America Latina' (*Str.* 33, 1–2)

Lanson, A., *Liberar a los oprimidos* (Buenos Aires, 1970)

Leturia, P. de, *Relaciones entre la Santa Sede e Hispanoamérica* (Rome and Caracas, 1959)

Lopez Rosas, E., 'Teología de la liberación: su profundización a partir de la experiencia peronista' (*Hechos e Ideas*, 1, 4, 1974)

Lopez Trujillo, A., *Liberación o revolución?* (Bogota, 1975)

Lopez Trujillo, A., 'Las teologías de la liberación en América Latina' (in CELAM (I))

Martin, J. P., 'Liberación, salvación y escatología' (in Karlic)

Medellín, *Documentos Finales* (Buenos Aires, 1972)

Mejía, J., 'La liberación: aspectos bíblicos, evaluación crítica' (in CELAM (I))

Mesters, C., *La palabra de Dios en la historia de los hombres* (Buenos Aires, 1972)

Miguez, J., *Polémica, diálogo y misión* (Buenos Aires, 1976)

Miguez, J., *Doing Theology in a Revolutionary Age* (Philadelphia, 1975; English edition: *Revolutionary Theology comes of Age*, London, 1975)

Miguez, J., *Christians and Marxists: the Mutual Challenge to Revolution* (London, 1975)

Miguez, J., 'Nuevas perspectivas teológicas' (in Assmann)

Miguez, J., 'El nuevo catolicismo' (in Padilla (I))

Miguez, J., 'El Reino de Dios y la historia' (in Padilla (II))

Miguez, J., *Theology and Liberation* (*IRM*, LXI, 241, 1972)

Miguez, J., *The Struggle of the Poor and the Church* (*Ec. Rvw.* XXVII, 1, 1975)

Miguez, J., *The Human and the System* (*Theology Today*, XXXV, 1, 1978)

Miguez, J., et al., *Jesus: ni vencido ni monarca celestial* (Buenos Aires, 1977)

Miranda, J., *Marx y la Biblia* (Salamanca, 1972)

Miranda, J., *El Ser y el Mesías* (Salamanca, 1973)

Miranda, J., *Marx and the Bible* (New York, 1974)

Miranda, J., *Being and the Messiah* (New York, 1977)

Moncada, C., et al., *Liberación en América Latina* (Bogota, 1972)

Moncada, C., 'Presentación' (in Moncada)

Morelli, A., *Libera a mi pueblo* (Buenos Aires, 1971)

Negré, P., 'Los cambios metodológicos de las ciencias sociales y la interpretación teológica' (in Assmann)

232   LIBERATION THEOLOGY

Negre, P., 'Biblia y liberación' (*Crist. y Soc.* 8, 1970)
Olaya, N., 'Unidad cristiana y lucha de clases' (in Assmann)
Oliveros, R., *Liberación y teología* (Lima, 1977)
Padilla, R., et al., (I) *Fe cristiana y Latinoamerica hoy* (Buenos Aires, 1974);
    (II) *El Reino de Dios y Latinoamerica* (El Paso, 1975)
Padilla, R., 'Iglesia y Sociedad en America Latina' (in Padilla (I))
Padilla, R., 'El Reino de Dios y la iglesia' (in Padilla (II))
Padilla, R., *'Evangelism and the World' in J. D. Douglas, ed., *Let the Earth
    Hear his Voice* (Minneapolis, 1975)
Paoli, A., *El grito de la tierra* (Salamanca, 1977)
Paoli, A., *Freedom to be Free* (New York, 1976)
Peruvian Episcopate, 'La justicia en el mundo' (*Act. Past.* 4, 1971)
Pironio, L., 'Imagen del sacerdote posconciliar' (in Galilea)
Pironio, L., 'Teología de la liberación' (*Criterio*, XLIII, 70–1)
Ribeiro, d'Arcy, *Los Américas y la civilización* (Buenos Aires, 1972)
Rivera, F., 'Sobre el socialismo de Santiago' (*Rev. Bib.* 34, 1, 1972)
Rivera, F., 'La epístola de Santiago como modelo de halaka cristiana' (in
    SAPSE)
Rivera Pagán, L. N., 'Teología y praxis de liberación' (in Assmann)
Rivera Pagán, L. M., 'Aportes del Marxismo: apuntes para el tema implica-
    ciones socio-políticas e ideológicas del lenguaje de la liberación' (in Ass-
    mann)
Ruiz, S., 'Teología bíblica de la liberación' (in CELAM (I)
Sacerdotes del Tercer Mundo, *Pólemica en la iglesia: documentos de obispos argen-
    tinos y sacerdotes del tercer mundo: 1969–70* (Avellaneda, 1970)
Santa Ana, J. de, *La iglesia y el desafío de la pobreza* (Buenos Aires, 1978)
Santa Ana, J. de, 'Notas para una ética de liberación a partir de la Biblia'
    (*Christ y Soc.*, 8, 1970)
SAPSE, *Mito y Hermenéutica* (Buenos Aires, 1973)
Sartor, R., 'Exodo-liberación: tema de actualidad para una reflexión teoló-
    gica' (*Rev. Bib.*, 33, 1971)
Savage, P., et al., *El debate contemporaneo sobre la Biblia* (Barcelona, 1972)
Scannone, J. C., *Teología de la liberación y praxis popular: aportes críticos para
    una teología de la liberación* (Salamanca, 1977)
Scannone, J. C., 'Teología y política: el actual desafío planteado al lenguaje
    teológico latinoamericano de liberación' (in Escoria)
Scannone, J. C., 'Situación de la problemática, fe y política' (in Karlic)
Scannone, J. C., 'Teología, cultura popular y discernimiento' (CIAS, XXIII,
    237, 1974)
Segundo, J. L., *Función de la iglesia en la realidad rioplatense* (Montevideo, 1962)
Segundo, J. L., *Iglesia latinoamericana: protesta o profecia* (Avellaneda,
    1969)
Segundo, J. L., *Teología abierta para el laico adulto* (Vols. I–V) (Buenos
    Aires, 1969–72)
Segundo, J. L., *De la sociedad a la teología* (Buenos Aires, 1970)
Segundo, J. L., *Qué es un cristiano?* (Montevideo, 1971)
Segundo, J. L., *Acción pastoral latinoamericana: sus motivos ocultos* (Buenos Aires,
    1973)

Segundo, J. L., *Masas y minorías en la dialéctica divina de la liberación* (Buenos Aires, 1973)
Segundo, J. L., *Liberación de la teología* (Buenos Aires, 1975)
Segundo, J. L., **Theology for the Artisans of a New Humanity* (Vols. I–V) (New York, 1973–75): *I *The Community called the Church*; *II *Grace and the Human Condition*; III *Our Idea of God*; IV *The Sacraments Today*; *V *Evolution and Guilt*
Segundo, J. L., ** The Liberation of Theology* (New York, 1976)
Segundo, J. L., 'Instrumentos de la teología latinoamericana' (in Moncada)
Segundo, J. L., *'The Possible Contribution of Protestant Theology to Latin American Christianity in the Future' (*LQ* 22, 1, 1970)
Tormo, L. y Alzpuru, P., *Historia de la iglesia en América Latina (III): la iglesia en la crisis de la independencia* (Fribourg, 1963)
Torres, C., *Camilo Torres: por el Padre Camilo Torres Restrepo* (Cuernavaca, 1966)
Torres, S. & Eagleson, J., **Theology in the Americas* (New York, 1976)
Valle, G. del, 'El papel de la teología en América Latina' (in Moncada)
Various, *Liberación y cautiverio; debate en torno al método de la teología en América Latina* (Mexico, 1976)
Villegas, B., 'La liberación en la Biblia' (*TV*, 3, 13, 1972)
Villegas, B., 'Exégesis técnica y anuncio de la fe' (in CELAM (II))
Zañarfú, M., *Desarrollo económico y moral católico* (Cuernavaca, 1969)
Zea, L., ** The Latin American Mind* (Oaklahoma, 1963)

NON-LATIN AMERICAN AUTHORS

Abbott, W. M., **The Documents of Vatican II* (New York, 1966)
Aguirre, J., et al., *Los problemas de un diálogo* (Madrid, 1969)
Antoine, C., **Church and Power in Brazil* (London, 1973)
Antonio, W. V. D. & Pike, F. B., **Religion, Revolution and Reform in Latin America* (New York, 1964)
Baird, J. A., ** The Justice of God in the Teaching of Jesus* (London, 1963)
Barr, J., **Old and New in Interpretation* (London, 1966)
Barr, J., ** The Bible in the Modern World* (London, 1973)
Barrett, C. K., **From First Adam to Last* (London, 1962)
Barthes, P., et al., *Interprétation de langage mythique et théologie biblique* (Paris, 1967)
Belo, F., *Lecture matérialiste de l'évangile de Marc: récit, practique, idéologie* (Paris, 1974)
Bennet et al., **Christian Social Ethics in a Changing World* (New York, 1966)
Black, M., **Romans* (London, 1973)
Boehrer, G. C. A., *'The Church and the Overthrow of the Brazilian Monarchy' (in Schmitt)
Bornkamm, G., **Early Christian Experience* (London, 1969)
Boven, F., et al., *Analyse structurale et exégèse biblique* (Neûchatel, 1971)
Brown, R. E., *'The Problems of Sensus Plenior' (*Ep. Th. Lov.*, XLIII, 1967)
Castillo, J., 'L'expérience démocrate chrétienne au Chili' (RGB, 11/12, 1967)
Childs, B. S., **Biblical Theology in Crisis* (Philadelphia, 1970)

Childs, B. S., *Exodus: A commentary* (London, 1974)

Clements, R. E., *Exodus* (Cambridge 1972)

Coleman, W. J., *Latin American Catholicism: a Self-Examination* (New York, 1958)

Considine, J. J., et al., (I) *The Church in the New Latin America*; (II) *Social Revolution and the New Latin America* (Indiana, 1967)

Converse, J., et al., *Raise a signal: God's action and the Church's task in Latin America today* (New York, 1961)

Daube, D., *The Exodus Pattern in the Bible* (London, 1963)

Deister, A., *El Antiguo Testamento y la moderna exégesis católica* (Barcelona, 1966)

Eagleson, J., *Christians and Socialism* (New York, 1976)

Eagleson, J., ed., *My Life for my Friends* (journal of Nestor Paz) (New York, 1976)

Eliade, M., *Aspects du mythe* (Paris, 1963)

Espinosa, A., *'Catholicism and the National Tradition'* (in Pike)

Forestell, J. T., *The World of the Cross* (Rome, 1974)

Fohrer, G., *Introduction to the Old Testament* (London, 1970)

Frank, H. T. & Reed, W. L., *Translating and Understanding the Old Testament* (Nashville, 1970)

Furnish, V. P., *The Love Command in the New Testament* (London, 1974)

Gadamer, H.-G., *Warheit und Methode* (Tubingen, 1965)

Garaudy, R. & Balducci, E., *El cristianismo es liberación* (Salamanca, 1976)

Geffre, C., *'Editorial: a Prophetic Theology'* (*Conc.* 6, 10, 1974)

Glasson, T. F., *Moses in the Fourth Gospel* (London, 1963)

Grelot, P., *Bible et Theologie* (Paris, 1965)

Gremillian, J., *'The Church goes into the Market Place'* (in Considine (I))

Griffin, C. C., *The Enlightenment and Latin American Independence* (Ithaca, 1961)

Grillmeier, A., *'The Divine Inspiration and Interpretation of Sacred Scripture'* (in Vorgrimler)

Haring, G. H., *'The Church–State Conflict in 19th century Brazil'* (in Pike)

Herring, D., *A History of Latin America from the Beginning to the Present* (New York, 1963)

Hooker, M., *'Adam in Rom. 1'* (*NTS*, vi, 1959–60)

Houtart, F., *La iglesia latinoamericana en la hora del concilio* (Freibourg, 1962)

Houtart, F., *'The Roman Catholic Church and Social Change in Latin America'* (in Landsberger)

Houtart, F. & Pin, E., *The Church and the Latin American Revolution* (New York, 1965)

Hubner, J. I., *'Catholic Social Justice, Authoritarianism and Class Stratification'* (in Pike)

Hyatt, J. P., *Exodus* (London, 1971)

Hyatt, J. P., et al., *The Bible in Modern Scholarship* (London, 1966)

Illich, I., *The De-schooling of Society* (New York and London, 1972)

Illich, I., *Tools for Conviviality* (New York and London, 1973)

Kadt, E. de, *'JUC and AP; the Rise of Catholic Radicalism in Brazil'* (in Landsberger)

Kirk, J. A., *Jesuscristo: revolucionario* (Buenos Aires, 1974)

Kirk, J. A., *Theology encounters Revolution* (Leicester, 1980)

Kirk, J. A., 'La biblia y su hermenéutica en relación con la teología protestante en América Latina' (in Savage)

Kirk, J. A., 'La presencia y ausencia de Dios en la revelación de su ira según Rom. 1:18ss' (*Cuad. de Teol.* II, 1973)

Kirk, J. A., 'The Bible in Latin American Liberation Theology' in *The Bible and Liberation: Political and Social Hermeneutics* (a Radical Religion Reader), (Berkeley, 1976)

Kirk, J. A., 'The use of the Bible in interpreting salvation today' (*Ev. Rvw. Th.* 1, 1, 1976)

Koch, K., * *The Growth of the Biblical Tradition* (London, 1969)

Knowlton, R. J., *'Clerical response to the Mexican reform: 1855–75' (*CHR*, 1964–5)

Landsberger, H., et al., * *The Church and Social Change in Latin America* (Notre Dame, 1970)

Landsberger, H., 'Time, persons, doctrine: the modernization of the Church in Chile' (in Landsberger)

Lapointe, R., *Les trois dimensions de l'herméneutique* (Paris, 1967)

Larrain, D., & Gagliano, J. A., *'The plagues that followed freedom' in Considine (II))

Latourette, K. S., *Christianity in a Revolutionary Age*, Vol. LII, VI (New York, 1958)

Leaney, A. R. C., *'Form criticism and the historical Jesus' in *The Pelican Guide to Modern Theology*, Vol. III (London, 1970)

Levie, P., * *The Bible: Word of God in Words of Men* (New York, 1971)

Lindblom, J., * *The Bible: a Modern Understanding* (Philadelphia, 1973)

Lohfink, N., *Exegesis bíblica y teología* (Salamanca, 1969)

Lubac, H. de, *Catolicismo: aspectos sociales del dogma* (Barcelona, 1963)

McGrath, M., *'The Church and social revolution' (in Considine (II))

Maritain, J., * *The Peasant of the Garonne: an old layman questions himself about the present time* (London, 1968)

Meecham, L. B., *Church and State in Latin America* (Chapel Hill, 1934)

Moule, C. F. D., *'Fulfillment words in the New Testament: use and abuse' (*NTS*, XIV, 1967–8)

Munro, D. G., * *The Latin American Republics: a History* (London, 1961)

Murphy, R. E. & Peter, C. J., *'The role of the Bible in Roman Catholic theology' (*Int.* 25, 1, 1971)

Mutchler, D., *'Adaptations of the Roman Catholic Church to Latin American development: the meaning of internal church conflict' (in Schmitt)

Navarette, F., *'Conflict in Mexico ... defense of the clergy' (in Pike)

Noth, M., *Exodus: a Commentary* (London, 1962)

Orlinsky, H. M., *'Nationalism–universalism and internationalism in ancient Israel' (in H. T. Frank & W. L. Reed)

Pannenberg, W., *Basic Questions in Theology*, Vols. I & II (London, 1970, 1971)

Pattel, R., *El catolicismo contemporaneo en Hispanoamérica* (Buenos Aires, 1951)

Pike, F. B., et al., * *The Conflict Between Church and State in Latin America* (New York, 1964)

Poblete, R., *'The great resurgence' (in Considine (II))

Popper, K., *Conjectures and Refutations: the Growth of Scientific Knowledge (London, 1969)

Portes, E., *'Conflict in Mexico ... 1854–1876: defense of civil power' (in Pike)

Rahner, K., Befreinde Theologie: Der Beitrag Lateinamerikas zur Theologie der Gegenwart (Stuttgart, 1977)

Rahner, K., et al., La Respuesta de los teólogos (Buenos Aires, 1970)

Rasmussen, D. S., *Mythic-Symbolic Language and Philosophical Anthropology: a Constructive Interpretation of the Thought of P. Ricoeur (The Hague, 1971)

Ricoeur, P., De L'interprétation (Paris, 1968)

Robinson, J. M., *'Scripture and Theological Method' (CBQ, 27, 1, 1965)

Rossell, M., *'A pastoral letter on Catholic social justice and the struggle against Communism' (in Pike)

Rostagno, S., *'Is an interclass reading of the Bible legitimate?' (WSCF dossier, No. 2, Oct. 1973)

Sarna, N., *Understanding Genesis (New York, 1966)

Sartre, J.-P., 'Jean-Paul Sartre répond' (L'Arc, 30, 1966)

Schild, E., *'On Exodus iii.14 – "I am that I am"' (VT, 4, 1954)

Schlier, H., *The Relevance of the New Testament (London, 1968)

Schmitt, K. M., et al., The Roman Catholic Church in Modern Latin America (New York, 1972)

Stendahl, K., *'Method in the study of Biblical theology' (in Hyatt)

Stephenson, K. D., *'Roman Catholic biblical scholarship: its ecclesiastical context in the last 100 years' (Encounter, 33, 4, 1972)

Thiselton, A. C., *'The parables as language-event: some comments on Fuch's Hermeneutic in the light of linguistic philosophy' (SJT, 23, 4, 1970)

Tibesar, A., *'The Peruvian Church at the Time of Independence in the Light of Vatican II' (in Schmitt)

Turner, F. C., *Catholicism and Political Development in Latin America (Chapel Hill, 1971)

Vallier, I., Catolicismo, control social y modernización en América Latina (Buenos Aires, 1971)

Vanger, M. I., *José Battle y Ordoñez of Uruguay: The Creator of his Times (London, 1963)

Reit, G. van, 'Exégèse et réflexion philosophique' (Ep. Th. Lov. XLIII, 1967)

Vargas, P., 'El episcopado en la emancipación sudamericana' (in Houtart & Pin)

Vaux, R. de, *'Method in the study of early Hebrew history' (in Hyatt)

Vawter, B., Biblical Inspiration (London, 1972)

Vekemans, R., Teología de la liberación y cristianos por el socialismo (Bogota, 1976)

Vekemans, R., 'Panorámica actual de la teología de la liberación en América Latina: evaluación crítica' (Tierra Nueva – Bogota – 5, 17, 1978)

Vorgrimler, H., et al., *Commentary on the Documents of Vatican II (London and New York, 1969)

Wells, D., *Revolution in Rome (Downers Grove, 1972)

Williams, E. J., *Latin American Christian Democrat Parties (Knoxville, 1967)

Winter, D., *Hope in Captivity: the Prophetic Church in Latin America* (London, 1977)

Wright, A. G., *'The literary genre Midrash' (*CBQ*, 28, 1966)

Yoder, J. H., * *The Politics of Jesus* (Grand Rapids, 1972)

Yoder, J. H., *'Exodus and exile: the two faces of liberation' (*Missionalia* (Pretoria) 2, 1, 1974)

Yoder, J. H., 'La pertenenicia del concepto bíblico del reino para la hermenéutica' (in Padilla (II))

Zimmerli, W., * *Man and His Hope in the Old Testament* (London, 1971)

Zuck, J. E., *'The new hermeneutic on language: a critical appraisal' (*J. Rel.* 52, 4, 1972)

* Books and articles written or translated into English

INDEX OF SUBJECTS

INDEX OF NAMES

INDEX OF BIBLE REFERENCES

NEW TESTAMENT